The Life of Sir Herbert Gibson, Bart, KBE
(1863–1934)

Published by

MELROSE BOOKS

An Imprint of Melrose Press Limited
St Thomas Place, Ely
Cambridgeshire
CB7 4GG, UK
www.melrosebooks.com

FIRST EDITION

Copyright © Iain Stewart 2008

The Author asserts his moral right to
be identified as the author of this work

Cover designed by Matt Stephens

ISBN 978-1-906561-34-5

All rights reserved. No part of this publication may be reproduced,
stored in a retrieval system, or transmitted, in any form or by any means
electronic, mechanical, photocopying, recording or otherwise,
without the prior permission of the publishers.

This book is sold subject to the condition that it shall not,
by way of trade or otherwise, be lent, re-sold, hired out or
otherwise circulated without the publisher's prior consent
in any form of binding or cover other than that in which
it is published and without a similar condition including this
condition being imposed on the subsequent purchaser.

Printed and bound in Great Britain by:
CPI Antony Rowe, Chippenham, Wiltshire

AUTHOR BIOGRAPHY

Born in Edinburgh, Iain Stewart grew up in Dundee and attended the city's High School. After studying languages, he completed a doctorate in Argentinian cultural history at the University of St Andrews, where he also taught for a number of years. He has a particular interest in links between Scotland and the countries of the River Plate region, and has previously published *From Caledonia to the Pampas: Two Accounts by Early Scottish Emigrants to the Argentine* (East Linton: Tuckwell Press, 2000), as well as numerous articles on the history and literature of Argentina, Uruguay and Paraguay. Iain's other interests include computing (he holds a Master's degree in the subject and is a professional member of the British Computer Society), motor sport and looking after his British Shorthair cats.

TO THE MEMORY OF GEOFFREY GIBSON, IN WHOSE FOOTSTEPS I HAVE DARED TO FOLLOW.

CONTENTS

List of Illustrations viii
The Gibsons ~ A Partial Family Tree, 1771–1934 ix
Foreword xi
Introduction and acknowledgements xiii
Chapter 1 ~ Forebears 1
Chapter 2 ~ Schoolboy 21
Chapter 3 ~ Apprentice 50
Chapter 4 ~ Manager 84
Chapter 5 ~ Man of Letters, 1892–1911 119
Chapter 6 ~ Husband and Father 142
Chapter 7 ~ Commissioner 171
Chapter 8 ~ The Turbulent Twenties 192
Chapter 9 ~ The British Exhibition 215
Chapter 10 ~ Man of Letters, 1911–1934 237
Chapter 11 ~ The Final Years 253
Bibliography 263

LIST OF ILLUSTRATIONS

Los Yngleses by Thomas Gibson
    (figure in doorway may be artist himself) 115
Estancia buildings by Thomas Gibson......................116
Wagon train carrying wool to the port of Ajó
    by Thomas Gibson 117
Argentine rural scene by Thomas Gibson 118
Photograph taken in 1860s by George Corbett, showing
    Thomas Gibson (tall, bearded figure standing by wagon)
    and his brother Robert (figure holding pole) marking out
    the boundaries of Los Yngleses. Clementina Gibson,
    Thomas's wife, stands in the background with children.
    Baby Herbert is in her arms. 233
Thomas Gibson (seated) with three of his sons
    (Herbert on right) 234
Herbert and Maddie 235
Herbert (seated) with his sons standing behind
    (from left to right, Cosmo, Gerald, Chris and Clem) 235
Gibsons' house at Linconia 236
Herbert and Maddie's 'cottage' at Bella Vista 236

The Gibsons ~ A Partial Family Tree, 1771–1934

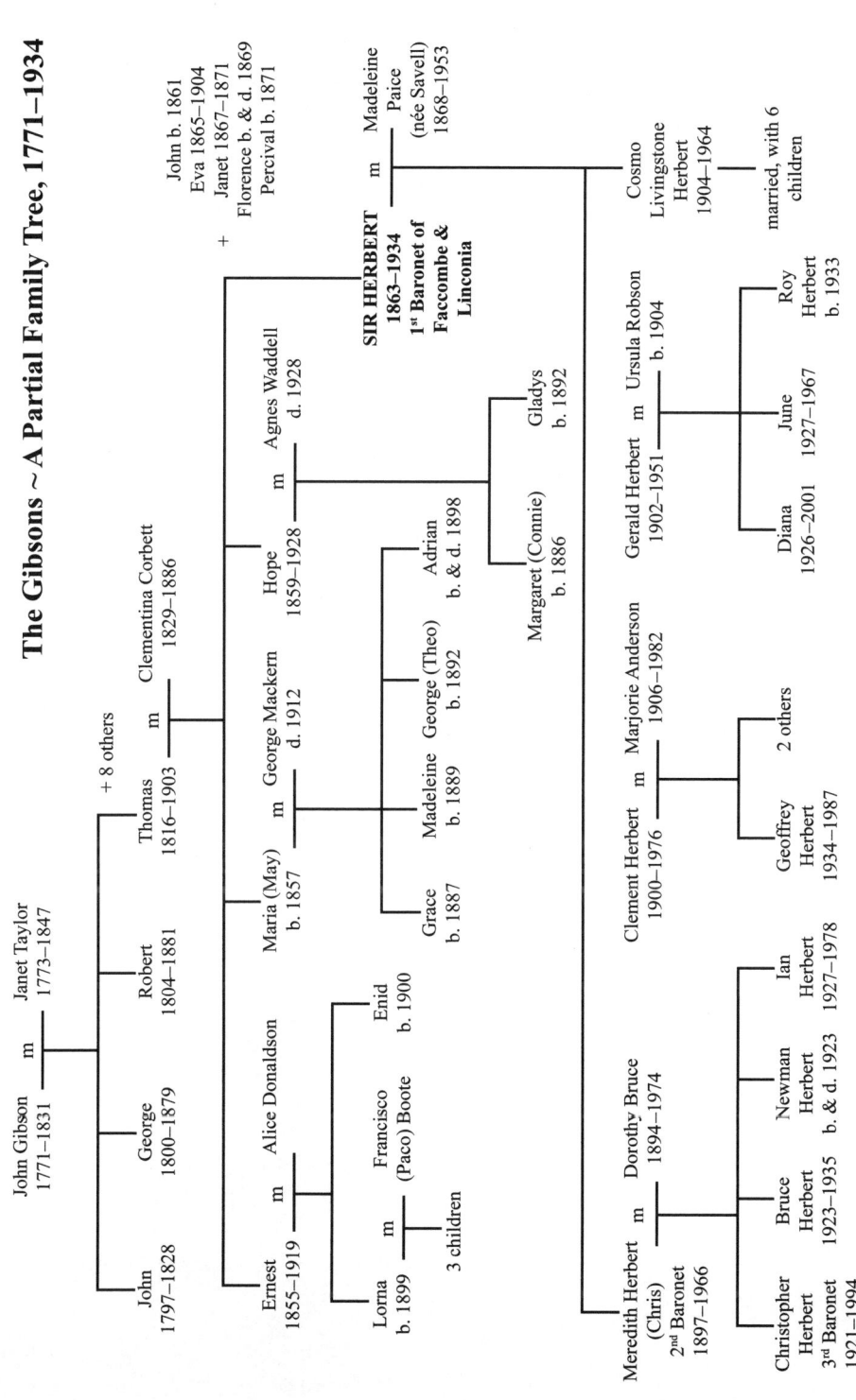

FOREWORD

My brother Geoffrey was half way through writing the biography of our illustrious grandfather Sir Herbert Gibson when he died of cancer in 1987 at the age of 54.

In 1994, I sent Dr Iain Stewart a copy of Geoffrey's unfinished biography of Sir Herbert for use in his research into Scottish families in Argentina. Then, a decade later, I was fascinated to read about the early history of the Gibsons in Iain's 'Living with Dictator Rosas: Argentina through Scottish Eyes'[1]. Not only was it a thundering good read but it made me realise that quite a lot of the family story as passed down by word of mouth was inaccurate. Here was a scholar who knew a lot more about my ancestors than I did. Where had he found all his information? Well, it transpired that my uncle Sir Christopher Gibson had sold a considerable portion of the family papers to an Argentine bibliophile, Alberto Dodero. On Dodero's death, his family sold his library in 1966 at Sotheby's and everything related to the Gibsons had been acquired by the National Library of Scotland.

For some time, Iain had been in touch with Minnie Boote, wife of John Boote, the son of Lorna Gibson who had inherited, along with his two sisters, Los Yngleses, an original Gibson estancia (ranch). Minnie and John were living at the property and managing it. Minnie was deeply immersed in, and knowledgeable about, the history of Los Yngleses and the family in general.

It was through Minnie that I originally met Iain. Although very busy with his own academic endeavours, Iain mentioned to me in a letter written on 6 September 2004 that he 'might still be interested in such a project', the 'project' being a history of the Gibsons in Argentina. Crucial, however, would be access to Sir Herbert's diaries. Luckily, my nephew Robert had most of these for they had been the main source of material for his own father's half-finished biography. Once Iain had read these he believed that in Sir Herbert he had found the subject for a fairly exceptional history. A prodigious writer and intellect who was deeply

---

1 'Living with Dictator Rosas: Argentina through Scottish Eyes', *Journal of Latin American Studies, 29* (1997), 23-44.

involved in the development of trade between Argentina and Great Britain, Sir Herbert was the greatest advocate his adopted country could have wished for. He was a man equally at ease with a waiter, an intellectual, or a prince and balanced his public life with a deep concern for his family's welfare.

It is with enormous gratitude, therefore, that I thank Iain for showing this man with such clarity, honesty and skill.

Thomas Gibson
London, December 2007

INTRODUCTION AND ACKNOWLEDGEMENTS

Some observers have suggested that Argentina resembled an unofficial dominion of the United Kingdom during the nineteenth and early twentieth centuries. While Britain probably never enjoyed sufficient political influence for such a claim to withstand close scrutiny, the trading links between the two countries were certainly strong, with the result that significant numbers of British citizens developed commercial interests in the young South American republic. The Gibsons, who originally hailed from the Glasgow area, were among the earliest of their compatriots to set up business in Buenos Aires and, moreover, went on to enjoy an unusually enduring connection with Argentina, a relationship that continues to the present day. Originally merchants dealing in textiles and animal hides, they wasted little time in becoming landowners and soon established themselves as one of Argentina's foremost ranching families. Sir Herbert Gibson (born in Bridge of Allan, Scotland, 1863; died in Buenos Aires, 1934) was undoubtedly the outstanding member of the line, becoming an influential public figure in both his native and adopted homelands.

A man of considerable intelligence and vision, Herbert possessed a deep affection for all aspects of Argentina's culture as well as an unrivalled knowledge of her rural industries. After establishing himself as an expert sheep-breeder, he went on to develop strong interests in areas such as the history, politics and economics of Argentina, topics on which he wrote and lectured frequently. As his reputation grew, so did the scope of his business interests and he was to become a leading player in the country's vital railway industry. Another field in which Herbert was particularly active was that of forging ever-closer ties between Britain and Argentina. It is no exaggeration to say that he gave exemplary service to both nations throughout his adult life, winning the respect and friendship of many in the process. He moved in the highest circles and his opinions came to be valued by those in positions of authority, including several Argentine presidents and the Prince of Wales. Knighted in 1919 in recognition of his services to the Allies as a Wheat Commissioner during the First World War, he was awarded a baronetcy in 1931 for his leading role in the organization of a major British export exhibition in Buenos Aires.

Herbert's is a story that would have been worth telling even were it not for the fact that he recorded his experiences over many years in a series of detailed and fascinating diaries. The existence of such diaries is, of course, a positive boon to any biographer, as they provide a minute account of the subject's daily activities and permit extraordinary access to his innermost thoughts. Given that Herbert was endowed with a good measure of literary talent, his musings are frequently entertaining as well as enlightening and, to put it simply, make for a jolly good read. I offer no apology, therefore, for putting his journals centre stage and quoting from them liberally throughout this study.

Of course, many other sources were to prove invaluable in preparing Herbert's biography. Chief among these were scrapbooks of press cuttings relating to Herbert's life, two bound volumes of his published writings, his notebooks on agricultural and anthropological topics, and numerous files of personal and business correspondence. It is fortunate that all these documents had survived in the possession of Herbert's descendants, many of whom still reside in Argentina. Most were gathered on my behalf by Thomas Gibson, one of Herbert's grandsons, and others were provided by Minnie Magrane de Boote. To Thomas and Minnie I extend my very sincerest thanks; this book would certainly never have been written without their inspiration, encouragement and unstinting collaboration. A full inventory of documentary sources is included in the bibliography.

I also owe a particular debt of gratitude to the late Geoffrey Gibson. Although we never met and my interest in the Gibson family history did not develop until many years after Geoffrey's death, we shared the conviction that Herbert's experiences should be recorded for posterity. In his last years, Geoffrey began to write the biography of his illustrious grandfather, only for his efforts to be cut short by illness. The few chapters he managed to complete, under the working title 'The Chivalrous Shepherd', helped to shape my view of Herbert's family background and early life.

Father Sir Christopher Gibson, a great-grandson of Sir Herbert and the fourth baronet of Faccombe and Linconia, generously provided electronic copies of the many family papers and photographs in his possession. Other members of the extended Gibson clan who contributed to this project in various ways were Anthea Gibson, Miles Gibson, Robert Gibson, Peter Gibson Mackern, Cecilia Perkins Correa, and John Boote. Thanks to them all. I am also grateful to Michael Corbett for information on Clementina and George Corbett, Herbert's mother and uncle.

Two people deserve special mention for their personal support: Muriel Stewart, for her unwavering enthusiasm for my South American researches, and Katherine Smith, for her friendship and historical insights. Warmest thanks to you both, and to Maisie for keeping me company while I wrote.

CHAPTER 1

FOREBEARS

When Thomas Gibson, Herbert's father, entered his marriage in the family Bible in 1854, he recorded his occupation as 'sheep farmer at Los Ingleses, Department of Ajó, Prov.ce· of Buenos Ayres'. Such a description, while technically accurate, hardly did justice to Thomas's status as the scion of a wealthy Scottish dynasty whose presence in Argentina stretched back thirty-five years, and which would continue to play a prominent role in the commercial and public life of that nation for the foreseeable future.

Towards the end of the second decade of the nineteenth century, John Gibson, a flourishing textile merchant from Garnet Hill, Glasgow, was seeking to expand his operations into emerging markets. Inspired by the favourable trading conditions that followed Argentina's achievement of independence from Spain, he resolved to open a branch there. Prior to 1810, the year in which the bold citizens of Buenos Aires declared their intent to throw off the yoke of colonialism, the restrictive practices of the Spanish authorities had made the Viceroyalty of the River Plate a difficult place for foreign citizens to do business. A handful of British merchants had prospered there, but all were expelled in 1807 following an ill-fated military venture by their countrymen to annex Buenos Aires to the Empire. The backlash from the so-called 'English invasions' was short-lived, however, and some British traders were soon readmitted under special licences granted by Viceroy Liniers. By the outbreak of the revolt against Spain, it is estimated that 124 British citizens were residing in the Viceroyalty, with a total capital of between £750,000 and £1,000,000.[2] With the liberalization of trade that followed independence, the community expanded rapidly, numbering 1,355 by January 1824, and including many artisans and labourers as well as merchants and their clerks.[3]

---

2 H. S. Ferns, *Britain and Argentina in the Nineteenth Century* (Oxford: Clarendon Press, 1960), p. 68.

3 Ferns, p. 76.

By the time John Gibson's interest in Argentina was developing, therefore, the foundations of a substantial and thriving British community were in place. John had been born into a family of small farmers from Bothwell, Lanarkshire, in 1771, and had entered the textile business in association with his cousins, the Dunnetts, in Paisley around 1793. Paisley was just becoming a centre for the manufacture of cotton, wool and muslin goods, and Gibson & Company grew rapidly, setting up overseas branches in Brussels and Singapore. John's reputation as a pioneer among Glasgow's commercial establishment is exemplified by the following anecdote. According to family legend, he returned from a European business trip shortly after the Battle of Waterloo bearing a bank draft from Rothschild of Frankfurt; unfortunately, it proved impossible to redeem the draft in Scotland since nobody had yet heard of the issuer!

In 1796, John Gibson had married Janet Taylor, daughter of a farmer from the Fife village of Ceres. It is thought that twelve children were born of this union between 1797 and 1826, but only the four eldest will feature prominently in our story: John (1797–1828), George (1800–1879), Robert Taylor (1804–1881), and Thomas (mentioned above, 1816–1903). It was John junior who was entrusted by his father with establishing the Argentine branch of the family business. One day in 1818, so the story goes, young John was summoned to the study, where he found his father revolving a globe. Pointing to the Argentine, the elder man declared: 'We will go there.' At the end of that year, John junior embarked upon the long voyage to the River Plate.

On arriving in Buenos Aires, John opened his office in Calle Potosí, importing textiles and exporting local goods such as hides and nutria pelts. The business proved highly profitable and John began to seek opportunities to reinvest his proceeds, settling, like many other members of the mercantile community, on real estate. Before making any purchases, he travelled home in 1822 to win his father's approval for the scheme, which was duly granted. Once back in Argentina, John took advantage of the prevailing low land prices and began to purchase *estancias* (ranches) in rural Buenos Aires Province. It seems likely that the venture was initially one of speculation rather than an attempt to move the company's interests seriously into ranching; indeed, the first estate to be bought, in a wooded area then known as the Montes Grandes, was soon sold on to John and William Parish Robertson as the site for their Scottish agricultural colony.[4] However, John quickly realized that ranching could be a lucrative

---

[4] On the Monte Grande colony, see Iain A. D. Stewart (ed.), *From Caledonia to the Pampas: Two Accounts by Early Scottish Emigrants to the Argentine* (East Linton: Tuckwell Press, 2000) or James Dodds, *Records of the Scottish Settlers in the River Plate and their Churches* (Buenos Aires: Grant and Sylvester, 1897).

business in the early 1820s, and turned his attention to the stocking and management of the new properties. To assist with this, he brought out to Argentina a young employee from the company's Glasgow office, Richard Newton, who would go on to become a wealthy *estanciero* (rancher) in his own right and the first president of the Argentine Rural Society.

In 1824, George Gibson arrived in Argentina to join forces with his brother. Together, they acquired large tracts of land in southern districts of Buenos Aires Province, stretching from just south of the metropolis down to the town of Chascomús and eastwards to the Atlantic coast of Samborombón Bay. The Gibsons' final investment of this period, bought on 7 May 1825, was the Carmen *estancia*, also known as Rincón del Tuyú. This property was located on the southern margins of the territory governed by Buenos Aires; beyond the ranch lay only the domain of the indigenous tribes. Indian raids were a frequent hazard to the early occupants, and among the first provisions sent to Richard Newton when he was appointed manager of the *estancia* were 'gunpowder, two cannons, eight muskets, twenty sabres, lead and stone cannonballs'.[5]

By 1826, the Gibsons owned five *estancias*, more than 60,000 head of cattle, some 4,000 horses, many mules and a few slaves. In November of that year, Robert Gibson set sail from Liverpool to assist his elder brothers in Buenos Aires, having recently qualified in medicine at Edinburgh University. Like many travellers of the era, Robert kept a journal throughout the voyage. In addition to the meteorological remarks and records of the ship's progress typical of the genre, his log contains an account of the captain's death following a 'severe inflammation of the chest, attended with considerable fever'. The poor seaman perished in spite of Robert's best attempts to save him, which included the administration of various medicines and bleeding him 'to a pretty large amount' on two occasions from different arms.[6] Perhaps the most fascinating section of the journal is Robert's description of his first impressions of South America, which includes the following commentary on the ostriches (more accurately, rheas) that abounded in the River Plate region at the time:

> On our journey through the Banda Oriental [the territory lying to the east of the River Plate, now Uruguay], among the many different kinds of birds which we saw, we occasionally fell in with flocks of Ostriches. – These birds are of a grey leaden colour with a large

---

5   Herbert Gibson, *The History and Present State of the Sheep-Breeding Industry in the Argentine Republic* (Buenos Aires: Ravenscoft and Mills, 1893), p. 243.
6   Robert Gibson, 'A Journal of a Voyage from Liverpool to Montevideo and Trip Thence to Buenos Ayres in 1826-27', 5-6 December 1826.

> body set upon very long legs – their necks are also of a great length. The long feathers of the wings and tail are used principally for <u>dusters</u> of furniture – These birds are not to be compared with the <u>African Ostriches</u>, being much smaller, and the feathers not nearly so large nor so beautiful –
>
> There are Ostriches on the Buenos Ayres side of the river also, although not in such numbers, I believe, as in the Banda Oriental – The eggs are very large and the yolk is very good eating, although a little strong tasted.

Until this time, the Gibsons' record in Argentina had been one of sound financial progress. However, shortly after Robert's arrival in 1827, their fortunes took a turn for the worse. All sectors of the economy were feeling the adverse effects of a conflict that had broken out with Brazil over sovereignty of the Banda Oriental. The port of Buenos Aires was blockaded and the Argentine unit of currency, the peso, had undergone a catastrophic devaluation from four shillings to just over one penny. Such circumstances severely compromised the trading side of the Gibsons' business, as they had to pay for imports that escaped the blockade in hard currency (that is, gold), yet received only devalued pesos in the Buenos Aires market. To make matters worse, the ranching aspect of their enterprise was suffering from a particularly severe drought, which had begun in 1824 and continued for around four years. The south of Buenos Aires Province, where the Gibsons' *estancias* were located, was the most severely affected area; it was reported that the 'dry beds of the San Borombón [sic] and Salado rivers were filled with the carcases of dead cattle from bank to bank'.[7]

The combination of economic and environmental calamities could alone have struck a devastating blow to the Gibsons, but these were compounded by John falling into ill health. Suffering from a lung complaint, John, accompanied by Robert, set sail for Scotland in an attempt to recuperate and also with the intention of persuading his father to supply funds to prop up the failing Argentine enterprise. Sadly, John's condition deteriorated into pneumonia during the voyage and he died in April 1828 during a stop at Gibraltar, where he was buried.

John Gibson senior, greatly distressed at the death of his eldest son and troubled by the crisis in the River Plate region, decided to cut his losses, ordering George and Robert to liquidate all their Argentine assets and return home. Selling land was, of course, difficult in the turbulent economic climate, but the brothers eventually managed to dispose of all but the Rincón del Tuyú estate and a smaller area near the Samborombón river. Finding a buyer for the Tuyú

---

7 'Old British and American Firms', *The Standard* (Buenos Aires), 1 May 1930.

ranch proved impossible, as its remote location and low-lying terrain made it an undesirable purchase. The *estancia* was frequently cut off from Buenos Aires by flooding; the alternative was to approach by sea, but landing was made awkward by capricious wind and tides.

By the mid 1830s, the brothers seem to have given up on the idea of selling the land and reconciled themselves to persevering in Argentina as ranchers. Such was the remoteness of Rincón del Tuyú that George Gibson did not even visit it until February 1835. His description of the journey makes clear the difficulties of access:

> The vessel arrived at the mouth of the Salado on Sunday the 8th, but in consequence of a strong wind blowing right into the harbour she could not get out again till Tuesday morning. We were then kept beating about for two days with a head wind, without being able to make a mile in our course. At the end of that time we got a fresh breeze from the North, which sent us spinning along at a good rate, so that in twenty-four hours we were anchored off the coast of the 'Tuyu', 4 or 5 miles distant. Here again we were kept three days before we got into the river or creek, waiting till both wind and water answered, as both at once are necessary to get in. On the bar at the entrance there are seven feet of water at the highest tides, and only about a foot at low tide. When we did get in the wind was again contrary to proceeding up the creek; we therefore started next morning in the boat for the berth the vessel usually occupies, about 15 miles up from the mouth, which we reached in about two and a half hours, and landed on the estancia. We despatched a sailor on foot to the steading, but he met Don Mariano (the manager) and a peon, and we soon had horses and left for the station, a distance of 12 miles by the roundabout road necessary to avoid the deep marshes.[8]

Despite his trying journey, George goes on to express his appreciation of the attractive landscape:

> I was highly delighted with the appearance of the woods, which greatly exceed the idea I had formed of them. [...] They are beautiful, and some of them magnificent, forming many of the finest sylvan scenes

---

8 George Gibson to Robert Gibson, 18 February 1835. Quoted by Herbert Gibson, *Sheep-Breeding Industry*, pp. 248-49. Original in National Library of Scotland (henceforth NLS), Edinburgh, MS 10326.

I ever looked upon. I will try to describe one of these to you, which I believe will answer for the others. Imagine yourself to be in the middle of an immense park about two miles in diameter, bounded with fine woods, not in a continuous line but with open spaces here and there forming delightful recesses, these again bounded by more distant woods, and in the centre of these, stretches of open land with fine circular clumps of trees. In the area of this great park are scattered various clusters of timber, under whose shade if the day be hot you will see cattle standing or lying down on the grass. There are also single trees standing here and there. To complete the scene, a herd of deer bounds across before you, from one wood to another. (18 February 1835)

At the time of George's arrival, the main activities at the *estancia* were the breeding of cattle and horses. A few sheep were kept for food, but, in the words of Herbert Gibson, 'were utterly disregarded' and many 'died with the wool of five or six years on their backs'.[9] This situation was by no means unusual; excluding a few isolated and largely unsuccessful ventures, no serious attempt had yet been made to undertake sheep breeding in Argentina. It was not until the 1840s that sheep began to feature prominently on the landscape of Buenos Aires Province, and the Gibsons, together with a few other British (predominantly Scottish) landowners, were truly pioneers in the field. Before even seeing Rincón del Tuyú for himself, George Gibson had decided to diversify into wool production; on arrival, he quickly set about introducing merino rams to interbreed with the existing substandard stock. In the following months, he further expanded the flock by offering calves to neighbouring ranchers in exchange for ewes.

Around the same period, Rincón del Tuyú began to be known as Los Yngleses (The Englishmen), almost certainly a designation first bestowed upon it by the local population in recognition of its British owners.[10] Notwithstanding its inappropriateness, given their unambiguously Scottish origins, the Gibsons seems to have adopted the new name readily, although Herbert Gibson notes that until 1859 the *estancia* was still listed as Rincón del Tuyú in the company's invoice books.[11]

---

9 Herbert Gibson, *Sheep-Breeding Industry*, p. 248.
10 The letters 'y' and 'i' were frequently interchangeable in older Spanish so some documents record the *estancia*'s name as 'Ingleses', a spelling that follows modern orthography. The traditional 'Yngleses' is favoured by the current owners.
11 Herbert Gibson, 'Agricultural & General Notebook, 1899-1912'

In 1838, the fourth of the Gibson brothers, Thomas, set foot in Argentina for the first time. According to a number of accounts, he had just qualified as an engineer in Glasgow. Which branch of engineering he specialized in and where he learned his trade is unclear, but it seems likely that he would have trained through an apprenticeship. He certainly demonstrated a sound grasp of the requirements of the engineering profession many years later when he gave his son Herbert some career advice:

> I was very glad to learn you were taking a liking to becoming an engineer, which is a grand profession & a very remunerative one. You are but young yet to fix & meantime before fixing you wo'd need to find out if you have the capacity for learning the intricate subjects trigonometry, landsurveying and levelling. That is both the capacity and liking for them. Because you cannot be an engineer without.[12]

Thomas was also a keen and talented artist who would go on to paint some fine views of the Argentine landscape, as well as a self-portrait. Many of his works, numbering around twenty in total, in both watercolour and oils, are still in the hands of members of the Gibson family today.[13]

Between them, the three remaining Gibson brothers, George, Robert, and Thomas, guided their Argentine enterprise through the turbulent decades of the 1830s and 1840s. For some of this period, George Gibson returned to Scotland to take charge of the firm there; Robert, meanwhile, remained principally in the city of Buenos Aires; and Thomas spent much of his time running Los Yngleses, ably assisted by his relative Matthew Dunnett. Both the city and rural sides of the Gibsons' business suffered from the effects of political unrest. Between 1829 and 1852, Argentine politics was dominated by the colossal figure of Juan Manuel de Rosas, a conservative, staunchly Catholic landowner who ruled the developing nation with a rod of iron. His enemies were depicted as 'vile', 'filthy', 'savage' and 'perverse' in government propaganda and were routinely murdered by cut-throat death squads. Despite, or perhaps because of, the repression, there was a vibrant opposition movement, composed chiefly of young, liberal thinkers. Rosas's protectionist policies and open interference in the affairs of

---

12 Thomas Gibson to Herbert Gibson, 21 June 1877. Quoted by Geoffrey Gibson, 'The Chivalrous Shepherd', p. 7. In Thomas Gibson's obituary in *The Standard* (Buenos Aires, 8 December 1903), it is stated that 'as a young man [he] had been engaged in the construction of the first railway from Liverpool to Manchester', but I have been unable to verify this assertion.

13 'La obra pictórica desconocida de Tomás Gibson y la estancia Los Ingleses en el Tuyú', *La Prensa* (Buenos Aires), 15 May 1938.

neighbouring Uruguay also drew Argentina into international conflict, both as a major player in the Uruguayan civil war between the forces of Manuel Oribe, allied to Rosas, and his opponent Fructuoso Rivera, and as an antagonist of British and French schemes to open the region to trade. France first blockaded the port of Buenos Aires between 1838 and 1840, and an Anglo-French fleet did so again from 1845 to 1848.

On two occasions, Thomas Gibson inadvertently became embroiled in the political mêlée. Towards the end of 1839, an anti-Rosas uprising broke out in southern Buenos Aires Province, first in the town of Dolores and then spreading to Chascomús. As one summary of the Gibsons' history records, 'it was at the Estancia Los Ingleses that the last chapter of the famous Southern Revolution of '39 was enacted'.[14] The leaders of this rebellion were not the urban liberals of Buenos Aires, many of whom had now fled into exile in Montevideo or Chile, but the *estancieros* of the south, whose prosperity had been undermined severely by the economic ramifications of the French blockade. Indeed, among the rebels was Gervasio Rosas, younger brother of the dictator, a friend and neighbour of Thomas Gibson. In a letter to his brother George, Robert Gibson gives his view of the situation from the city of Buenos Aires:

> A great many of the principal Estancieros of the south appear to have been in it, as you will observe from the representation they made to the French admiral and besides these there were many more who did not sign that document. From all accounts they appear to have collected about 3000 to 3500 men altogether. They were joined by the officer and troops stationed at the Salado (about 300 men), the troops at the Atalaya without their officer, and they counted upon an officer called Granada joining them with his force, about 600 or 800 veterans (those from the Salado and Atalaya were only militia). This last however, together with Prudencio Rosas, fell upon the insurgents at Chascomús and completely routed them, killing a number of their chiefs.[15]

Despite the close proximity of the rebellion to Los Yngleses, Robert goes on to express confidence that nothing 'will have happened to Thomas or our own people at the Estancia', adding that 'had anything happened to him I should certainly have heard of it, as news of this sort generally travels fast'. Thomas's subsequent account reveals that, while the *estancia* escaped the fighting, it was significantly affected by the aftermath:

---

14 'Old British and American Firms', *The Standard* (Buenos Aires), 1 May 1930.
15 Robert Gibson to George Gibson, 23 November 1839. NLS, MS 10326.

> The insurgents gave battle at Chascomus, and, being defeated, retreated to the coast and encamped upon our place. Here they remained three or four days, getting or taking over 40 steers per diem. Report reached them that the Government army was on their track, and they moved on to Ajó creek, whence they embarked for Monte Video. We, however, anticipating an action and all its consequent disorders, left the head station by night and travelled down to an isolated corner of the *estancia*, taking with us a bullock cart which served as house and store-room. A few days later we heard of the flight of the insurgent army, and returned to the head station. On the same afternoon the whole eastern horizon became serrated by the Government army, 3200 strong, including 400 Indians, the infantry of course mounted; they brought immense troops of spare horses, and had one or two pieces of artillery. The General, Don Prudencia [*sic*; should read 'Prudencio'] Rosas, and his staff, accepted the offer of our house, and the army encamped about the steading. They slaughtered 120 steers upon arrival, the General apologising for not being able to save the skins, as the soldiers needed *carne con cuero* [meat with the skin still attached, a traditional Argentine dish] on the successful termination of the campaign. They remained with us two or three days, consuming over 60 steers per diem.[16]

Robert Gibson's account of the fate of one of the leading rebels plainly illustrates the harsh methods of the Rosas regime: 'Pedro Castelli, one of the principal movers in the affair, was taken in the Montes Grandes [...] and shot, and his head was taken off and sent to Dolores'; he further notes that 'a number of people have been brought into town [...] what their fate will be quien sabe [who knows?]. Rosas surely can't shoot them all' (23 November 1839).

A later incident placed in jeopardy the life of Thomas himself. For much of the 1840s, the export of foodstuffs from Buenos Aires to Montevideo was prohibited, as that city was in the hands of Rosas's enemies. The punishment for transgression of this decree was death. From around 1843, one of the activities at Los Yngleses was the 'boiling down' of sheep carcasses to produce fat for both culinary and industrial purposes. The two grades of fat were classified as *sebo*, which was suitable for human consumption, and *graza* (tallow), which was exported to Europe for greasing industrial machinery and making candles. In 1847, Thomas Gibson obtained an export permit to send *graza* to Europe via the port of Montevideo, but *sebo* was mistakenly entered in some

---

16 Quoted by Herbert Gibson, *Sheep-Breeding Industry*, pp. 27-28.

of the documentation. As a result, Thomas was arrested, charged with attempting to export edible produce, and taken to Buenos Aires as a prisoner. After a few days living under the threat of imminent execution, he was released, partly thanks to the intercession of Gervasio Rosas, who, one must assume, was once again *persona grata* at his brother's court, and partly through the testimony of the expert witnesses who found that the consignment of tallow was unfit for human consumption.

Throughout the 1840s and 1850s, Thomas Gibson worked tirelessly to turn Los Yngleses from a remote and inhospitable backwater into a modern, profitable sheep-breeding concern. The pumas and packs of wild dogs that wrought a terrible toll on the stock were exterminated; Virginia tobacco was planted to make a dip for curing scabies; baths for dipping and presses for wool-baling were constructed, the first of their kind in Argentina. At the same time, constant experimentation to find the breeds best suited to the climate and terrain was the order of the day; following attempts with the Cheviot, Cotswold, Leicester and Romney Marsh varieties, the Lincoln established itself as the most viable breed, both for its adaptability to local conditions and the value of its wool.

On 9 May 1854, Thomas Gibson married Clementina Corbett at a ceremony in Buenos Aires. Clementina (1829-1886) was the daughter of an Edinburgh dental surgeon and granddaughter, on her mother's side, of Robert Spence, who had served as dentist to George III during the King's visits to Scotland. According to Herbert, Thomas and Clementina's fifth child, the union had at first been opposed by his mother's parents, who were appalled at the 'idea of the granddaughter of a court-physician throwing herself away on a penniless farmer', but they later recanted when Thomas told them 'that they measured his land by the square mile and that his flocks numbered over five-thousand'.[17] Doubtless, they would have been even more impressed had they known that by around 1880 Thomas would own some 200,000 sheep and lands stretching from the southern grasslands of Buenos Aires and Pampa Central Provinces to Mendoza and Córdoba in the foothills of the Andes and northwards into the Paraguayan Chaco. It is true that many of Thomas's acquisitions consisted of poor land of comparatively little value, but the proprietor of land well in excess of one million acres could hardly be considered 'a penniless farmer'.

During the 1850s, both George and Robert retired from the Argentine side of the business and returned to Britain, leaving Thomas in sole charge. George married Louise Platton, settled in King's Lynn, Norfolk, and had four children: George, John, Matilda (known as Milly), and Louise. Robert returned to

---

17 Diary of Herbert Gibson, 26 April 1881.

Glasgow, where he lived at 14 Hamilton Park Terrace with his two unmarried sisters, Eliza and Jessie, dying a bachelor in June 1881.[18]

On 25 April 1855, having turned seventeen less than two weeks earlier, George Corbett, youngest brother of Thomas Gibson's wife Clementina, arrived in Buenos Aires to try his hand at *estancia* life. Starting as an apprentice at Los Yngleses, he quickly earned his spurs and, by 1862, the year in which his brother-in-law retired from living in Argentina on a full-time basis, was ready to take over management of the *estancia*. Corbett proved to be a highly capable, if somewhat conservative and cantankerous, general manager. In August 1877, the firm of Gibson Brothers presented him with a gold watch 'as a mark of appreciation of his services in saving flocks of sheep from the floods'.[19] Corbett remained in the post for more than a quarter of a century, before leaving Los Yngleses with his wife Helen, whom he had met on a trip home to Scotland, to run the impressive array of *estancias* he had by then acquired on his own account.

Thomas Gibson's retirement from Argentina in 1862, occasioned by ill health, did little to diminish his involvement in the country and he continued to visit his properties on a regular basis until 1891, at first annually, later every two or three years. By the time they returned to live in Scotland, Thomas and Clementina had four children: Ernest, born in Buenos Aires, 8 July 1855; Maria Spence (known as May), born in Glasgow, 9 June 1857; Hope, born at Los Yngleses, 23 May 1859; and John Constant, born in Buenos Aires, 31 March 1861. Rather than settling his family in one location, Thomas chose to live a somewhat itinerant life, renting furnished properties for a few months at a time, mainly around the Edinburgh area. The motivations for this lifestyle are unclear, although it is reasonable to assume that Thomas was reluctant to tie himself to Scotland so long as he still visited Argentina regularly; indeed, he may even have been contemplating a full-time return there. Moreover, Thomas was known for his penny-pinching ways, so thrift might well have played its part in his reluctance to commit to the purchase of an appropriate family home.

Clementina gave birth to five more children in the following nine years: Herbert, born at Henderson Place, Bridge of Allan, 8 July 1863; Eva, born at Pitt Street, Portobello, Edinburgh, 30 August 1865; Janet Maud (known as Nettie), born at Melville Street, Portobello, 13 September 1867; Florence, born at East

---

18 According to his nephew Herbert, Robert had been 'particularly handsome' as a young man, 'was accounted to be about the most graceful horseman in Buenos Ayres', and 'as is usual with handsome men who die bachelors there is a tale of a girl whom he honoured with his love but who preferred a crusty old party with a good bank book, & there are the thousand and one tales of ladies who fell victim to his comeliness but who loved him in vain'. Diary of Herbert Gibson, 6 June 1881.

19 Inscription on watch now in possession of Michael Corbett.

Brighton Crescent, Portobello, 3 May 1869; and Percival (known as Percy), also born at East Brighton Crescent, 3 June 1871.

By the mid 1860s, Clementina, known affectionately in family circles as 'the little mother', was much worn down by the combination of the hardships she had endured at the remote Los Yngleses and the household's frequent moves after returning to Scotland. Already suffering from a spinal curvature, she nearly lost her life giving birth to Eva and was warned that future children would be born prematurely. As a result, Nettie and Florence were not strong and lived only short lives, dying at the ages of three and a half years and six weeks respectively. The death of Nettie, in particular, had a devastating impact on Clementina, who was pregnant with Percy at the time. Whether because of his mother's emotional collapse, his premature birth or, as one family tale holds, as a result of being drugged by his wet-nurse, Percy suffered from a serious mental handicap. Further beset by childhood ailments, he nonetheless survived to a ripe old age. Herbert, in a letter written to his fiancée in 1895, described Percy thus:

> He was born the last one of my family and is much the youngest. My mother was in the poorest of health and the child was a very sickly plant. He only lived through the united skill of the best doctors in Edinburgh; indeed I recognise now that nature had not intended him to live and what remained was but the shell. In infancy he had one illness after another; and by the time he was three years old it was seen that he was totally lacking in his mental faculties. After some years at home he was taken by my mother to Brighton and there put under the care of a Dr. Scatliff. […] He is quite happy there, but he is nothing but a child, and never will be anything else. […] It is a great blow to my father to have this son.[20]

While we must suppose that Thomas was genuinely affected by the plight of his youngest son, the final sentence may also hint at the taboo regarding mental frailty in nineteenth-century society, which probably contributed to the decision to send Percy to the other end of the country. Certainly, Percy's disability does not seem to have been so severe by modern standards as to require lifelong confinement; one of Thomas's grandsons has even suggested that had it not been for the 'Victorian shame at simplemindedness', Percy 'might well have been happier with a horse on the Pampas'.[21]

---

20 Herbert Gibson to Madeleine Paice, 10 May 1895.
21 Geoffrey Gibson, p. 48.

The other children of Thomas and Clementina displayed the usual range of personalities and aptitudes within a large family. Ernest, a shy, quiet child who loved poetry, suffered under the harsh regime at his boarding school, Dirleton, near North Berwick, and was equally ill at ease when sent by his father to spend a year as an apprentice at the Smith & Wellstood engineering works in Bonnybridge. He subsequently travelled to Argentina to take up the family business, becoming an enthusiastic and knowledgeable ornithologist who corresponded with the renowned W. H. Hudson on the subject of River Plate bird life. May, a somewhat highly strung girl with an exceptionally strong bond to her father, lived a long life troubled by frequent bouts of depressive illness.

Hope, John and Herbert, after starting at Dirleton, all moved to the Norfolk County School on the recommendation of their uncle George, who had been horrified at the conditions Ernest endured. On leaving school, Hope was apprenticed to a company of dock engineers in Sunderland, from where he joined the James Watt Dock at Greenock and was later employed by a London firm on a contract at Kingston, Jamaica. While in the Caribbean, he contracted malaria, from which he suffered for many years after. At varying times, both Hope and John played important roles in managing the Gibsons' Argentinian interests, the former being particularly influential. Hope grew into a kind-hearted, loyal man and proved to be a key ally of Herbert throughout his adult life. John, on the other hand, who qualified as a chartered accountant, seems to have been a rather cold individual who developed into a very capable, hard-nosed businessman and later quarrelled bitterly with his siblings over matters of their inheritance.

According to Boz Donaldson, a childhood friend whose twin sister Alice went on to marry Ernest Gibson, Eva was a 'commanding spirit to whom we all turned for help, advice or information [...] an exceptional girl [...], handsome, mentally quick, clever and original with quite advanced views on subjects which were then [...] at the controversial stage'.[22] Sadly, the vivacious Eva was to die prematurely of appendicitis in 1904, leaving a husband, James Nicolson, the son of a wealthy Edinburgh brewer, and two children, Leslie and Nancie.

As was by no means uncommon for the times, the Gibson children grew up in an environment in which faith played a central part, although, more unusually, the family did not adhere rigidly to one denomination. According to Herbert Gibson, his father was a 'God-fearing Presbyterian';[23] this may certainly have been true in his younger years, but in later life Thomas seems to have favoured the Scottish Episcopal Church. Indeed, Clementina once described him as being 'as much Church of England as Church of Scotland',

---

22 Memoir of Boswell Secundus Donaldson, vol. 1.
23 Diary of Herbert Gibson, 27 April 1881.

adding that 'he likes a warm church where he can hear a practical discourse'.[24] Throughout Herbert's childhood, the family were regular attenders at Sunday worship, frequenting churches of both types, but with an increasing preference for the Episcopalian version. Undoubtedly, Clementina's membership of the latter would have played a role in this. She had been brought up in a staunchly Episcopalian family, although her mother and father later 'defected' to the Established Church of Scotland, blaming the High Church atmosphere of St Paul's in Edinburgh for the decision of one of their sons, William, to convert to Catholicism and become a Jesuit priest. While William's choice of career led to total estrangement from his parents, Clementina remained devoted both to him and her childhood faith.

Thomas Gibson ruled over his family like a true Victorian patriarch. His sons accepted his plans for their futures unquestioningly, even when the chosen path was not to their liking, such as Ernest's engineering apprenticeship. Similarly, there is a story in the family that Hope's ambitions to join the medical profession were suffocated by Thomas's lack of enthusiasm for the lengthy university education involved. One supposes that Clementina too had to bend to her husband's will in most areas of family life. By the late 1870s, relations between the couple seem to have become strained and Clementina's health, both mental and physical, had fallen into a precarious state. At the end of November 1879, Thomas and his eldest daughter May travelled to Southampton to embark for a visit to Buenos Aires, only to be recalled to Edinburgh on account of Clementina having suffered some sort of breakdown. Herbert, still a schoolboy in Norfolk, recorded the incident in his diary: 'Received a letter from May from Edinburgh to say that on their arrival at Southampton they had found a telegram from Hope saying that Mama was so upset that they had better return which they did, May immediately & Papa in a drawing room Pulman [sic] car on Wednesday'.[25]

Letters written by Clementina to Herbert, then in Argentina, in the early 1880s hint at her own unhappiness, Thomas's frustration at being so distant from his Argentine affairs, and a growing tension between the couple:

> Ah! dear how your dear letters bring back the happy days [...]. Things are not always so bright [...] this winter I am finding Papa rather irritable.[26]

---

24 Clementina Gibson to Herbert Gibson, 6 October 1885, quoted by Geoffrey Gibson, pp. 45-46.

25 Diary of Herbert Gibson, 4 December 1879.

26 Clementina Gibson to Herbert Gibson, 31 December 1882, quoted by Geoffrey Gibson, p. 43.

> I see he [Thomas] is worrying very much at his wool no longer finding favour in the Antwerp market.[27]

> You know the father gets very uneasy & anxious about business, if it does not go perfectly right & he is no longer a young man.[28]

> The father is very well but I do know him aged and changed [...] the deafness troubles him & his memory is also bad [...] the father's heart is much out at his beloved Ingleses.[29]

By then, Thomas and Clementina were spending much time apart, he living mainly in Edinburgh and she staying mostly in Brighton to be near Percy. Early in 1885, Thomas purchased an impressive home at 1 Eglinton Crescent, Edinburgh, which Clementina described, in a somewhat disparaging tone, as a 'large grand swagger house'.[30] Clementina seems to have played little or no part in choosing the property, and in a letter written when she returned to Edinburgh later in 1885 for Hope's marriage to Agnes Waddell, it is hard to discern the true nature of her feelings:

> We are <u>swells</u> now real & bona fide, I don't feel like walking in this house, without my nose cocked right up in the air. It's so grand, I feel quite subdued & humble & feel inclined to beg the carpets pardon for walking on them! [31]

Within a matter of weeks, Clementina's mild discomfort turns to despair as she feels that neither her husband nor children welcome her presence in Edinburgh:

> I am sorry to say Bertie neither John, May or Eva are kind to me but the very reverse, & the father tho' he sees & knows it, will not put matters right. It is very hard for me & I am often very lonely. I often wish I was back in Brighton again and near my dear wee Percie.[32]

---

27 Clementina Gibson to Herbert Gibson, no date (probably 1883), quoted by Geoffrey Gibson, p. 43.
28 Clementina Gibson to Herbert Gibson, 7 July 1884, quoted by Geoffrey Gibson, p. 44.
29 Clementina Gibson to Herbert Gibson, no date (probably early 1885), quoted by Geoffrey Gibson, p. 44.
30 Clementina Gibson to Herbert Gibson, no date (probably early 1885), quoted by Geoffrey Gibson, p. 44.
31 Clementina Gibson to Herbert Gibson, 7 September 1885, quoted by Geoffrey Gibson, p. 45.
32 Clementina Gibson to Herbert Gibson, 6 October 1885, quoted by Geoffrey Gibson, p. 45.

> You must have gathered from my late letters, that what should have been my home, was no longer so; I bore the unkindness day after day but saw it must come to an end, as they did not wish me at home.[33]

What happened next, according to Clementina's account, is shocking in its cruelty:

> On the morning of the 15th your father – after consulting his lawyer Mr. Fraser & Dr Halliday Croom of 25 Charlotte Square, who was so unkind to me in my illness of ten months ago – came about 9.30a.m. & told me I must at once pack up my things & bundle neck & crop out of his house that night & go anywhere; Brighton if I chose, or Dr. H. Croom & another man, or Doctor, would come that night & put me in a lunatic Asylum. (25 October 1885)

Faced with this horrific dilemma, Clementina fled to the sanctuary of Brighton with her loyal maid Bella and just £37 given to her by Thomas to pay her expenses. She was met at Brighton station by Dr Scatliff, Percy's guardian, who called in 'one of the best Physicians of Brighton', and both doctors assured her that she was 'perfectly sane' and in no danger of being committed to an asylum (25 October 1885).

Despite her apparent mistreatment in Edinburgh, Clementina is reluctant to lay all the blame at Thomas's door, viewing it instead as the product of his manipulation by some of the children, especially her daughter May:

> I was not wanted in the grand new house; May took the head of the table, held the keys, money etc etc & I was treated with the greatest disrespect; but May, Eva & I am afraid John also worked on your father, who not having much love for me, was easily persuaded & has taken this very grave step, for once turned out, I shall never go back & May by her action in this has taken a fearful responsibility on herself. (25 October 1885)

When Thomas writes to Herbert and Ernest to inform them that he is paying Clementina an allowance of £500 per year (which Clementina later alleged that he cut to £400), he makes no reference to her claims of being forced out under threat of committal and, indeed, expresses the hope that she will return to Edinburgh 'when the irritation with the children – & even myself – passes

---

33 Clementina Gibson to Herbert Gibson, 25 October 1885, quoted by Geoffrey Gibson, p. 45.

away'.³⁴ It seems unlikely that the full story will ever be known: did Clementina exaggerate, or even imagine, the circumstances of her separation, or was she truly the victim of a vile cabal involving ungrateful offspring and a hard-hearted husband? It may be significant that Herbert makes no mention of the episode in his diaries and that references to his father continue to show Thomas in a positive light; perhaps Herbert recognized that in such situations it is unusual for either party to be wholly faultless or scrupulously fair in their version of events. Clementina lived out the short remainder of her life in Brighton, where she died on 30 August 1886.

Thomas remained at 1 Eglinton Crescent, normally with at least one of his offspring in residence. In his final years, his sons and daughters took it in turns to stay with him, a trying experience for them at times as Thomas fiercely maintained his independence and bitterly resented anything that he considered to be interference. Until the very end of his life, he kept up a keen interest in the Gibsons' Argentine operations. He would frequently write to his sons, making enquiries about aspects of the business and offering authoritative, and usually unsolicited, advice. Even small details, such as the exact date on which shearing started at Los Yngleses in a particular season, were of concern to the patriarch. As late as the 1890s, he would not hesitate to reprimand his sons when he considered they had acted unwisely, despite the fact that they were by then experienced hands with a firmer grasp of local conditions and day-to-day affairs than he could possibly have claimed. On one occasion, overcome by frustration at his sons' failure to respond to one of the detailed questions he had asked in an earlier letter, Thomas suggests a method by which such oversights might be avoided in future:

> The best way is to have your pocket pencil in your hand when you read business or indeed any letters, as I do, & note by a stroke on margin anything requiring answer […]; sometimes there will be nothing to ans^r, sometimes 1 or more points. This saves much trouble because we can have little time to read over letters at answering, it is often a bore. You will find this a useful hint, as thus the letters need not be read over at all.³⁵

The rather patronizing tone of the above fragment is to be found in much of Thomas's later correspondence; another notable example is when he gives precise instructions as to how ram lambs should be castrated to avoid mortality:

---

34 Thomas Gibson to Ernest and Herbert Gibson, 14 November 1885, quoted by Geoffrey Gibson, p. 47.
35 Thomas Gibson to Herbert and Ernest Gibson, 24 February 1897.

> The deaths from castration may have been from rashly wrenching out the testicle when the lamb (though small) is just perhaps a fortnight too old for that, in which case it should be cut out as we do with the old lambs. The rule should be if the testicle is 3/8ths and 1/16th of an inch in diameter to cut it out as if it were a big lamb. The men should be so directed from me, and to have patience in the cutting out, suppose that each lamb takes 1½ minutes longer, and indeed humanity requires it.[36]

While Thomas's sons seem to have borne their father's meddling and criticisms of their methods with great patience and good grace, signs of frustration creep into their later correspondence. In February 1899, Hope writes to his brothers from Edinburgh that Thomas 'is carried away in his old age with an exaggerated opinion of himself and a mistaken idea of the youth and ignorance of his sons'.[37] The following month, Hope reports that Thomas's '<u>physical</u> health is good'; the underscoring speaks for itself.

A further trait of Thomas's character, his extreme frugality, is illustrated in his response to a request from his sons for a fresh consignment of tea to be sent out to Argentina:

> I have your request for tea but you are getting it so often that I wish first an explanation of the large consumption before sending it. Since that sent 2 Decr 95 this wod have been the 3rd time in less than 2 years; the first was in 9½ mo^s, then another 6 mo^s it was sent, then this wo^d have been in other 6! When people have much of a thing they are apt to use it too freely.[38]

This recalls an occasion in 1884 when Thomas, like any caring parent, expressed concern for Herbert's health when working outside in bad weather and sent him a 'warm poncho for the cold days'. Nothing remarkable in that, but the postscript to his letter reads, 'Poncho cost $300 wh I charge to your a/c in Edn [Edinburgh]'.[39] In 1895, Herbert makes his own comment on Thomas's increasing miserliness in a letter to his fiancée:

---

36 Thomas Gibson to his sons, 19 September 1898.
37 Hope Gibson to his brothers, 7 February 1899.
38 Thomas Gibson to his sons, 24 November 1897.
39 Thomas Gibson to Herbert Gibson, 8 May 1884.

> The poor father like all men who attain a great lonely old age is becoming a victim to the scars left by his hard-working life; his ideas of economy taught him by a lifetime spent in rebuilding his father's shattered fortune have now become fads of parsimony which he preaches at all hours.[40]

For a man in his eighties, Thomas enjoyed fairly robust health until the final months of his life. Indeed, apart from one or two bouts of something like influenza, the only genuine cause for concern among the family seems to have been an aggressive growth in an unspecified location, which was removed at the end of 1898:

> The surgical operation was successfully performed y'day, and altho' the father had a restless night last night he has no fever and the wound (as well as his general health) are very satisfactory.
> The growth had developed with great rapidity during the last few days, and the portion removed was larger than I had expected. It was about 1½" long by say ¾" wide and as there is not only a main artery but about half a dozen smaller vessels at the spot which had to be severed, it became necessary to give him chloroform. He was under it about a quarter of an hour. Suffered no pain: but the vessels showed great vascular activity and generally speaking the result of the operation has gone to prove that he is organically as sound as a bell, has a better circulation than he professes, and a vast amount more vitality than I had given him credit for.[41]

By 1899, it is clear from his correspondence that Thomas was becoming quite frail: some of his letters were dictated; the handwriting of those that were not is rather spidery and difficult to read. In terms of content, the letters are coherent enough, but reveal a man ever more obsessed with minutiae. In 1898, Hope, John and Herbert had appointed their father Administrator of the Gibson properties with an honorarium of £750 per annum. Rather than accept this gesture in the spirit it was intended, as a commemoration of the sixtieth anniversary of his arrival in Argentina, Thomas seems to have interpreted it as an invitation to redouble his efforts to oversee as many aspects of the business as possible. In rather ungenerous fashion, one of his first actions in this new capacity was to cut the commission payable to Gibson Brothers, the city branch of the firm,

---

40 Herbert Gibson to Madeleine Paice, 11 June 1895.
41 Hope Gibson to Ernest and Herbert Gibson, 12 December 1898.

for acting as agents for the family *estancias*. Ernest Gibson writes scathingly to his brothers of the unwelcome effects of Thomas's new position, which seem to have included a considerable boost to his ego:

> Your sudden and unexpected change as to an allowance of £750 a year to the father as 'Administrator' is suitably rewarded by him in that capacity in his ultimatum cutting down our commission by 1/3. Your homage to him in connection with his Jubilee has so turned his head that he tenders his advice on such subjects as the recent strike to the Archbishop of Canterbury and the Editor of the 'Times'.[42]

Thomas continued in similar vein right to the end, his remarkable life coming to a close in 1903 in its eighty-seventh year. His obituary in the leading English-language newspaper of Buenos Aires hailed him as 'one of the last, perhaps the very last, of the early British residents who were contemporary with those who had fought for the independence of the country' and records that General Bartolomé Mitre, one of the great intellectual figures of nineteenth-century Argentine politics, on hearing of some of Thomas's early experiences in the country, once remarked that 'he, too, has been a defender of the "patria" [homeland]'.[43] This is a fitting note on which to close our account of the Gibson ancestry; the forthcoming chapters will reveal the extent to which Herbert not only lived up to, but also surpassed, his father's example as a loyal friend and servant of the Argentine nation.

---

42 Ernest Gibson to Gibson Brothers, Buenos Aires, 13 February 1898.
43 'The late Mr. Thomas Gibson', *The Standard* (Buenos Aires), 8 December 1903.

CHAPTER 2

SCHOOLBOY

'Memoranda I bought this book at that shop on the South Bridge opposite the University' (10 September 1879). Thus opens the first extant volume of Herbert Gibson's diaries. The long summer vacation was coming to a close; five days later, sixteen-year-old Herbert would entrain south to return to the Norfolk County School at Elmham, near King's Lynn, where he was a boarder.[44] Why Herbert chose this particular date to commence recording his everyday experiences, a habit that would last throughout his lifetime, is unclear; we do know, however, that he had dabbled with the diarist's art in the past, but on an irregular basis, and none of his earlier writings have survived. In reflective mood some years later, Herbert wrote:

> It was after a few desultory efforts in very early boyhood that I first resolved to keep a diary of my life: such a diary as would far surpass the minuteness of Pepys or the comprehensiveness of Evelyn. Half afraid lest my future biographer should lose some of the details of my life, & not having perfect understanding of all things from the very first, miss some of the most salient points in my career, I resolved to furnish him with what should be a very olio of my existence.
>
> From 1878–1879 I kept a small pocket book, in which I pencilled every day the most noteworthy events of the preceding one. In 1879 I blossomed into a regular diarist, purchasing when home for the summer holidays, a substantial note book with a brass clasp. How well do I remember that occasion! A sixpenny piece was to me a very

---

44 The Norfolk County School was founded in 1873 to serve the educational needs of the sons of farmers and artisans. It closed in 1895, but was re-established briefly in 1901 by E. H. Watts. After Watts' death, the school was turned into a home for orphans and destitute boys under the charge of Dr Barnardo, and was used for the training of selected boys for a life in the Royal or Merchant Navy.

valuable coin, and when I invested it in the small stationers shop on the South Bridge Edinburgh, I felt my bosom swell with pride in the sacrifice of wealth for honour! (3 April 1888)

As well as giving the history of his journals, this passage reveals an awareness on Herbert's part that he would go on to lead a sufficiently interesting and significant life to one day warrant the attentions of a biographer. Whether this was the product of a sense of destiny or simply youthful vanity is unimportant; it shows a young man confident of his future and ability to make his mark on the world. Throughout all Herbert's diaries, there runs the impression that they were never intended as solely private documents, but rather as a record for posterity, with the conviction that the author's life story would one day reach a wider audience.

Returning to 1879, the opening pages of the diary are filled with Herbert's preparations for returning to school: packing, acquiring a new set of 'tails', and receiving his allowance (twenty shillings) for the term ahead. En route to the school he calls, as he often did, on his Uncle George's family at King's Lynn and quips that 'the Kings were not at Lynn but a young lady – a Miss Leslie I think – was there' (15 September 1879). Life at the Norfolk County School seems to have proceeded at a leisurely pace, leaving the boys with plenty of time for recreational activities, such as bathing in the lake in summer, skating in winter, and visiting the village shop in Elmham. On these excursions, Herbert and his friends frequently bought fruit and cakes to supplement their diet, sometimes consuming prodigious quantities:

> Bought some apples, nuts etc. I was seized with a tremendous appetite and eat [sic] 11 good sized apples, 1½ pints nuts, two Dilly buns, 25 pears, and a huge hunk of cake when I got home. I ate a very good tea after it all. (17 September 1879)

> Went down to Elmham again with Putty. Bought <u>splendid</u> greengages at 4^d per lb and had 5lbs bet. us. Mr Watson [the Reverend William Watson, Headmaster of Norfolk County School] told us that we had bought 5lbs of belly ache. Sour grapes! (23 September 1879)

On other occasions, Herbert's voracious quest for fruit was satisfied by collecting plums and damsons on walks along country lanes, often in the company of one of his best friends, Harry Brereton. Schoolwork does not figure very prominently in his diary, except around examination times, but there are frequent reports on cricket and rugby matches. Another regular activity, gathering firewood, came to a tragic end in October 1879:

> Went out carting in the afternoon. We first went to Fulcher's and got a waggon. We then took it to the field close to Broom Green bridge which – the field – belongs to Mr. Nicholson. Having got half a load, we proceeded home but were told we might get some faggots from a field which is some little way off Broom Green. Having taken all there was we started home again, running down the hills and walking sharply. As we got to the entrance of the drive leading to the school, we started running again but this time the boys got so excited that they tore along at a tremendous pace. The little fellows began to lag, stumble and fall. I tripped over a boys [*sic*] leg and fell and just narrowly escaped being run over. Savory L was saved by Loynes who was in the shafts steering the waggon clear of him. Lloyd was saved in a similar way tho' he would have nevertheless been killed had he not turned head over heels backwards and got clear. Charlie Durrant also tumbled and was nearly run over, but little Wilson, whom nobody noticed, fell and was instantly under the wheels. Both of the wheels went over him and left him shrieking. (11 October 1879)

Poor Wilson was carried into the school and the doctor summoned, who duly set the boy's dislocated thigh. Initially, it seemed that Wilson's injuries were not life-threatening, but at breakfast the next morning one of the masters announced his death 'from some internal hurt' (12 October 1879). Understandably, the mood among the boys was one of gloom, but Herbert took solace from the peaceful manner of Wilson's passing:

> He died easily, he had been kissing Miss Fulcher [the nurse] and she saw that the end was close at hand. Mrs. Watson [the headmaster's wife] who was in the room rushed off to fetch Mr. Watson, but she had scarcely got beyond the door before the little boy kissed Miss Fulcher once more and then turning on his side he died. (12 October 1879)

An inquest was held the next day and Wilson's demise recorded as accidental death, although, according to Herbert, the 'jury decided that the boys should not have been allowed so heavy a waggon' (13 October 1879).

The following Sunday, the headmaster preached an emotional sermon (nearly breaking down in the process), in which he expressed the view that 'grief was a laudable thing', but implored the boys 'to take a lesson from Wilson's death and think that he is in heaven' (19 October 1879). The sermon was subsequently printed and a copy distributed to each boy (26 October 1879).

Among Herbert's other extracurricular activities, there featured singing in the choir, contributing to production of the school magazine, *The Norfolcian*, and participating in something known as 'penny readings'. The latter took place at seemingly irregular intervals, usually on a Wednesday evening, and consisted of a session of music and recitations by the boys, masters, and occasionally masters' wives. Herbert records the programme of one particularly successful event:

>   Song – May day – choir
>   Reading – Handy Andy – H. Hickman
>   Song – Hearts of Oak – Doy
>   Recitation – Popping the Question – W. Hilton
>   Song – A warrior bold – Mr. Sharp
>   Song – The Iron founders – Choir
>   Reading – Dora – Mr. Holt
>   Song – Trab, Trab – G. Wingate
>   Recitation – Vulgar boy – C. J. Lownds
>   Song – As I'd nothing else to do – Mrs. Holt
>   March pianoforte – Roll Call – A. Beck
>   (12 November 1879)

Apart from the headmaster, the Rev. William Watson, the teachers do not play a particularly prominent role in Herbert's schoolboy recollections. The former is portrayed as a kindly, paternal figure in the main, although prone to occasional bouts of temper with little apparent provocation. Herbert records:

> Watson got in a wax with me for no mortal reason. (18 November 1879)

> Was on the Saturday roll for late for the 5 p.m. roll. Mr. Watson was in an awful wax. Set me 250 lines. Let every one off but me. Let me off 150 eventually. […] Mr. Watson spoke very kindly to me at seven o'clock however. (22 November 1879)

> Late in the morning and Mr. Watson looked very black. Got late again for morning lessons. Mr. Watson got blacker and my face being very

clean the reflection of his face on mine caused him to accuse me of dirtiness. (7 December 1879)

In December 1879, Herbert sat the so-called Cambridge Exam, a series of externally examined papers covering the whole school curriculum. It is at this point in the diaries that we begin to discern that young Herbert is a pupil of considerable academic ability who performs creditably across the board:

> Strange to relate we began the exam. punctually at two with the same examiner Mr. Marshall. Both our papers were easy and I am tolerably satisfied with my performance. Awful hard work in the evening!! of course!!!! (15 December 1879)

> Arithmetic and Shakespeare in the morning. Arithmetic was hard and too many sums for the time, Shakespeare was pretty easy. Euclid in the afternoon, very easy. (16 December 1879)

> Latin, Geography and Algebra, all pretty easy papers. (17 December 1879)

> Latin Grammar, and French. I believe I am plucked in my Grammar for Mr. Marshall piddled up the time and all of a sudden I discovered that I had only 5 minutes to spare. I scribbled fast but had not time to finish my analysis. (18 December 1879)

> Drawing from the flat, Composition, History. Drawing from the flat very easy. (19 December 1879)

> Drawing. Did a passing paper but shaded it on the wrong side through carelessness, which I am afraid will put my candle out. (20 December 1879)

When the results are about to be announced the following term, Herbert appears understandably nervous, but is relieved to discover that he is among the top performers in a strong showing by his school:

> At 12.20 p.m. Watson came in to the class room where Brisbois was taking us. He asked permission to have us all in the schoolroom, and being assembled there he brought in the class lists of the Cambridge

> Exam. I felt very blue. Watson went on to say that though the standard had been raised, still the list is very creditable to us. Only two seniors had passed. Brereton and myself. I felt considerably relieved, though I was very sorry for poor Harry. In the juniors, Garrett M had got first class honours, Girling had got second, Cooper, Large, Bird & Bulcher R. S. had third, and there were 19 passes. I think it was a most unexpected list. I never expected half these boys to pass. (15 March 1880)

Immediately after finishing the final paper of the 1879 Cambridge Exam, Herbert left the school for the start of the Christmas holidays, spending a few days with his cousins in King's Lynn before travelling on to Edinburgh. Two notable events, one of a family nature and the other of wider significance, occupy much of Herbert's thoughts around the turn of the year. The first is a leg operation carried out on Herbert's brother John, the second a national tragedy:

> The operation. A nurse, Drs. Spence and Balfour and Mr. Peddy and an assistant. Such a sensation, John the coolest in the house. The doctor came down to say it is all right. The doctors went up 12.13, came down 12.54. John complains, a good deal, of pain.
>
> Yesterday there happened one of the most fatal accidents that ever occurred in Scotland. A very high gale was blowing, so fierce that several Dundee gentlemen went to see if the 7.20 train would venture across the Tay bridge. They saw the lights of the train enter the south west end of the bridge and come along a little distance. Just then a fierce blast came down the valley. The watchers could hear nothing for the roar of the wind, but they saw a brilliant light fall and presumed it to be the coals out of the engine fire. Then a distant rumble came across the water.
>
> Sir Thomas Bouch with several engineers and others left Edinburgh at 12.25 a.m. this morning for the bridge.
>
> The number supposed to have been drowned was 300. (29 December 1879)

By the next day, it has become clear that the casualty figure from the Tay Bridge disaster is much lower than initially feared:

> Happy to say that the number surmised to have been drowned and killed has been reduced from 300 to about 75. The Queen telegraphed

to Edinburgh yesterday enquiring particulars. It appears that 13 great spans have been broken, this makes a distance or gap of 1000 yards. One body of a woman supposed to have been in the train was washed ashore further up the firth. (30 December 1879)

As an engineer, Herbert's brother Hope was much excited by the bridge collapse and set off for Dundee to see the sight for himself. The catastrophe seems to have provoked a rather different mood of melancholy reflection in Herbert and likely influenced the moralizing tone of his diary entry for Hogmanay:

Last day of the year. This ought to be a day of thought. How many will signalize the last day of the year by getting intoxicated and hail the advent of the new year from the very street gutter. (31 December 1879)

During the holidays, Herbert devoted much of his time to trawling Edinburgh's second-hand bookstalls, indulging his developing passion for antiquarian volumes:

Went out book buying and got a good copy of Ovid's Metamorphosis [*sic*] also a life of Cicero (27 December 1879)

Bought a volume of the Citizen of the World 1776, which should be very valuable but it only cost me 1^d. (30 December 1879)

Went out as usual a tour round the bookstalls and picked up the 2nd volume of Robertson's History of Scotland under Mary of Scots & James VIth. (5 January 1880)

Went my usual tour. Bought a Winchester School book 1670 and the first volume of Plutarch's Lives. (6 January 1880)

Bought a large book containing a translation of Josephus for 1/3 which I consider very cheap. My little library has now mounted up to 12 volumes. (9 January 1880)

After returning to Norfolk for the new term, Herbert kept up his interest in old books by beginning to examine the Holmes Collection kept in the school board room:

> Went in to the Board room and looked at the old books. There is enough there to interest me for months. I notice that they pronounce Caius Col. Key's col. because it was founded in the XVIth cent. by a Dr. Kaye or Caius. (14 February 1880)

Over the course of the next nine months, Herbert worked intermittently at compiling a catalogue of the collection. He also became increasingly involved in preparing issues of the school magazine:

> Went in to Mr. Sharpe's study and assisted him in getting the Norfolcian ready. It is to be sent off to-night, the proof sheet will be sent on Wed. and the paper come out on Sat. (14 February 1880)

Life in the school continued at the same leisurely pace as before. Although he never openly says so, one gets the impression that Herbert is sometimes bored, reduced to filling idle days with futile activities, such as the following:

> I amused myself by trying to kick up to the lamp shade in the prefects [*sic*] room, and almost succeeded. The lamp is about 6ft 3inc off the ground. (13 February 1880)

In March 1880, Herbert was embroiled in a serious dispute with the headmaster over the issue of bullying. As a prefect, one of Herbert's responsibilities was to protect the boys in his dormitory from abuse. The Rev. Watson, however, accused Herbert, unfairly in the latter's view, of turning a blind eye to the victimization of one younger, vulnerable pupil by failing to investigate or report an incident at once. Herbert seems to have done little wrong and the humiliation Watsons' heaped upon him in front of his peers, without first having established all the facts of the case, could be considered a form of bullying in itself. Herbert records the headmaster's harsh words on entering the classroom:

> "Gibson you have woefully failed in your duty as a prefect. You have been placed in charge of a room and have permitted a small boy to be bullied there. I will say a boy who has allowed this has shown himself unworthy of his place; I will go further and say a boy who has allowed this is a <u>coward</u>." And so on all to the same effect. (8 March 1880)

Herbert finds Watson's next action, the appointment of another pupil as senior prefect, particularly hurtful:

> "James I make you senior prefect, you are a big boy and I hope you will do well in your office." I felt that. I who have been here 4½ years longer, am 1½ years his senior with respect to wearing a tassel [the mark of a prefect], am head boy of the school and have never been in a serious scrape, was passed over for an accusation that had not yet been proved. It was a hasty step and I blame Watson for it. (8 March 1880)

Only after this snub is Herbert taken to the headmaster's study and allowed the opportunity to defend his actions. Several pages of his diary are taken up by his refutations of the charge against him and it seems that Watson's attitude towards him soon mellows: 'Watson is very kind to me. I believe he regrets what he has done a little' (9 March 1880). A week later, the headmaster speaks to Herbert about the incident again in a much gentler fashion and suggests that his failing was 'only a little looseness, perhaps mere good nature in not being more vigilant' (16 March 1880). Watson extends the olive branch further by explaining why he chose James as senior prefect and hinting strongly that Herbert will soon fall heir to the position: '"James leaves at Midsummer", and then he laughed & said he couldn't speak plainer' (16 March 1880). We also learn that Thomas Gibson had written to Watson to complain about him calling his son a coward, a charge that Watson tries to evade by claiming that what he said was not directed at Herbert personally but to the boys in general (17 March 1880). Whatever the truth, the whole affair then seems to have reached a natural end and Herbert's relationship with the headmaster returned to its previously amicable state.

Soon Herbert's thoughts turned to politics and the forthcoming general election. His interest was whetted by attending a luncheon given by his aunt in King's Lynn to some leading local Conservatives:

> Came to Lynn. [...] Aunt had a swell luncheon at which were Sir L. Jarvis, Lord & Lady Claude Hamilton M.P., Hon Bourke M.P. and others. Lady Claude Hamilton is very pretty. (25 March 1880)

On 30 March, just two days before the election, Herbert attended a rally:

> Went to the theatre to hear a Conservative meeting. Some of the speeches were capital but I did not think much of either of the two

> candidates speaking. Some of the Liberals got in towards the end & created a disturbance. (30 March 1880)

The excitement of polling day is overtaken by disappointment, however, as the scale of the Conservative defeat emerges and Gladstone is swept to power in place of the incumbent Disraeli:

> Polling day. The Cons. are very quiet but the Liberals go about with flying colours. However on dit that the Conservatives are already 400 ahead.
>
> 8.30 p.m. Perfidious rumour! After waiting close on 1 hour and a half we hear that Sir William Ffolkes (L) is head of the poll, 2. Hon Bourke (C), 3. Lord Hamilton (C), 4. Lockwood (L). Poor Hamilton! He has represented Lynn for 11 years, and is now superseded by that jackass Ffolkes. (1 April 1880)
>
> Liberals are gaining everywhere. Poor Sir James Bain (C) is altogether out of it at Glasgow, being last of 5, 3 of whom were L and 2 C. (3 April 1880)

A few days later, Herbert's place as the best pupil in the school was confirmed when he topped the mark list for the internal examinations: 'Order of the exam read out, I am first 960 marks, 2nd Garrett M 914, 3rd Girling 700, 4th Hilton 665, 5th James 620' (8 April 1880). He retained his position with even greater ease in the next round of exams: 'I am first in the school by the last exam, having kept my place with 155 marks to spare' (24 July 1880). Further proof of his intellectual capacity is found in his victories over the headmaster at chess: 'Played two games of chess with Mr. Watson, and beat him both times' (28 April 1880).

Herbert generally fared less well at games, performing modestly at rugby, slightly better at cricket, and participating keenly but without any great distinction in athletics: 'Ran the 220 but stopped in the middle (this is rather Irish) as my knees were sore from my being unused to practice. I ran the mile however in very fair time viz 6.20 secs, for I did not take my coat off' (30 April 1880). Although he briefly broke into the first XI at cricket, his chief role when the school played external opponents was to write match reports for publication in *The Norfolcian*.

At the end of June 1880, Herbert received news that he had been granted a significant academic accolade by his school: 'Yesterday I heard that I had got the Prince of Wales Scholarship. Of course it was a very pleasant surprise to me' (27 June 1880). This appears to have been awarded to the pupil who had performed best in the Cambridge exams. He had a long wait for his financial reward, however, for the letter sent by the clerk of the Norfolk County School Association with the £10 cheque is dated 25 January 1881, by which time Herbert had left school![45]

The Prince of Wales Scholarship was probably the most important prize Herbert received as a schoolboy, but was far from being his only honour. Extant letters from the School Association's clerk show that he also received the Marquis of Cholmondeley Exhibition (14 January 1879) and the Wellingham Exhibition (15 January 1880), both worth £5.[46] During his final term at the school, he scooped numerous academic prizes and was awarded 'the Bible' by the votes of his peers:

> The Bible was voted for today by all the VI & Remove and they did me the honour to award it to me voting being 27 for me 3 for Girling 1 for Beck and 1 for Winearls, the latter of whom I voted for myself. (4 October 1880)

> Speech day! [...] I had to go up 7 times, 5 for prizes, 1 for bible 1 for medal. [...] There were some more speeches by various long winded gentlemen but I did not listen to them. The only thing I remember was that some one advocated the exceedingly brilliant notion of having boys and girls together in one school. (13 October 1880)

As the end of the summer term of 1880 approached, Herbert was struck down by a debilitating bout of rheumatism. He recorded this in detail in the pages of his diary, thus establishing a precedent of describing closely the ailments that afflicted him throughout life, most of which were nothing more serious than colds or the occasional toothache:

> Had a bullfight in the night and I, very foolishly, lay on the top of my bed in nothing but my night-shirt. I do not mean that I generally lie under my bed, but I lay on the bed outside the clothes. I got into bed stiff in my shoulders. (29 June 1880)

> I had a bathe at 3.30 thinking that it would do me good. I might have taken warning that there was something beyond mere stiffness in me,

---

45 J. S. B. Glasier to Herbert Gibson, 25 January 1881.
46 J. S. B. Glasier to Herbert Gibson, 14 January 1879 and 15 January 1880.

> for once or twice a sharp pain shot through my shoulder. However, in I went. I could not use my arms, but I swam about a little time on my back or chest without my arms. When I came out my shoulders were extremely painful, so that I could scarcely lift my arms. I got dressed in about an hour and went up the hill. [...] Went to bed with my belly full, and my back sore. (30 June 1880)
>
> I got up with difficulty but was obliged to go to bed soon after. My rheumatism is very bad now in the shoulders, just as if the blades were broken. I had a mustard plaster on for some time. (1 July 1880) The doctor saw me & made me get up. That will not do much good for I am scarcely any better than I was yesterday. (2 July 1880)
>
> Through practising cricket my rheumatism is becoming much better. (13 July 1880)

By 25 July, Herbert had recovered sufficiently to attend the final Sunday High Table supper of the school year and pass humorous comment on this tradition:

> Went to the high table to supper where there was a tremendous squash, 18 of us seated round a table which could not be more than 8ft by 6ft. I have gone to supper at the high table every Sunday both this term and last.
>
> In case I may forget what this high table was when I grow older, I may state that it is not any higher than any other table but derives its name from the fact that the masters or high people sit there. Now every Sunday evening there is a goodly spread on this table, consisting of beef and tarts; and Mr. Watson always asks some happy beings to come and eat. The masters never eat anything on these nights (except tart which being unwholesome for boys they demolish with a kindly interest for their welfare) but look on with curiosity as people do when seeing the wild beasts fed at a menagerie. (25 July 1880)

Two days later Herbert is en route home for the long summer vacation, completing the journey in a single day by getting up at 5 am and reaching Edinburgh at 9 pm. He has just enough time over the next few days to do some general shopping and complete his usual tour of the bookstalls before the family decamp en masse for a rented house in North Berwick:

Went into town and got measured for clothes, also had my hair cut. (28 July 1880)

Went round the book stalls and picked up an Algebra 1736, and a book on law with Adam Smith's bookplate in it.

> ADAM SMITH

How simple it is! As the book only cost 4d it would be a haul for some collector of bookplates. (29 July 1880)

Everything in a turmoil for we leave for N. Berwick today. All the house is shut up and Mama Papa & I lunched in the hall. May, Eva & Percie went down in the morning. Mama with the rest of us went by the 2.20 train. Very crowded. Arrived at N. Berwick at about 3.30. Like the new house very much. We have a capital sea view. (31 July 1880)

Even the family cat makes the trip and promptly causes great consternation by vanishing, probably keen to explore his summer territory. To the relief of all, and especially Clementina, he turns up again the next evening:

Budge the cat which has looked very shy ever since we brought it down, made its escape at 11 p.m. (31 July 1880)

Great lamentations over the loss of Budge. [...] At about 9 p.m. Mama cried out "there's my Budge" & rushed into the garden. I followed and there was Budge on the top of the wall. It looked half inclined to run away again but however it was captured. Universal rejoicings. (1 August 1880)

Herbert's main holiday activity was playing golf, punctuated by long walks along the coast and the occasional excursion further afield. Hardly a day went by without him heading to the links to get in at least one practice round (much needed on the evidence of his errant aim and decidedly mediocre scoring):

> Got my clubs and commenced playing by myself; enjoyed it immensely. At the first start off I broke my driver, which is very slim and long. Went over the four mile course three times. (3 August 1880)
>
> Golfing all day. My average per hole is 7 5/8. (5 August 1880)
>
> Played golf most of the day. (9 August 1880)
>
> Got up before breakfast to golf and broke my golf iron. Knocked about the place all day. (14 August 1880)
>
> As usual played golf & unfortunately also as usual I broke a golf club. (18 August 1880)
>
> Played golf and succeeded better than usual. Nearly knocked a boys [*sic*] head off as I can not aim straight. (30 August 1880)
>
> Played my last game of golf for this year. […] My average of averages in golf is 6 1193/10710 per hole. (11 September 1880)

On a walk, Herbert passes Dirleton, where he had attended school for a brief spell eight years earlier, but states that he 'did not recognise much' (8 August 1880). Probably the highlights of this holiday are two grand picnics, one on the Isle of May and the other at an artificial lake:

> Went to the Isle of May in a small tug. The vessel was overcrowded and very uncomfortable. Rounded the Bass Rock where there are myriads of Solan geese. Picnic'd on the Isle of May. The water was intensely clear. Stewed in the sun coming home. (12 August 1880)
>
> A !Picnic! 16 of us started squashed up in a drag for a place 13 miles off. Songs on the way also wasps buns and heat. Arrived at our terminus, an artificial lake surrounded by trees etc. Very beautiful, full of lemonade bottles, paper bags and gooseberry skins. Picniced [*sic*]. Then boating and tea. Drove home, more wasps, songs, & more room for I was on the box. "Enjoyed the whole thing immensely." (19 August 1880)

By 13 September, Herbert was returning to school to begin his final term. Back in Norfolk, he resumed his customary activities: a lot of doing nothing productive, a bit of sport, and continuing to work his way through the school's old book collection:

> Stayed in and intended to do some writing but played marbles instead. (30 September 1880)

> Did nothing except getting turned out of the classroom by Mr. Aborn for not working. (2 November 1880)

> Paid a visit to the Holmes Collection of Old Books for the 2nd time this term the 1st being yesterday when I got the keys.
> In 'Religio Medici' a 12mo volume 1659 I noticed amongst the advertisements 'The Counter Scuffle and the Counter Ratt.' Now in the Antiquary for August this year I notice this book mentioned by C. Walford as one of the books which he never expects to see and gives the date 1670. But a correspondent in November mentions that he has a copy & that the 1st ed. came out in 1628. If there have been so many editions why is it so rare? (25 November 1880)

> Had a game of [rugby] football. I kicked 2 goals & a try. The second goal was a close thing; Faulke was placing it and I ran forward to show him how to place it; he thinking I was going to kick laid it down & I had to kick it standing still, however it was a goal. I always have thought that in trying to kick goals the great mistake is kicking so hard; the object is not to send the ball a great distance but to send it over the goal bar, a fact which most players forget. (29 November 1880)

> My catalogue of the Holmes Collection of Old Books which I commenced in the middle of last term and got half way through was finished today. (30 November 1880)

> Did nothing and it took me the whole afternoon to do it. (7 December 1880)

The most significant event of this period is the arrival of a letter from his father, proposing that Herbert's future after leaving school should lie in Argentina:

> In the evening I had two letters one from pater and one from the mater. The paters [*sic*] had an offer in it to send me to S. America in

> October (he did not say whether he meant 1880 or 1881). The reason he gave me was that he now owned 9 tracts of unstocked land the smallest of them 15 square miles. And that Ernest was not enough by himself to be able to stock them, so the pater wishes me to go over, learn the business and help him. (8 October 1880)

After very brief consideration, Herbert wrote back the next day accepting the proposition and enquiring exactly when he would depart: 'I wrote a letter to the pater in which I accepted his offer. I shall know by Wed. night whether I am to sail this year or next' (9 October 1880). He soon received confirmation that he was not to set out until the following year: 'Oct. of next year of course. You will not return to Elmham after Xmas, but attend some spring lectures in Edin[burgh] & perhaps learn Spanish'.[47]

Herbert left Norfolk County School for the last time at the start of the Christmas holidays, immediately after completing his final exam. He expresses disappointment at the send-off he received from the headmaster, but looks back upon the years he had spent at the school with fondness:

> I had only time to say a hurried goodbye to the masters. Mr. Watson was sitting at the far away end of the exam. room. He merely shook hands with me and said goodbye. Perhaps considering that I had been under him for 8½ years we might have been a little more intimate. But I was always shy and reserved and I may have appeared to him taciturn and sulky. It was a clear frosty night and the moon was full. The old school stood out clearly in the moonlight as we drove past it on the road to the station. I already felt that I had said goodbye to the happiest days of my life. (17 December 1880)

As Herbert's grandson Geoffrey would go on to write, 'anybody claiming schooldays as the happiest of their life must be suspect of filtered memory or a miserable existence thereafter', although there is no reason to believe that Herbert suffered from either of these afflictions.[48] It may be significant that Herbert never returns to eulogize his schooldays and it certainly seems that he derived greater contentment and fulfilment from some of his subsequent activities, despite the burdens that go with adulthood. While we may attribute Herbert's hyperbole partly to his emotional state on reaching one of life's milestones and partly to his

---

47 Thomas Gibson to Herbert Gibson, 11 October 1880, quoted by Geoffrey Gibson, 'The Chivalrous Shepherd', p. 13.

48 Geoffrey Gibson, 'The Chivalrous Shepherd', p. 7.

youth and inexperience of the world, it suggests at least that his time at Norfolk County School was more pleasant than that endured by many contemporaries at similar establishments.

Having returned to Edinburgh, Herbert was left with some ten months to fill as a 'gentleman at large' before his scheduled departure for Argentina to 'commence business' (31 December 1880). For the first few months of 1881, he filled his time by writing sketches and poems and sending them off to various publications, chiefly *The North British Advertiser* and *The Ladies' Journal*, and by attending lectures on Natural Philosophy and English Literature at Edinburgh's Watt Institute:

> Wrote a poem of 23 verses entitled Retaliation and sent it off to the N. B. Advertiser. (29 January 1881)

> Commenced attendance of lectures on N. Philosophy at the Watt Instit^e. (2 February 1881)

> Came home & wrote 'The true aspect of a Picnic' a sketch which I think rather good. (28 February 1881)

> Yesterday my 'T. A. of a Picnic' appeared in the Ladies Journal. (5 March 1881)

> Went to the lecture as usual. Subject "Longfellow and Tennyson". There is to be an essay written for a prize; time given 3 weeks; subject "The effects of a study of literature on our everyday life". I am going in for it. (11 March 1881)

> Wrote a pretty long sketch entitled "Father & Son" and sent it off to the N.B. Advertiser. I also in the evening wrote a poem "Jobs from Bilingsgate". (16 May 1881)

> "Father and Son" appeared in today's N.B. Advertiser. (20 May 1881)

> Yesterday, I forgot to say, there appeared in the N.B. Advertiser a poem by me entitled "Door Knocks". (28 May 1881)

Herbert, who is at this point nurturing ambitions of a literary career, spends much time preparing his entry for the essay competition and has high hopes for its success. His optimism is to prove unfounded, however, and he reflects bitterly on his failure to make the prize list:

> And now I have to record the depth of my degradation. I went as usual to the English lecture. At the close of it the result of the essays was read out. I was not so much as mentioned! This I suppose is a wholesome check on my dreams. But really, seeing who it was I competed with, it was so very ambitious expectation to think I stood a chance. And when I read the essay again I cannot help thinking there is some mistake, more especially as Alexander <u>Gibson</u> who was first looked as stupid a fool as I have ever seen. (8 April 1881)

> First was "Mr Alexander <u>Gibson</u>" who stood up. A youth scarcely older than myself with a blank, vacant, idiotic countenance; there was less intellect visible in that face than there was in the stupidest of dogs. His face was a stolid, mountain-like, eruptive, grinning mass of stupidity. And this dolt was first! (8 April 1881, supplementary diary)

From 1 January to 10 June 1881, Herbert kept two diaries; one was a small clasped notebook identical to that he had kept during his final year at school, the other a more substantial quarto volume costing two shillings.[49] In the smaller book, he continued to keep a basic record of his daily activities; the larger one contained elaborations upon these and extended musings on historical, philosophical or literary topics. Between them, the two diaries present a fairly comprehensive picture of young Herbert's interests and character.

As well as writing and attending lectures, Herbert frequently visited the theatre during the first few months of his post-school career. His tastes in dramatic and musical entertainment were catholic, ranging from serious theatre and opera to light farces and amusements of the burlesque genre. His developing interest in matters of the heart was fuelled by attendance at the theatre and his admiration of some of the leading ladies of the day:

> In the evening I went to the Pirates of Penzance of which both the music and jokes (I can't say the plot) were excellent, especially the music. One of the actresses who took the part of Ruth was very pretty

---

49 'For now have I not invested the sum of 2/- in a goodly volume containing some four hundred pages. From this chrysalis state of a cheap notebook I am about to merge [*sic*] into the butterfly state of a quarto volume.' (31 December 1880)

and I in a manner fell in love with her. But if I go to the theatre next week she will be supplanted by some other beauty. I say "in a manner" because, having seen her once, I build up an ideal with her as a base and fall in love with this creation. My love therefore is of the mildest species for even if I have a chance I never care to exert myself to see the loved one again. Verily, I am a strange youth, or as some more candid and less polite would say, an awful ass. Remember Mr. Diary all I have said is in the strictest confidence and you must not blab. For between you and I if ever this most eccentric of mortals does fall in what is called love with a woman in reality he will prove a more faithful lover than the other 999. And perhaps his choice will not be so bad, old black & white; she must be fair outwardly and fairer, far fairer, inwardly. [...] I have committed myself I perceive. I the staid H Gibson who pores over fusty old books, who is more modest than even young Marlowe, talking of love. And you are chuckling and shaking your clasped sides you old villain of a diary. [...] However I'll not confide in you any more Mr. fat memorandum book. I'll put down the driest old remarks I can make. You've had the first and last glimpse into my mind; and so now you'll learn to restrain your hilarity when it isnt [sic] wanted.

What rot! (20 January 1881)

Another dance at this house, & also music. I did not present myself but went to the Chippendale Company, where Miss M. de Grey formed the basis for a new ideal. Don't grin. They acted Sheridan's School for Scandal. Came home & wrote 'The true aspect of a Picnic' a sketch which I think rather good. (28 February 1881)

Went to the Chippendale Company again. This time to see 'She stoops to conquer'. Miss M. de G. 'stooped', but don't imagine I went again through any desire… you understand? It was to escort my mater, sister & Miss Drysdale there. (1 March 1881)

In the evening I went to the Princess Theatre to see "Crutch & Toothpick" followed by a burlesque on "The Corsican Brothers". The first piece was very good and amusing, and to my taste the last was simply perfect. But then I have such a shocking bad taste that probably as usual I am greatly mistaken. We never have good actors – the leading men, that is to say – in Edinburgh, and unlike other people

> I don't go to the theatre to criticize medium players, I go to swallow their faults and enjoy, to the best of my ability, the play. And I never go to see an opera or anything of that sort here for I object to hearing good music murdered. (5 April 1881)

> In the evening saw the Chippendale Company at the "Royalty" in "Extremes" & a burlesque "Black Eyed Susan". Excellent. (16 June 1881)

During his time as a 'gentleman at large', it becomes clear that Herbert is developing into a vigorous young man of wide-ranging interests and powerful intellect. He throws himself wholeheartedly into his assorted activities and seems committed to living life to the full. In early February 1881, his excessive expenditure of energy brings a minor, but nonetheless alarming, breakdown of his health:

> Had a fit of extreme stupidity, a loss of the meaning of words, which was preceded by a dimness of eyesight & followed by a severe headache. (3 February 1880)

> Had another fit of dimness of eyesight & headache. (5 February 1881)

> Had another fit at dinner of the same complaint. (6 February 1881)

> Doctor called in. Pronounced the cause of the fits to be over-work. Beastly crack. Never overworked myself in my life. Perhaps its [*sic*] my old books. Doctor ordered me perfect rest, diet of medicine etc etc. Confounded nuisance. Mayn't write or exert my brain. Hopes of a literary fame dying away in the distance. (7 February 1881)

Soon after recovering from this affliction, Herbert learned that his Aunt Eliza, who lived in Glasgow with her brother and sister, Robert and Jessie Gibson, was seriously ill. His mother rushed to the house in Hamilton Park Terrace and arrived 'just in time to see Aunt Eliza alive' (3 March 1881). Two days later, the family heard that Uncle Robert had also fallen 'dangerously ill' (5 March 1881). Although Robert seems to rally slightly, he is described as 'intensely weak and ill' on the day of his sister's funeral (7 March 1881) and survives just three months more, coming, in the words of Herbert, 'to a most peaceful end' (6 June 1881). While special authorization had been obtained 'by dint of pleading & influence' (7 March 1881) to open the closed burial yard of Glasgow Cathedral for Eliza to be interred in the plot belonging to her father, Robert had to be buried in the family's new vault in the Necropolis instead. The funeral was a grand affair and, as was customary at the time, was followed immediately by the reading of the will:

> At two we went over to 14 Hamilton Park Terrace for the funeral. About 30 guests. A very handsome procession consisting of eleven carriages. The burial place is at the Necropolis, permission not being obtainable to use the Cathedral ground as formerly. The new place in the Necropolis is a vault constructed to hold twelve bodies. Aunt Eliza's remains are to be removed there.
>
> Then we returned to 14 Hamilton Park Terrace & the will was read. Small bequests were:- £500 for charitable purposes, viz £100 to Royal Infirmary, £100 to west ditto, £100 to small stipends of the Church of Scotland fund, and the remaining £200 to be disposed of as the trustees shall think fit. £100 was left to Miss Taylor; £100 to Miss Ann Taylor; £500 to Matthew Dunnet. An annuity of £20 to Miss Taylor; £20 to Miss Ann; £20 to Miss Maria Spence Corbett; £50 to Etta; £200 to Robert Smith, the latter two only to last till they receive their shares following. The whole remaining estate is to be divided into 15 parts, 6 of which are to go to Uncle George's children, 6 to my fathers [sic], 2 to Robert Smith & 1 to Etta. Aunt Jessie is to have the life rent & every facility is to be given to my father by the trustees for buying up the stock, renting the land etc. (10 June 1881)

Between attending the funerals of his aunt and uncle, Herbert continued his usual activities and even developed new interests, such as attending debates at the popular Edinburgh Parliamentary Society, a forerunner of sorts, albeit without any statutory authority, of today's talking shop at Holyrood:

> Went to the "Stranger's Gallery" of the "Edinburgh Parliamentary Society." This is a Club which represents Parliament. Each member sits for some constituency. They have a prime minister and all the government officers. Several of the speakers were gray bearded men; and the spirit of the thing is well kept up. One of the orators of this night was an Irishman, well known in the house, whose caustic remarks & humour were inimitable. Another was a Scotchman of the real Scotch type, lank brownish red locks brushed carefully down on each side of his head, a thin and shrewd face and a lank form. He spoke with a strong

Scotch accent, & his sarcasm kept the whole House in convulsions of laughter. If I get the chance I will join this society, but I suppose I am too young. There are some 1200 members at present. (10 March 1881, supplementary diary)

Another amusement was watching a shooting contest:

To night I went to see the shooting competition between Dr. Carver and Carl Jough, at the Waverly Market. It is to see who hit the most out of 1800 glass balls, they shoot at 300 apiece every evening. To night Karl Jough hit 279 & Dr. Carver 274. The balls are about the same size as a small cricket ball & are started two at a time from a trap in front of the marksmen who hits them one after the other before they reach a large white board 25 paces off. (18 May 1881)

Herbert also made several trips during this period, the first to his birthplace, Bridge of Allan, Stirlingshire, with his mother to select a rented house for a holiday they were going to spend there:

Went with mater to Bridge of Allan to select house for us when we go there in the middle of next month. […] Mater left me at the Queen's Hotel whilst she went to call on Miss Smith, an old maiden friend of hers. I had my lunch at the hotel & then walked up and down the street waiting for her. I walked for a mortal hour and a half, when she reappeared with Miss Janet Miller. […] I was born here on July 8th, 1863 and a numerous but select company beheld my baptism, consisting of the aforesaid Miss Smith, my father and mother, and the clergyman.

My father used to come to this village as a boy, some 50 or 60 years ago. He "hung out" in a little white washed – it is yellow washed now – three storied (!!) cottage at the side of the bridge from whence the village gains its name.

I had neither time nor inclination to appreciate all this when I was there, for I was divided betwixt indignation at the length of time I was kept waiting, and violent indigestion the result of hastily eating cold roast beef and then walking up and down with a glaring sun shining on me – albeit in the shade it was almost freezing – all of which conspired to give me a most melancholy stomach ache. (29 March 1881)

On 13 April, Herbert, Clementina, Percy, and a maid travelled to Bridge of Allan for their vacation, where Herbert's other siblings John and May joined them. Herbert spent much of his holiday on long country walks:

> At 11 a.m. I started for the "Rumbling Bridge" "on my mare shanks" and covered the 15 or 16 miles in 4 hours, not that I either intended to or did walk fast, for I enjoyed myself, and enjoyment & rapidity are incongruous. The rumbling bridge is over a mountain stream that descends about 200ft. in a fall or rapid just beneath the bridge. [...] By the bye those rapids or falls are nearer 20ft. than 200. The scenery is majestic and interesting. (22 April 1881)

> In the afternoon a walk by the banks of the Allan at which time I indulged in my first cigarette. (26 April 1881)

The whole party returned to Edinburgh on 27 April in preparation for Herbert and his mother to travel to Southampton to meet Thomas who was due to arrive from Argentina. Before leaving Scotland 'by the flying Scotchman' (30 April 1881), Herbert had an interesting encounter with a travelling salesman:

> In the evening an old Italian came to sell some plaster busts. The mater bought all his stock but one & gave him some claret & cake. He talked for a long time on religion, having once been a Roman Catholic and become a Protestant. His ideas were far more widened than many a Scotch clergyman, his doctrine being that all who were good went to heaven, whether they were R. Catholic or Protestant. I thought him an exceedingly worthy old man & I hope he will pay us another visit when the governor [Thomas] is here. (29 April 1881)

Both en route to Southampton and on the return journey, Herbert passed several days in London, seeing the sights, attending various entertainments, and spending time with his younger sister, Eva, who was at school in the capital:

> Visited St Pauls [sic] Cathedral in the morning & attended service there.
>
> Afternoon, Westminster Abbey & saw Dean Stanley stand in a pulpit for ¾ of an hour, but heard nothing. (1 May 1881)

> Still the most exquisite weather, & woke up with the most exquisite toothache. The latter I have been expecting for some time but I had hoped it was going to have the decency to wait until I returned to Edinburgh.
>
> To alleviate the pain I went into the Smoking room and indulged in a mild cigarette. […]
>
> Toothache excruciating and almost made up my mind to have a tooth drawn only unfortunately all one side of my jaw aches.
> Brought Eva from school & consulted a very pleasant chemist at Swiss Cottage, who opined that the toothache proceeded from the stomach being out of order & gave me a draught which did me an immense deal of good.
>
> Went with Eva to Mme Tussaud's and was greatly disappointed in the whole affair which I thought feeble in the extreme. (7 May 1881)

> In the evening I went to the Lycaeum [sic] & saw Henry Irving, Edwin Booth & Ellen Terry all together in "Othello". Grand. (9 May 1881)

Back in Scotland, Herbert prepares for the arrival of Harry Brereton, the old school friend who is coming to stay in Edinburgh for a holiday.[50] Together, the two young men tour large parts of the country in remarkably short time; Herbert's accounts of their travels serve as a tribute to the efficiency of public transport in the Victorian era:

> Went by the Chancellor to Loch Long and ascended that inlet to Arrocher [Arrochar] walked over to Tarbet, took boat there, went all the way down Loch Lomond to Balloch, thence train to Dumbarton & to Helensburgh, then boat to Greenock. (20 June 1881)

> Started by the 8.30 a.m. train to Callendar [Callander] for the Trossachs. Had half an hour at Dunblane, did Cathedral. Arrived at Callendar at 11.15 a.m. Took coach to Trossachs through the most exquisite scenery and in real Highland rain. Had half an hour at the Trossachs Hotel. Lunched. Then another mile & a half brought us to the head of Loch Katrine. Sailed down there to Stronachlacher [Stronachlachar] in a cockle shell. As we were to spend the night somewhere on the route did not take the coach to Inversnaid but walked, intending to return to

---

50 By 1883, despite his tender years, Brereton had graduated from Cambridge, been ordained, and received the appointment of Headmaster of the North Eastern County school.

Stronachlacher Inn if there were no room at Inversnaid Hotel. Came to Inversnaid just as the boat was starting & could not resist the temptation of rushing & catching it. Resolved to do whole route in one day. Boat all way down to Balloch. Train to Glasgow. 40 minutes there. Train to Edinburgh. Arrived at home 10.50 p.m. (28 June 1881)

In early July, as his eighteenth birthday approaches, Herbert begins to make the first preparations in advance of his departure for South America. He starts to take lessons at Scott's Riding School in Edinburgh (4 July 1881), but initially shows little indication of the expert horseman he would later become on the Argentine pampas:

Had my first riding lesson at 10 a.m. this morning, got jolted horribly. (4 July 1881)

No riding lesson this morning as I have ridden myself sore. (18 July 1881)

Had my sixth and last riding lesson. A precious tough one too, as a wind up. Was thrown twice. (25 July 1881)

For his birthday, Herbert receives practical gifts for the future ranch-hand, a 'jack knife [...] for estancia life' from his mother and a flask from his father (8 July 1881). On the same day, he performs the solemn duty of arranging the exhumation of the remains of his late sisters, Florence and Nettie, from the cemetery at Portobello in order for them to be transferred to the burial ground recently purchased by his father in Edinburgh's Newington Cemetery:

Was down twice at Portobello to arrange about the disinterment of Florence & Netty, for as we are now having a tomb in the Newington cemetery they are to be laid there. (8 July 1881)

Three days later, the family attend the reburial:

In the morning May Hope and I attended the reinterment of Nettie and Florence in our new burying place in Newington Cemetery. Pater & Mater took a cab to Portobello and followed the hearse all the way up to Edinburgh. (11 July 1881)

Iain Stewart

In the weeks leading up to the family's annual holiday at North Berwick, Herbert spends a lot of time in the company of a friend called Megget, including the following misadventures on Arthur's Seat, the hill overlooking Edinburgh:

> Under the Salisbury Crags I did two peculiarly idiotic things. First I saw an easy place to ascend to the top and went up ¾'s way. But I determined to go down again firstly because Megget wouldn't follow and next because the ascent was troublesome & I was not going to be foolhardy. But in discending [*sic*] I placed my foot on a rock which gave way and a large piece fully 12 or 14 lbs in weight went crashing down straight for Megget's head. He ducked but it appeared to me to go straight onto his head and then spring off rushing madly down the scaur to the foot. I was considerably relieved to hear him swear at me roundly and found that providentially it had missed him.
>
> Near the end of the crags I took it into my head to rush violently up a small slope and down the other side on to the path again. But in rushing down I slipped and fell on the stony path, cutting my trousers, my leg, my elbow and my hand. The sentence unanimously pronounced on this performance was "serves me/you jolly well right". (14 July 1881)

On 1 August, the family set off on their pilgrimage to the coast with a vast quantity of baggage:

> At half past one the pater, mater, Eva & Val started in the carraige [*sic*] and pair to drive to N. Berwick, May & I with the maids taking the luggage 32 parcels not to speak of the things we <u>carried</u> to the station to go by train. (1 August 1881)

In addition to his usual summer activities, Herbert attends a golf tournament at North Berwick and records his impressions of one of the finest players of the era:

> Saw a great deal of "Johnny Ball, (tertius)" a great golf-player from Hoylake where [Harold] Hilton stays. An amateur player. At the early age of seventeen he astonished all the golfing world by challenging David --- somebody or other, the champion Scotch professional, to a game and beating him hollow. He can scarcely be more than 22 now, I heard someone say he was only 20, but he has beaten all our crack men, amateur & professional, here. He plays extremely gracefully, is

a splendid drive, & to boot a very handsome young man, a well built and improved edition of Donald Fergusson. (8 August 1881)

By 24 August, Herbert has returned to Edinburgh to watch a spectacular military review attended by the Queen herself. An event of even larger scale than today's Military Tattoo, its description takes up no less than twenty-one pages of Herbert's diary; a few extracts from his observations are reproduced below:

> It cleared a little in the evening and I went out to view the scene of action, the Queen's Park. The troops begin to the east of Holyrood Palace and extend all the way south west to the other extremity of Salisbury Crags. They will number 40,200 men in all.
>
> The grand stand is a magnificent erection, fully ¼ mile in length, gorgeously decorated.
>
> Already the ground was a slough of despond, ankle deep in mud. (24 August 1881)
>
> The morning broke fine and even sunny but before 1 p.m. it commenced to rain & increased in heaviness until at 4 p.m. (the time of the review) it was descending in a deluge. [...]
>
> The Canongate had never seen such splendour since the bygone days when the aristocracy inhabited its narrow closes and flung their slops out of the top windows. Gay bunting, flags of every description, pictures of Sir Walter Scott & Robert Burns. [...] And such was the pitch of loyalty in the city that these thrifty Scots, regardless of expense, <u>actually left these gorgeous decorations untouched when it came on to rain!</u>
>
> By twelve o'clock Arthur's Seat was becoming dense with people and already some had taken their seats in the Grand Stand. The crowd gradually thickened, and various philanthropic gentlemen, to while away the time, kindly put up our country cousins to a wrinkle or two concerning the vicinity of a pea under three thimbles, and one or two jokes with three cards; nay, I even saw one who, determined to get rid of his superfluous cash, was prodigally putting golden sovereigns in handsome leather bags, & selling them for the small consideration of half-a-crown. [...]
>
> The firing of a gun shows the Queen to have left Holyrood. A royal salute is poured forth from the Leith Battery. The Queen in an open carraige [*sic*], with his deputy majesty John Brown Esq

supporting an extensive gingham over her royal bonnet, drives round all the volunteers, and comes to a halt in the centre of the Grand Stand under the fold of the Royal Standard.

Then commences the <u>wade past</u>, all the regiments marching past her. What followed I cannot say for by this time I was seated in front of a fire at home enjoying the bliss of a dry suit of clothes. (25 August 1881)

Herbert then returned to North Berwick, spending the whole of September engaged in his habitual programme there. By the beginning of October, he was back in Edinburgh making final preparations for his voyage to Argentina in three weeks' time: 'Bought a great number of things en autres – a set of boxing gloves for estancia use' (4 October 1881). He also undertook a day excursion to the racetrack, but found the sport of kings and its adherents distasteful in the extreme:

> Started to go to Musselburgh races, this being the second day. Passing along the train to find an empty seat a turfy looking fellow (who was alone in a coup) cried out "Plenty of room here, sir". I passed on & got into another empty smoking coup. A low looking man was in after me and the same one who accosted me followed him, shutting the door and leaning over it to check ingress of any strangers. Not anticipating a particularly pleasant journey in this companionship I speedily got an opportunity of finding out that the train was for Musselburgh (one of the fellows was very talkative and horsey but was meanwhile taking a mental survey of my person & "contents") and instantly rose stating with desperate mendacity that I was booked for Queensferry (which lies on an exactly opposite route). Thus heroically I escaped. The one leaning on the door, as I left, regretted that we were not to be fellow passengers, whereupon I, being safe, in order to exonerate my character and remove a little of the shame of retreat replied that that was impossible seeing that <u>he</u> was booked for Hades. Having fired this shot I went away with a lighter heart.
>
> I got into another carriage and arrived at Musselburgh. Commend me from the turf! It is the most abominable amusement that I have ever seen. Mixing with roughs and blacklegs of the lowest description, the aristocratic patrician, the earnest commoner, & the honest and industrious commercial man all endeavour to cheat one-another. I am no preacher of morals and never will be but I presume it is from my father I inherit a thorough contempt for the turf and have not the

least desire to mingle with the howling crowd offering "2 to 1 bar 1" "Even on the fi-eld"; and I cannot understand the existence of this mania in respectable man.

Holy Moses! I intended to describe the Musselburgh Races and instead I have wandered into a vague dissertation on the spirit of gambling. (7 October 1881)

In the middle of the month, Herbert, in common with many of his countrymen, celebrated the arrest of Charles Stewart Parnell, leader of the Irish Home Rule faction: 'Parnell is arrested. Hooray! As all Britain & half Ireland have this day cried or felt' (15 October 1881). Just five days later, domestic politics was probably far from Herbert's mind as he finally set off on his maiden journey to South America, accompanied by his father and sister May:

Started by the 10.30 a.m. train for London – the Midland route. They were all down to see us off, Mater, Hope, John and Eva. The pater and May travelled in the Pullman Car. I went third and pocketed the difference, a suggestion of the pater's. (20 October 1881)

Thus began the defining phase of Herbert's life; departure for Argentina marked the dawn of adulthood and was his first true step on the path that would lead to numerous achievements. It is an appropriate point in this story at which to open a new chapter.

CHAPTER 3

APPRENTICE

On reaching Waterloo station en route for Argentina, the Gibson party, comprising Herbert, his father Thomas and sister May, met up with the Raeburns, also bound for Buenos Aires. The son of this family, Eric, was to assume a post at the Gibsons' Los Yngleses *estancia*, where he would train alongside his close friend Herbert. Together, they made their way to Southampton, from where their steamship, the *Trent*, set sail on the afternoon of 24 October 1881. Also on board were members of another prominent Argentine-Scottish family, the Drysdales, the patriarch of which was a good friend of Thomas Gibson.

In addition to his usual diary, Herbert would keep a more detailed journal of the voyage, the opening pages of which are much concerned with the inexperienced sailor's discomfort:

> At 2 p.m. the "Trent" chartered for Buenos Aires loosed from her moorings and steamed down Southampton Water. At 5 p.m. I began to think that the beer I had taken before starting had disagreed, and from this cause – and nothing else; – the motion of the ship in no way contributed to it. (Journal, 24 October 1881)

> Got up and looked out of the port-hole. The horizon was behaving in a most dissipated and irritating manner, now leering down at me from the heavens, now disappearing rapidly beneath the keel of the ship. I experienced a sensation which I never hope to experience again; (owing to that miserable beer) my head and my stomach parted company, my head preferring to retain its equilibrium, my stomach recklessly following the movements of the vessel so that at one moment I felt myself drawn out to a length of 20 ft, at another my heels & my head seemed to come in contact. (Journal, 26 October 1881)

> Got up. Considerably worse. Rushed up on deck and fed the fishes. Felt better. Breakfasted. (Diary, 27 October 1881)

Herbert's constitution quickly regained its balance and he was able to start appreciating his experiences with greater enthusiasm. The first major attraction of the voyage is Lisbon, which he describes with the inevitable awe of one who had never before ventured abroad:

> It was all so very different to anything I have seen before that I might go on for hours and never finish describing all we saw. The people, the shops, the houses, the churches – they were all so unreal. The ladies were all powdered, like second-rate characters in a second rate theatre. [...] Everything looks rickety, one is afraid to lean up against a wall for we are morally certain it would give way – like the scenes in the harlequinade at the pantomime. And yet these paper walls are made of unpolished marble! [...]
>
> Our guide, a foundling 16 years old who spoke English with tolerable fluency, informed us that there was a bullfight every second Sunday and added with unction that last Sunday 4 men, 9 bulls & 13 horses were butchered. Such sport! (Journal, 28 October 1881)

As the *Trent* neared Tenerife, the unfamiliar climate began to take its toll on the diarist: 'Phew!!! How hot its [*sic*] getting. Too hot to walk or to play deck quoits – feeblest of feeble amusements – and yes, certainly, much too hot to write' (Journal, 31 October 1881). Little of note occurred during the Atlantic crossing, save for Herbert's discovery of an unfortunate flying fish as they approached the Equator:

> Found a flying-fish lodged on our porthole which was open. It is not so large as a herring but not unlike it in appearance. The lamp last night had probably attracted it, being of the same nature as bats and moths, unable to resist the attraction of a flame. (Journal, 7 November 1881)

The *Trent* finally made land at Pernambuco in north-eastern Brazil. Arriving in this lively town brought welcome relief from the tedium of almost two weeks on the open sea. Herbert's journal becomes more expansive as he eagerly records his first impressions of South American life:

> And now most lenient and gentle reader I would crave your attention for a few minutes while I have a quiet talk about this Pernambuco and other Brazilian towns. No doubt you have pictured to yourself a place with little more than a name, a judge, ten niggers and a fishing smack. Just listen to these statistics – the population is over 100,000 souls and the commerce and shipping equals that of Leith. Don't know anything about Leith don't you. Well, I'll bring it nearer home – it surpasses the shipping of Yarmouth, while the town is half as large again as Norwich. It has post offices, railway stations, churches, tramway cars etc etc. And it isn't the first nor the second, nor the third town in Brazil. It isn't even capital of its province, Bahia. (Journal, 10 November 1881)

Bahia, the next stop, provides even more interest on account of its unusual location, the main part of the town being built atop a high escarpment, the remainder lying below:

> Now you must know that Bahia is a curious town. Half of it is down below, half of it above. There is no gradient, the houses and walls suddenly rise perpendicularly to a height of 2 or 3 hundred feet. The difficulty of transition from the lower to the upper town was formerly got over by having sedan chairs which are still used. Niggers carry them, running at a jog trot, and keeping up a curious melancholy cry as they go. They go by a zig zag road, very steep and slippery. But for the past 10 years a much better ascent is managed, they have a magnificent and capacious hydraulic lift – "elevador" as they call it. (Journal, 12 November 1881)

However, the attractions of Bahia were far surpassed by those of Rio de Janeiro, where the Gibsons spent a memorable night in a luxurious hotel among the hills overlooking the city:

> Got a car and ran out of town in it. Then a carraige [sic] (it now being dark) and drove away up among the hills to the hotel at "Ti Juca". Wonderful place! (Diary, 15 November 1881)

> I have exhausted my notes of admiration or I would have peppered them down here broadcast.
>   Picture to yourself – no you can't, the thing is impossible. Look here, just run down to Southampton, get into the first boat, and come

and see it yourself.

We are away down in the valley, with the mountains rising from our very feet, a stream babbling past us, and amongst such foliage! Oh! its [*sic*] no use none whatever; I must give it up as a bad job. [...]

I shall carry the recollection of that place with me all my life – and my father will carry his bill with him, as a proof of how much an hotel can charge without blushing. (Journal, 16 November 1881)

While in Rio, Herbert's curiosity begins to be aroused by the diverse inhabitants of South America. His observations begin with some rather unflattering and, by modern standards, politically incorrect comments on members of the city's substantial black population:

What a curious habit those negresses have of kissing one another's hands when parting in the street. Niggers have several peculiarities, one of them is to put their hands in other people's pockets in a sportive way, also to run away with the contents in a sportive way. Bless their dear innocent harmless souls. And do you know my dear friend that then half of these same niggers you and I have been looking at for the past half hour, are actual slaves. Not so illtreated as Uncle Tom perhaps, but just as real slaves, whose earnings all go into their masters [*sic*] pockets. You see we are not so far off Wilberforce and his times after all. (Journal, 16 November 1881)

The next focus for his critical gaze is the Uruguayan envoy to Brazil, who boards the *Trent* on his way back to Montevideo:

We have shipped "his excellency the ambassador from Monte Video to Rio", and a more ruffianly hairy ferocious monster I never set eyes on. Are they all like that I wonder? He might palm himself off as a Pitcairn Islander and make his fortune at the Westminster Aquarium. (Journal, 18 November 1881)

As the ship nears the Uruguayan capital, it emerges that Herbert's remarks about the ambassador may well have been influenced by a preconceived and overwhelmingly negative view of that nation:

Land ho! Here we are starting up the famous River Plate with the Banda Oriental on our right. Then a rock surmounted with a

> lighthouse – "Monte Video" – "I see a hill". And finally the town itself, capital of the inflated, pompous, bellicose and microscopic republic of Uraguay [*sic*]. [...]
>
> By the bye we unshipped the Pitcairn Islander here. He was received by another ruffian, in military costume, more ferocious and shaggy than the other. His most benign supreme and all other adjectival excellency, General Santos, President of the omnipotent republic of Uraguay, general of the republican forces, etc etc etc. What a monster to govern a civilized country. (We have since learned that we were fully justified in this estimate of him.) (Journal, 20 November 1881)

Contrary to Herbert's assertion, General Máximo Santos did not ascend to the presidency until March 1882, but it is true that he was already the most powerful figure in the turbulent country, simultaneously occupying the posts of Minister of War and Chief of the Army. As the *Trent* sails away from Montevideo, Herbert elaborates upon his earlier remarks:

> Now we are out of the power of the government let's indulge in a little high treason. As I remarked before Santos is a villain, so is every[one] else so that balances. Every morning the inhabitants look at the papers to see who is president & how many revolutions have occurred during the night. Every man's hand is against every one else. The whole country is a seething mass of sedition, treason and ambition. An ordinary Englishman would never sink 5 paper dollars in the place. (Journal, 20 November 1881)

While this analysis of Uruguay's condition may contain some exaggeration, it is broadly supported by historical record. Santos's presidency was effectively a military dictatorship, characterized by ferocious repression of free speech, gross economic incompetence, corruption, and ostentatious displays of power. Several unsuccessful efforts were made to overthrow Santos, culminating in an assassination attempt in 1886. The president survived, disfigured by severe facial injuries. Shortly afterwards, he resigned and travelled to Europe in search of medical treatment, but little could be done to help him. On his return to South America, he was denied entry to Uruguay and lived out the brief remainder of his life in exile, dying in Buenos Aires in 1889 at the age of forty-two.[51]

---

51 Juan Carlos Pedemonte, *Los presidentes del Uruguay*, 4th edn, (Montevideo: Ediciones de la Plaza, 1992), pp. 49-51.

Following his assessment of Santos's character, Herbert proposes a radical solution to Uruguay's current predicament:

> There is one living soul who could rectify this, who has rectified it once, and who (please God!) will do so again. His name – Colonel Latorre. This man once upset the government, took the town, governed despotically i.e. without aid, introduced and retained military law and tranquillised the country. In those days as in King Harold's a man could hang a bag of gold on a tree, leave it, and come back in a month to find it still there, untouched. Everyone respected their neighbour, bless them! not out of their nature but because they couldn't help themselves. This lasted for some months and then Latorre thinking he had tamed them, and civilized them, reintroduced the old form of government and started an election. He was elected President. So far so good. But in 6 months he tendered his resignation, pronouncing his country ungovernable by reason, and left the republic. And what we all say is – Hail the day when he returns a la militaire and kills off half the country to tame the other half – There, reader, this is a S. American republic, though thank heavens! the worst specimen. Here you have a country rich in soil, mineral and climate: and absolutely hopeless – at present at least. What a melancholy fact, what a stern reality to face in this our enlightened nineteenth century. (Journal, 20 November 1881)

Latorre, although undoubtedly an authoritarian leader, was of a much more reasonable disposition than Santos. Supported by rural landowners and the metropolitan elite, he strove to put in place the apparatus of a modern, efficient state. Latorre endured as constitutional president for slightly longer than Herbert's six months, resigning just over a year after his election. In his resignation statement, Latorre spoke of his disillusionment and famously told his fellow citizens that 'nuestro país es un país ingobernable' ['our country is an ungovernable land'].[52]

The *Trent* soon arrived at its final destination. By 1881, it was still impossible for large vessels to reach the port of Buenos Aires itself, on account of the shallowness of the Plate channel, so passengers transferred to smaller craft for the final approach. The Gibsons completed the journey in the private tender of their friends the Drysdales:

---

52 Cited by Benjamín Nahum, *Manual de historia del Uruguay*, (Montevideo: Ediciones de la Banda Oriental, 1994), p. 194.

> Woke up with Buenos Aires in sight, almost below the horizon though. Mr. Drysdale's tender, decorated with bunting, came alongside at 11 a.m. & we left the ship at noon, were a long time getting ashore – the distance being 13 miles. We had forgotten the Custom House officer and when about 8 miles from shore had to turn round and fetch him. (Diary, 21 November 1881)

Herbert's first impressions of Buenos Aires are highly favourable, and he praises the city's architecture and some of its culinary delights:

> As we neared the shore we began to agree that this was decidedly the finest town in the architectural way we had seen since leaving Edinburgh. Built like a chess board, white and healthy, at first sight and indeed always it has an imposing appearance. (Journal, 21 November 1881)

> Looked in at the "confiteria" windows – sweetie shops. It is astonishing to learn that the confections here are said to equal and even surpass those of Paris, which is of course, far beyond all the rest of the world in that line. (Journal, 21 November 1881)

Herbert closes his supplementary journal on 23 November and spends the next few days finding his bearings in the metropolis and visiting some of its attractions:

> Went to the Zoological Gardens in Palermo, just outside the town. A splendid large park and a fair collection of animals chiefly S. American. The guanacos attracted us. They are the size of medium deer, perhaps larger, with several of the sheeps [*sic*] characteristics, a long neck, and a camels [*sic*] head. One came up to us, quite docile, and leaned over the railings in a very friendly way. It watched us some time in a meditative manner and then suddenly expectorated about a half a pint of half digested grass over [Eric] Raeburn's head and shoulders. It appears this is a customary habit they have, and do it in a playful manner without any ill feeling. (25 November 1881)

On 3 December, the Gibson party begin the long journey south from Buenos Aires to the Yngleses ranch, arriving late the next day:

Woke up at 4.30 a.m. to find Raeburn thumping at the door opening into the next room, with a boot. It appears the Germans who sleep there, returning at 3 a.m. kicked up such a tremendous dunder that he awoke. He had passed the previous hour kicking up a row and make [*sic*] unearthly sounds by way of retaliation.

    5 a.m. Got up. Breakfasted at the Amistad Cafe and left the Central Station at 6.15 a.m. Pleasant journey but very dusty. Passed the 18 leagues of camp, formerly belonging to Gibson Brothers, splendid camp, large lake in the centre viz. "Laguna de Chascomos" [Chascomús]. Saw a great deal of game. Two or three horses lay by the side – killed by previous trains. One was still alive, 40 yds from the line, with its left hind leg completely severed at the knee. Poor beast! (3 December 1881)

Up at 5 a.m. In the diligence – a small one for ourselves; the big one and two others making four in all going – behind 6 horses, and scampering out of Dolores by 6 a.m. This is travelling! No regard for springs, no regard for person, no regard for anything be it man, beast or mud. Over swamps 3 ft deep in mud and into 2 or 3 ft of hard mud, no obstacle stopping us, we charge. (4 December 1881)

Having reached Los Yngleses, which he describes as 'the best estancia in South America' (4 December 1881), Herbert sets to work straight away and eagerly embraces the routines of ranch life:

Up at 4.30. Greased sheep shears till 8. Shot parroquets [parakeets] and pulled tobacco for washing the rest of the day. Had a very jolly time of it and like the place immensely.

    People here are – Uncle George Corbett, manager, wife and family. Ernest. Cairney. Runciman – a guest – . Todd. Casbos. [Cousin] George. (5 December 1881)

Mended sacks, stuck up a coral [corral], inked in a map and did other odd jobs.

    I like the business here immensely. Plenty of hard work and no time to weary and yawn. Splendid change after 10 months of idleness.

    My contract signed. (8 December 1881)

> Lay in bed till 8 a.m. [...] Never appreciated a Sunday more in my life. (11 December 1881)
>
> Commenced "outside" work viz work in the camp. (14 December 1881)

Herbert's contract, referred to above, set out the terms of his engagement as apprentice for the period of four years:

> The following agreement has this day been made by Messrs Gibson Brothers on the one hand and Mr. Herbert Gibson on the other hand.
>
> 1st. Mr Herbert Gibson hereby engages to serve Messrs Gibson Bros as apprentice in their sheep business in the Province of Buenos Ayres South America, for the term of four years commencing on the day of his arrival in the city of Buenos Ayres, and to obey the orders of their manager there and faithfully to discharge his duty in everything connected with the work, and to make himself generally useful.
>
> 2d. Messrs Gibson engage to pay his expenses at Buenos Ayres and thence to the farm, and also to pay him a salary Thirty Pounds for the first year, Thirty Five Pounds for the second year, Forty Pounds for the third year, and Fifty Pounds for the fourth year. – In addition to which he will have board and lodging free of any charge, also washing.[53]

Like most large Argentine sheep-breeding establishments of the time, Los Yngleses operated on a *puesto* system. The term *puesto* (literally a 'post' or 'position' in Spanish) signifies a portion of an *estancia* entrusted into the care of an individual known as a *puestero*. At Los Yngleses, each *puesto* consisted of an allotted parcel of land, a flock of sheep, and a simple house for the *puestero*, or shepherd, and his family. In return for his services, the *puestero* received a fraction of the profits from his flock, usually around a third or a quarter; this method of remuneration ensured that there was plenty of incentive for the shepherd to take good care of the animals under his charge. On some *estancias*, *puesteros* shared in the ownership of the flocks with the ranch owners, but this does not appear to have been the case at Los Yngleses. While some *puesteros* were local Argentinians, many were immigrants, hailing from Spain (especially the Basque country), Italy, France or Great Britain (including Ireland). In the case of Los Yngleses, a number were of Scottish origin.

---

53 Cited by Geoffrey Gibson, *The Chivalrous Shepherd*, p. 22.

Much of Herbert's early work consisted of helping with the supervision of the *puestos*. Routine tasks included distributing animals to the *puesteros*, counting the flocks, hand curing sheep for scab, parting animals selected for killing, and marking the flocks (this was done by cutting a series of notches in the unfortunate beasts' ears, a different pattern for each *puesto*). It was hard labour involving long hours on horseback. Although he clearly enjoyed the work, Herbert soon remarked that the 'effects of being so much in the saddle have not been conducive to much physical comfort' (16 December 1881) and expressed some surprise at the nature of his duties: 'Seems to me that the peons [workers] do the bossing and the capitazs [*capataces* – foremen] the manual labour in this country.' (21 December 1881).

Herbert's life in Argentina was one of simple pleasures. Although his first Christmas away from home was spent in unmemorable fashion, and the days preceding it were marred by severe toothache, he appreciated the holiday more than ever before:

Got very bad toothache from eating unripe pears. Half frantic with pain the rest of the day. (22 December 1881)

Toothache very bad, face swollen up like a pumpkin and body altogether weak & shaken. Didn't do much work. (23 December 1881)

Well! I don't know that this isn't the pleasantest Christmas Day I have ever spent. It has consisted of a programme of the most uninteresting items imaginable viz shooting and reading: but it has been without alloy. No Christmas dinner, no presents, no plum-puddings, no festival of any kind. Still it has been pleasant. As a child I found the foibles in my toys ere noon and remained quarrellsome [*sic*] the rest of the day. [...] Of course I hated going to church and of course I went. A hundred incidents cropped up during the day to mar my bliss and I generally returned to bed sulky. Today I had nothing to look forward to, and accordingly I have been happy. Dinner was wretched and my spirits still rose. At supper – where the fare was still worse – I was exuberance itself. – What was the cause of it? A week's hard work and a day of rest sir! (25 December 1881)

On Hogmanay, he once again contrasts his new and former lives in a manner that suggests he much prefers the present, in spite of its dull routine and basic values:

> Tomorrow I must date things in 1882. That perhaps defines the whole difference between this year and the next. Today I knock off work at sundown, tomorrow is a day of rest, and on Monday I resume work again at sunrise. No change. No variation.
>
> The year gone by has been a lost one. All but a month has been spent in idleness. Not quite perhaps. Did I not send forth a transient gleam of industry in the columns of the "North British Advertiser and Ladies Journal"? Did I not even threaten to shake the whole literary world when I sent a poem to "Punch" and another to "Judy"? But let me modestly draw a veil over these triumphs. Further vaunting them would constrain me to confess that these same poems were reject – were omitted. Oh! the utter blindness of some people, the bloated ignorance of those who refuse genius because she approaches without a name! […]
>
> I am in the first year of a new life. The preface is over, the introduction finished and Chapter I of the novel commenced. Its opening chapters will be indeed uninteresting, a steady routine of hard work, plain food and no holiday. (31 December 1881)

As well as marking the start of Herbert's first full year in Argentina, the arrival of 1882 brought a significant change at Los Yngleses with the construction of a new *estancia* house:

> Commenced the work of pulling down the principal dwelling house, including a dining room & 4 bedrooms. The house was built, the first part in 1827 and the rest some 15 years later by my uncles and father. Now a roomier and more comfortable edifice is to take its place. (28 December 1881)

By early January, work on the new dwelling is proceeding apace and a sort of time capsule is placed in the foundations:

> Bottle was put in the foundation of the new house, containing the following:-
> 1. "La Prensa" – Native paper for 1st January.
> 2. "Standard" – English B$^{s.}$ Ayrean paper for 1st Jan.
> 3. Almanac for 1882.
> 4. Price list for January of wool etc.
> 5. 1 dollar note and 5 dollar note.

6. Balance Sheet of the Estancia for 1881.
7. Paper stating the fol –
"Estancia de 'Los Ingleses'
Partido de Ajó
Buenos Ayres
January 9th 1882
Sala at Head Station. Built at the commencement of the year 1882 on the site of the old sala which was built in 1827. It is situated in the Estancia de 'Los Yngleses' the property of Messrs Gibson Bro^s in whose possession it has been since the year 1827. The only surviving partner of the firm is Thomas Gibson Esq. The extent of the estancia is 10 leagues:
the stock numbering in sheep 92,810; in cattle 4,427; and in horses 343. The manager is George Corbett Esq.; the sub manager is Ernest Gibson Esq.; the capitases [*capataces* – foremen] Messrs J. S. Cairnie, John Todd, José Casbas, George R. Gibson and Herbert Gibson Esquires."
The bottle was duly closed and buried. (10 January 1882)

Herbert's duties were nothing if not varied; as well as those tasks that directly involved the livestock, he had to ensure that the Sabbath was marked in an appropriate fashion, pull out damaging weeds, and assist with the digging of a watering hole for cattle:

> The pater wrote me requesting very earnestly that I should read prayers every Sunday morning, and accordingly we had them immediately after breakfast. (15 January 1882)

> Out "abrojo" gathering, a weed which bears a seed the size of a small walnut, full of prickles and very injurious to the wool. It comes up easily by the roots. We go down on our knees and work steadily towards the horizon leaving not a vestige of the plant behind us till we finish the patch of it. (18 January 1882)

> Started with George, Bob Nicholson, Simon and Cajetano to make a "hag well" [*jagüel* – pool] i.e. a well for the cattle. Got to the place, some 4 miles off the estancia and set to work, Don Jorge Corbett, J. Lean, and some six peons being on the ground before us. Water was struck at a depth of six feet; very good and cool. Then we set to work

to dig the hole 24 ft square, a terrific undertaking for 8 or 10 men. Were 4 ft deep by noon. Then dinner, two delicious asados cooked in the open air at a brushwood fire. Enjoyed it immensely. Then a cup of tea and we started to work again – no siesta. Found it very hard work. By sundown we were 5 or 6 ft deep the water beginning to rise up. – Though the hole is of such immense size, the well will be only 10 or 12 ft square; it seems an unnecessary expenditure of labour to me. (27 January 1882)

Galloped over with Ernest and George to the jaquel [*sic*] – not "hag well" as spelt formerly – where the box was already sunk a little way. The work now consists of digging round and inside the box, making it sink gradually, and keeping the water out by means of a "manga" a long watercloth sleeve lowered & raised by means of a pulley and rope pulled by a horse. The box was lowered some 4 or 5 feet today by this means. (30 January 1882)

Work kept Herbert fully occupied and his first couple of months at Los Yngleses flew by in a rush of activity: 'Veritate tempus fugit. I can scarcely realise that it is a month since New Year's Day' (31 January 1882). Soon, however, he starts to find more time for leisurely pursuits, often in the company of his brother Ernest, cousin George, and friend Eric Raeburn:

Went to a hajuel [*jagüel*] (the same as we made a fortnight ago) and had a bathe. Ernest, George, Raeburn & self made the party. A glorious little bath, 14 ft square & some 10 ft deep. (12 February 1882)

Spent a rather riotous night in our rooms, George having up a demijuana [demijohn] of something that shall be nameless from the port. Brewed cocktails in a teapot etc., etc. which ended in the course of two hours, in the lamps going out unaccountably, the crockery getting broken, and a general free fight with slippers and pillows. (15 February 1882)

In the evening got drunk and broke a window & water jug. First experience in that line. George and Raeburn the same. (1 March 1882)

In the evening went out shooting biscachos [*vizcachas*] by moonlight. Killed one myself. Raeburn shot a polecat. (3 March 1882)

On other occasions, he returns to his former hobby of writing, producing several pieces for his old school magazine:

> Did a creditable amount of writing, finishing, and I may also say beginning as well, a paper for the Norfolcian. (14 May 1882)
>
> Wrote a paper entitled "The Gaucho" for the Norfolcian. Sent it off.

He also starts to take an interest in South American history and anthropology, preferring to hunt for artefacts of Argentina's aboriginal inhabitants while his companions pursue the local wildlife:

> Wrote a letter in the morning and in the afternoon galloped over, in company with Ernest, Raeburn, & Todd, to a stretch of sand lying by V. Zemborain where pottery and flint arrowheads, remains of the aboriginal Indians are to be found. Was very successful in my search, finding a "bola perdida" [a rounded stone, thought to be part of the remains of a long-lost bolas], and a great deal of flint & pottery, two or three very good javelinheads amongst the flint, but the pottery very much broken. Here then is a pursuit & study which promises to fill up all my leisure time.
> Raeburn, Ernest and Todd left me "grubbing" and galloped to the Laguna Milan where they shot 6 or 7 swans & a number of ducks. (5 March 1882)

Anthropology would become a lifelong passion for Herbert, evinced by the series of notebooks he kept, the newspaper articles he wrote, and the public lectures he delivered on the subject. By the middle of March 1882, as Herbert's first southern winter approached, outside work at the *estancia* slackened dramatically and life moved on to a different timetable: 'Winter system of meals, viz coffee at sunrise, breakfast at eleven, tea at two & supper at sundown, commenced today' (18 March 1882). Herbert spent most of his time running the store that supplied provisions to all who live at Los Yngleses. In the following weeks, many of the ranch-hands were no longer required: 'Not much doing in the store. 6 fellows paid off today. Most of the boys gone' (3 June 1882). Activities remained at a low ebb until the shearing season began at the end of September.

During the winter months of comparative idleness, Herbert still finds isolated events of interest to record in his diary. A few examples are transcribed below:

> Tobacco from town for George, Todd and I here – 8 lbs! (27 May 1882)

> At about 3 p.m. the kitchen chimney caught fire but the gallant Brown – half intoxicated – extinguished it. (28 May 1882)

> Must have been bitten by a spider last night, for about 2 p.m. my lip swelled to the size of a walnut. In about 4 hours it began to go down again, and at bedtime it was all right again. (5 June 1882)

> George's party came to an untimely end [while out distributing sheep around the *puestos*]. He had left his two men, Hilario and Francisco, and galloped on to advise the puesteros of his intended delivery. No sooner had he left his peons than they agreed to settle a quarrel between them. Hilario made a hole in the other man's stomach, indented his head by way of variety & cleared. Francisco managed to get up to Salas' on foot, where George found him "weltering in gore". George came home as fast as he could to advise Don Jorge. (13 June 1882)

> Francisco in a very bad way. Wound has bled continually since last night. (14 June 1882)

The diary does not record the fate of poor Francisco.

Also during this period Herbert made his first visit to the nearby town of Ajó (usually referred to as 'the port' in his diaries), a place he would grow to know well over the coming years. Although he had never made the trip before, he had probably heard much about Ajó's limited attractions from his companions and had certainly received some supplies from the town:

> Raeburn, Dr Green and Runciman went to the port – Runciman getting for me a mate [a hollowed gourd, used as a vessel for *mate*, the green tea-like drink of the gaucho], bombilla [a silver 'straw' used for drinking *mate*] and 3 Basco pipes. These latter so closely resemble the pipes of Raleigh's time that, but for their brand – Violet, St Omer – they might be palmed off with success on some lion-hunting antiquary. (3 February 1882)

Herbert is underwhelmed by his first sight of the rather shabby town, but wastes little time in acquainting himself with the local bar-cum-grocery, Fugitt's, an establishment frequented by the young men of Los Yngleses:

> Started at breakfast time in company with Ernest to go to the port. Rode down there and entered by long straggling roads, without houses or even roadways, which are dignified by the name of streets. Then passing a few solitary huts we got into the principal squares, the houses being all detached and made mostly of wood as if the inhabitants expected to have to quit, any moment of their lives. Stopped at Fugitt's where we met Runciman, and "totted" all round. Fugitt's store is like the rest, a mere shanty outside but a decent enough general warehouse when inside. Then went over to the fonda [inn] where we had a glorious breakfast. (2 July 1882)

Just six days after his visit to Ajó, Herbert marks his birthday in modest fashion: 'My birthday! being now 19 years old. Bought a Dutch cheese for "Auld Lang Syne"' (8 July 1882). Now, in the middle of the Argentine winter, work at the *estancia* had reached a virtual standstill. Snow was a rare occurrence, but strong winds, cold driving rain, and harsh overnight frosts were commonplace, and Herbert reports 'suffering greatly from chilblains' on his hands and feet (31 July 1882). While most of his colleagues seem to fritter away the days, often with the aid of copious quantities of alcohol, Herbert strives to fill his time with more productive activities, a contrast illustrated by the following extracts from his diary:

> Mackechnie over again. How I dislike that rowdy, coarse young man, he is the very essence of vulgarity and bumptiousness. (29 July 1882)

> George & Mackechnie away shooting at the Tuyu coast.
> 8 p.m. The two back again half-intoxicated and noisy. George on the strength of leaving next week is making an utter fool of himself. Yesterday night he & Mackechnie were rioting over the camp after midnight, and tonight they are making a frightful row in the pateo, in company with Brown the carpenter who is of course drunk. (30 July 1882)

> Stayed up till 11 p.m. as usual – a habit I have taken to for the last week – writing and studying Spanish. (28 July 1882)

> Weeded my little garden and wrote a letter. By the bye one of the flower seeds that I brought out has struggled above the ground & I feel crowned with laurels. (15 August 1882)

By 25 September, with winter beginning to give way to spring, the annual shearing of the *estancia*'s sheep began. This was one of the main tasks of the year and would take around two months to complete. While much of Herbert's diary is taken up with the unremarkable daily routine of the shearing season, he also comments on an outbreak of cattle stealing, a successful mouse-hunt, the torturous removal of a tooth at the hands of his friend Runciman (who seems to have been an enthusiastic, if amateur and presumably untrained, practitioner of dentistry), and the first anniversary of his arrival in Argentina. It is interesting to note that many of the entries are now peppered with words of Spanish origin, reflecting Herbert's ongoing study of the language:

> There has been some pretty heavy carnearing (stealing cattle flesh, killing the animal on the camps) of cattle in the rincones [literally, 'corners', i.e. remote parts of the *estancia*] lately & some of the ladrones [thieves] are caught. (22 October 1882)

> A new juez de paz [justice of the peace] has been made, a German Henrich the old one having got the sack. Also a new comisariat [*sic*]. A great sensation on at present about some cattle thieves who have been caught. The principal part of the stealing is on this estancia. […] One or two puesteros are said to be connected with the thieves. (24 October 1882)

> Killed a mouse in my room, after having removed nearly every stick of furniture & hunted it high & low. Finally perceived it attempting to climb up between a chest of drawers and the wall.
> Had a tooth taken out. Terrible operation: tooth as firm as a rock. Very nearly punched the operator's head. (1 November 1882)

> In Runciman's hands nearly all day. Had my teeth properly fixed. (5 November 1882)

> This day last year I landed in Buenos Aires and to-day I commence the second year of my four year's [*sic*] contract. (21 November 1882)

Finally, at the end of November, the last of the flocks is shorn. Herbert records the details in his usual meticulous fashion and ponders what he has learnt from his first experience of the shearing season:

> Shearing commenced at puestos on Sept 27th: at the estancia on Oct 6th: finished to-day Nov 28th: Total number of days shearing exclusive of those flocks (3) shorn at puestos – 39, that is 1 14/39 flocks per day.
>
> The work has been very light, not at all what I expected. I have learnt a good deal however, can in some degree classify wool, have tried my hand at "bossing" the shearings, can work the big galpone [*galpón* – shearing shed] & in fact have worked in every branch of the shearing. (28 November 1882)

The following day he superintends the tidying-up operation:

> Took down all the corral by mid-day. Had everything sent up and the ground cleared & tidied by sundown.
> Very busy day.
> All the shearers cleared out by 12 o'clock. (29 November 1882)

With the activity of shearing over for another year, Herbert returns to keeping the *estancia* store, a tedious job he comes to resent, especially as a man appointed for this specific task is allocated other duties instead: 'This is a fraud! 3 months ago Don Jorge told me that after the shearing I was to be relieved by Smith as store man. But here I am, at it still' (16 December 1882). He continues by launching a bitter attack on Smith's character and capabilities:

> I suppose Smith is such a confounded nincompoop that he cannot be trusted with the store. He has been here 4 months & can't speak a word of Spanish yet. This is a man whose ignorance is so profound that he is not aware of it. He argues on every subject under the sun but I have not yet found any one thing on which he is even moderately informed. Examples are unnecessary: I have seen him holding on to the pommel of the saddle on a quiet horse at a moderate canter and then in the evening contradict men of 10 or 20 years experience in the country on the subject of horses & how to ride. Working in the corral I have found he cannot tell the age of a sheep from the mouth, nor the difference between a mestiza & Lincoln sheep, nor even between

a ram or an ewe till he puts it down, and that very evening volunteer information on the matter of sheep & their diseases to Don Jorge the manager for 20 years of this estancia. I wonder if there are many of his sort in the world.

He ends his tirade by contrasting Smith unfavourably with his good friend Eric Raeburn, whom he describes as a 'very clever & well read fellow, great at sports, at books & at general information. A perfect musician. The very antipodes of Smith'.

Herbert's invective against Smith evinces a trait running throughout the diaries. The personality projected through his writings is usually that of one who shows great generosity and tolerance towards his fellow beings; on the rare occasions he does take a dislike to someone, however, the result is often a fairly brutal outburst of condemnation.

The final weeks of 1882, after the end of shearing, pass otherwise uneventfully. Receipt of a copy of *The Norfolcian* containing his piece on 'The Gaucho' (7 December), a violent bout of sickness, attributed to 'eating native cheese & unripe cherries at the same time' (10 December), and witnessing a vicious fight between two bulls while out riding (1 December) are among the few noteworthy incidents. Probably the most significant event is Herbert's promotion to a more senior position on the *estancia*, by virtue of a number of other employees having absented themselves on either a permanent or temporary basis: 'By strange fortune I am now senior capitas [*capataz* – foreman], reckoning Mr Cairnie as mayordomo [overseer]. Ernest, George, Casbas & finally Todd having left I rise to this position – on £35 a year' (21 December 1882).

Christmas Day is spent as quietly as the previous year, but also just as contentedly from Herbert's point of view: 'Christmas passes like any other day, but that is not to be understood as a grumble. For we are so happy and free from care that every day is like Christmas' (25 December 1882). In reflective mood, he reiterates his contentment at Los Yngleses on the final day of the year and also hints at ambitions for the future:

> This year glided by very uneventfully. […] I am very contented; this life is pleasant, the work is agreeable and my health is good. […] Have any of my day dreams been shattered? Not one. I am still the same creature doing small things but imagining great ones. Not a pinnacle of my castle in the air has fallen, not a single crocket been broken nor a line in the plan been altered. (31 December 1882)

Life continues in similar vein for much of the early part of 1883. One unusual event does occur, the foundering of a British ship just off the coast of Los Yngleses:

> Went with Runciman to the coast to see the English vessel "Her Royal Highness" which has been recently shipwrecked there. She lies within a stone's throw of the shore – 1400 tons burden! The captain & mate were taken prisoner this morning, a grand climax to the system of leeching of these "furred law-cats" of the Republic. Visited the captain's wife, felt we were intruding, placed the estancia & establishment at her services & retired. (24 March 1883)

Subsequently, the *estancia* buys the wreck for timber and a major salvage operation commences:

> This morning Cairnie, Brown, 2 peons & a boy left for the coast to commence breaking up the wreck of H.R.H. which the Estancia has bought.' (30 May 1883)
> Went down to the wreck to see how they were getting on. [...] In the morning Brown had swam on board and taken a rope & fastened it. When on board he had tumbled down the hold and injured his foot pretty severely. Maimed for work at present.
> I took off my trousers and swam on board also. There are only ten yards or so of deep water, but a swift current swirls round and through the ship.
> Heaved all the timber I could find, overboard, to help them in making a raft. Another chap – Bilboa – followed me & the two of us took timber out of the hold for half an hour or so. (31 May 1883)

A further distraction from the daily routine of ranch life is the discovery of a man who vanished without trace as a boy some thirty years earlier:

> The missing Gilmour – the boy who was lost in 1853 & had never been heard of since – came with him [Don Jorge]. He was in the Sauce Grande, Nicolson suspected him to be a Gilmour, & Carruthers & Don Jorge identified him beyond a doubt. He has led a strange adventurous life almost too romantic to be believed. Speaks nothing but Spanish of course.
> His mother always said he would come back. (31 March 1883)

Herbert's diary from this time contains an interesting description of another occasional *estancia* task, the branding of cattle:

> Up at sunrise & went down to the cattle potrero at Gomez' to help Lean in the marking of the calves. Curious scene! The potrero, a wire fenced enclosure, must be fully ten acres. In this are enclosed about 3000 head of cattle, always kept moving by boys stationed outside. There are six men on horseback who enlasar [*enlazar* – lasso] the calves & bring them near the fire, where other twelve on foot pialar (lasso the feet) them & hold them down. They are then señaled [marked] & branded with the estancia mark. Terrible rough play & dangerous. Men covered with blood & almost naked whirling their lassos in all directions. Marked 900 & returned home after sundown. (11 April 1883)

Around this period, George Corbett, Herbert's uncle and manager of Los Yngleses, seems to have progressed from his usual irascibility into ever more unreasonable behaviour, as attested by repeated diary entries:

> Don Jorge not in an over amicable frame of mind. (14 March 1883)

> Don Jorge in need of a collar & chain. (3 April 1883)

> Don Jorge what one might call properly "enojado" [enraged]. (23 April 1883)

> Don Jorge in a passion as he has been all this fortnight. A very childish man when in a passion, foams at the mouth & screams. Would be rather amusing if he were not my uncle. (26 April 1883)

> Don Jorge in a very unbearable sort of humour. (31 July 1883)

> Don Jorge in a tremendous passion this morning. Amongst other violent deeds he gave Lavalle the sack. (8 October 1883)

> Don Jorge in a great passion. Gave Arranda the sack. (13 October 1883)

Quite what was wrong with Don Jorge is not stated, but he was clearly suffering from some sort of disorder. He became even more cantankerous early the following year when given notice by Thomas to resign as manager of Los Yngleses in order that Ernest could take over the post that he was now fully trained to occupy. While such a decision would likely be condemned as nepotism today, Herbert stoutly defended his father's move as the proper course of action:

> Ernest and Don Jorge had a bit of a yarn. Don Jorge alluded to his notice from the governor [Thomas] that he must resign on the 30th of September this year (3 months more than the stipulated warning between them) speaking of it as very abrupt, very injust [*sic*] etc. Accusing everyone of trying to supplant him etc.! By Jove! Does he really think it unjust of a father to make his eldest son "manager in his stead" when that son is 28 yrs. old and thoroughly competent in the work.
> Ernest wisely held his peace. (1 February 1884)

Poor don Jorge's woes were much amplified a short time later when his youngest daughter, Clementina, fell ill and tragically died at the age of six months:

> Don Jorge's youngest child seriously ill. Doctor La Serna up from the port to see her. (21 May 1884)

> Don Jorge's baby almost hopelessly ill. (25 May 1884)

> Don Jorge's youngest child, Clementina Gibson, died this morning at about 5 a.m. It was six months old.
> Lean went down to the port in the morning to make all the necessary arrangements for the interment which takes place today.
> He, Don Jorge and I went down in the volanta in the afternoon, the remains accompanying us. There were only three of us there. I read the burial service.
> Don Jorge very much broken down at this sad and unexpected event. (27 May 1884)

While his uncle's grief was surely understandable, Herbert expressed surprise at the depth of his despair, which showed no sign of lifting:

> Don Jorge continues very much cast down at his loss. Indeed he seems to feel it much more than one would expect, and walks about the place very dejectedly. (29 May 1884)

Don Jorge still ill & very depressed. (22 June 1884)

In the weeks following the loss of his daughter, Don Jorge appears to have become less prone to irrational outbursts, but increasingly downcast, to the extent that he spent long periods in bed. Finally, he travelled to Buenos Aires to consult a doctor and we learn that he underwent some sort of operation, a curious development in view of the fact that his ailment would appear to have been mental rather than physical (12 July 1884). It also seems that his marriage was on shaky ground, as, on one occasion, Herbert reports that his Aunt Helen 'broke out rather vehemently against D.J. [Don Jorge]' (12 July 1884). After this, we hear much less of George Corbett, presumably because the time came for him to hand over administration of Los Yngleses to Ernest.

Returning to 1883, a large part of Herbert's diary for August and September is occupied with the illness of his close friend and 'dentist' Runciman. The unfortunate Runciman is away from Los Yngleses when he becomes unwell, the news that he 'was very ill indeed' reaching the *estancia* on 16 August. Cairnie, the overseer, goes to investigate Runciman's condition and finds him lodged at the house of Dr Greene or Green, the 'merry stout Irishman' (2 February 1882) who often visited Los Yngleses in both social and medical capacities. When Cairnie returns, Herbert notes: 'Runciman is very ill, almost hopelessly so. What is worse is that he is badly housed and indifferently attended. Alas poor Yorick!' (17 August 1883). Runciman's illness drags on for the next couple of weeks, but by early September it is clear that he will not survive and Herbert, with two companions, journeys to Dr Greene's to see his friend for the last time:

> We arrived at the Doctor's place at 7 p.m. the sun having been in an hour. The road we took was 14 leagues long. [...]
>
> I was introduced to M$^{rs.}$ Greene and shortly afterwards we went in to see Runciman. He slept in the "Botica" the Doctor's drug store. It is a cold little wooden house. There are two rooms, the drug store & Runciman's. He was lying in a camp bed. What a change! The poor fellow had wasted away to a mere skeleton. He took my hand three or four times and muttered to himself "Bertie! This is Bertie!" He can only whisper and his cough is incessant.
>
> We stayed with him a few hours and then went to our room. A bleak sort of stable, with dilapidated camp beds. The wind blew chilly through the inch boards. It was freezing hard outside. I slept well, but Blichfeld & Carruthers passed a bad night. The rats were running under us and over us all night. (8 September 1883)

They remain with the wasted invalid, who is now attended by another good friend, for two days, before taking their sad farewell:

> Dan Cummings is with Runciman nursing him. He is a perfect attendant and as gentle & patient as a woman.
> We were with Runciman till late at night. It is apparent to all that he is sinking fast. He is still humorous and whispers a joke or an anecdote, broken by his want of breath & cough, but still showing his old wit & power of mimickry.
> The Doctor says that never, in his practise, either in the Hospitals or elsewhere has he seen so thin a man. It is a miracle to all that he lives, but the end is very near. (9 September 1883)
>
> Early in the morning we said goodbye to Runciman. He could only press our hands. It was a very painful sight: one I shall carry with me through life. (10 September 1883)

Later the next day, news reaches the *estancia* of Runciman's end and thoughts turn to his funeral:

> This evening at supper time a messenger arrived from outside. Runciman is dead.
> After supper Don Jorge, Cairnie & self discussed the burial etc. Dr. Greene's letter to Don Jorge was in Spanish and rather unfeeling in its tone. It was no doubt the wife's doing, the handwriting being hers.
> Dr. Greene suggested the interment should be either in Maipu, or in Buenos Aires. After discussing the question in all its aspects we decided that Ajó was preferable to either.
> Accordingly Cairnie is to be in the port tomorrow at sunrise, and return by 11 a.m. (12 September 1883)

Cairnie's attempts to arrange the funeral in Ajó do not proceed smoothly, as there is no precedent nor provision for dealing with the burial of a Protestant:

> Last night Cairnie and I revised all the deceased's papers. He had left no note of how his little property should be disposed. He had no relatives in the world.
> Cairnie returned after supper with Carruthers. They had had an immense trouble in obtaining permission to bury him in the port. The

> Juez referred them to the Doctor (native) the doctor to the priest, the priest to the Juez with an ineffable shrug and a "¿que [qué] tengo que ver yo con Protestantes?" ["what have Protestants got to do with me?"]. They all expressed extreme regret; Runciman had been their friend, there was nothing they would not do in their power. But their duties had to be observed, they had no precedent for interring a heretic in holy ground. At last they decided to permit it. Had the remains been of any other than the universally esteemed Runciman it had been more difficult. (13 September 1883)

It is evident that Herbert was deeply affected by Runciman's untimely demise, but at least he is able to take solace from reports of its peaceful manner:

> We learn that Runciman's end had been very gentle. The day before he had been out, sitting in the sun in an armchair, and felt better. That evening he gradually got weaker & towards dawn he whispered that he was dying. He took the Doctor's hand in his own and kissed him. Then he silently laid down in his last sleep. (16 September 1883)

Only a few months later, tragedy strikes again among the young men of Los Yngleses. On 9 December, Herbert discovers Eric Raeburn, who has been ailing for some time with consumption, in a state of great distress:

> I had occasion to go into the sala at 1 p.m. and saw Victoriana, the servant, standing at the passage door with a pale face. "What is this? What is this?" she was exclaiming, & at the same time I heard the sound of coughing and vomitting [sic] down the passage. I ran down hurriedly and found to my horror poor Eric standing over a bucket & vomitting blood like water. Luckily Lean was in Lavalle's room: I sent him to Eric's room & went over to Don Jorge. Then I returned to find Lean supporting Eric, the blood still flowing from his mouth. Aunt Helen appeared with water & Don Jorge made him a preparation of gallic acid and a red fluid for bleeding. The violent vomitting ceased and we lifted him into his bed.
>
> There was fully a quarter of a pailful of clotted blood. A horrible sight! He was greatly exhausted but sensible. […]
>
> As I sat fanning him later on in the afternoon he told me how it had happened. He went into Smith's room to pull off his top-boots which he had put on in the morning. As he was stooping he coughed & spat

blood. He at once went to his own room and was taking out some medicine when the attack overpowered him. (9 December 1883)

For the next three days, Raeburn remains in a precarious condition, sometimes appearing better, other times worse. He is nursed by Herbert's sister May, who has recently arrived at Los Yngleses on a visit, and Dan Cummings, who had also attended Runciman:

> Eric rather worse than better. His breathlessness has increased.
> Dr Greene arrived at 3 p.m. He pronounced the cause to be the bursting of an ulcer that had formed on the left lung. The present treatment is to be continued. (10 December 1883)

> Eric passed a better night. He is still very breathless, but quite sensible. He still spits blood.
> Thank God that May is here! She is a splendid nurse.
> Dan Cummings is here also as his nurse. (11 December 1883)
> Eric rather worse. (12 December 1883)

By the next morning, it is clear that the end is close:

> Eric passed a very bad night. He is sinking fast. Dan, May, Don Jorge & myself were up with him till 1 o'clock in the morning. Two or three times he seemed about to expire for want of breath. He would cry out help and struggle with his mouth open for air. It was a most pitiful sight! (13 December 1883)

Finally, at 11 am, Raeburn 'passed away peacefully, without a struggle' (13 December 1883).

The death had a profound impact on Raeburn's friends, especially on May, who had formed a very strong attachment to her patient. Herbert notes: 'Poor May is most dreadfully shaken by this sad event. She nursed him all through his illness and only broke down when it was over' (13 December 1883). The following day, May seems even more distressed and the high temperatures of the Argentine summer are beginning to take their toll on Raeburn's mortal remains:

> I had an anxious time with May. She is terribly upset, most alarmingly so. She made me take her into the room 3 times, to look at the diseased [deceased], and to cut off some hair. The heat of the day was

> great and towards the afternoon the smell became very offensive.
>
> A 10.30 p.m. Ernest and Don Jorge arrived. Ernest was terribly cut up too, poor fellow!
>
> The remains were at once chested and the coffin closed. It was a horrid ordeal to come through, the solitary lamp just making the darkness visible. (14 December 1883)

Worse is to come, for it becomes necessary to open the coffin again:

> The coffin had to be reopened for the body to be padded better. […] I got the face down to the eyes uncovered, to let Ernest see, as he expressed a great desire to look once at him. He was great shocked. Had he but seen the whole face! My God what a sight! (15 December 1883)

A few days later, Herbert headed off to Buenos Aires for a month's break in the city, which would include a good portion of time in the hands of the dental and medical professions:

> At the dentist's from 8 o'clock to half past eleven! (24 December 1883)

> At my dentist's again from 8 to 10 a.m. Had 3 teeth stopped, from one of which he extracted the nerves, and 3 extracted. The latter under gas.
> Very much shaken after it. (26 December 1883)

> Visited Dr. Alston to consult him about the symptoms I have; viz. very rapid action of the heart & a certain huskiness in the throat. I suspect that smoking, drinking, together with the shock of recent events are the causes of it. He sounded me, pronounced me alright and apparently agreed with me. He ordered me to steam 5 minutes every night over benzonine & hot water; and advised knocking off smoking and drinking. (4 January 1884)

The customary optimism of Herbert's previous end-of-year reflections is missing from his Hogmanay diary entry, as the deaths of his two friends still weigh heavily on his mind:

> This year has alas! been eventful. Two friends have died within 3 months of one another. I cannot close this year with any merry shout of "Ring out the old: ring in the new". What have I not lost this year!

My nearest friend; my light heart and all my ambition. God grant that 1884 may be a happier year for me. (31 December 1883)

While staying in town, Herbert and Ernest took a trip to La Plata, the city founded by Governor Dardo Rocha in 1882 to serve as capital of Buenos Aires Province. Construction was still ongoing when they visited, following the elaborate plan of the architect Pedro Benoit, who envisaged a city of wide avenues and diagonals along the lines of Washington, DC:

Went down to the new city of "La Plata" with Ernest. 3 hours journey by train brought us there. [...] Had dinner at the new hotel and knocked about. There are several very handsome buildings going up, and perhaps sixty or a hundred houses scattered over the place, but there is very little private enterprise. (9 January 1884)

By the end of January, Herbert was back in post at Los Yngleses, occupied with his usual round of activities. He returned to Buenos Aires for a short spell in late March, during which he and Ernest visited one of the new freezing plants that would soon transform the Argentine economy by making the export of meat a lucrative trade:

Up early and off to Campana to see the frozen meat establishment. [...] Arrived there shortly after ten & went up to the galpones.

No one at home, all at breakfast. Ernest went into the town and rooted up a "Mr. Angus" boss of the whole shanty. He trotted us round.

Everything interesting, but particularly the freezing rooms. We went into them through a door at least two-feet thick which fitted exactly into the panel. Inside, all was dark & there was a weirdness in the sight which sent a shudder of almost terror through us. By the light of a lantern we could see the long rows of carcasses (they looked like corpses) stretching out into the gloom.

We were walking through snow, above us hung icicles!

It was a wonderful sight to see at midday with 92° in the shade outside.

They were killing part of the 5700 wethers they bought of [sic] us. (22 March 1884)

Back at the *estancia*, one of the main talking points of the year was the sudden departure of Cairnie, the overseer, following a disagreement with George Corbett:

> Cairnie had a row with Don Jorge this afternoon. […] In the evening Cairnie told me that he was going to town by to-morrow's galera. From there perhaps home; & did not intend returning. I did all I could to persuade him to stay but failed.
>
> He said goodbye to the fellows here. I went with him to his room & he completely broke down there. I was half afraid that he intended to do something rash: but saw from his various preparations that this was not his purpose. So I went with him to the Palenque and said goodbye.
>
> I met Don Jorge at the big galpon just after he had gone. "Who is that leaving?" said Don Jorge. "Mr Cairnie" I replied. "Where is he off to?" "Home, sir." Then I explained. Don Jorge attributed it all, somewhat harshly, to drink. I had it on my lips to say "you drove him to it". But I did not. He is my uncle. (8 June 1884)

The drama intensifies when it is discovered that the Corbetts' ex-governess, a girl of suspect repute according to Herbert, has also left, and it soon unfolds that she and Cairnie have hastily married:

> Heard today that Miss Ward the ex-governess has also gone by yesterday's galera [stagecoach]. She went without warning anyone: but Mr Moore, smelling a rat, insisted on his wife accompanying her. Cairnie has paid all her debts in the port.
>
> This escapade has disgusted me with Cairnie: the girl is scarcely a respectable character & I don't think she can ever be received here as Mrs C. (9 June 1884)

> Weather continues very bad, and Don Jorge still in bed. Had a long interview with Aunt, who rather sticks up for Cairnie. (14 June 1884)

> At breakfast time Cairnie suddenly appeared. He was very excited & nervous. He shewed us his marraige [sic] certificate. Ernest and the pater are the witnesses. […] Ernest by no means enthusiastic about the marraige [sic] &c. (17 June 1884)

Cairnie returns to his post, despite some reservations on the part of George Corbett, but seems to be increasingly under the influence of drink, a long-standing weakness. When Herbert attends a sort of reception for the newly-weds in Ajó, Cairnie's conduct leaves much to be desired:

At sundown started with Hinchliff & Garrett for the port. Got to More's in due time & going inside were duly presented to M^rs. Cairnie. She is pretty but ---. [...]

Passed a splendid evening but Cairnie behaved atrociously. He bullied me into making a speech long after Garrett had proposed their health. He teased Hinchliff. He presented M^rs. Cairnie to the party several times. In fact he made an utter ass of himself. (21 June 1884)

In early July, Herbert turns his attention to marking his twenty-first birthday, doing so in the traditional drunken manner. As he acknowledges, the rather effusive diary entry for the momentous day, accompanied by a comical poetic composition, is best attributed to artificially elevated spirits:

My birthday. I now gracefully assume the "toga virilis" having attained my 21st year. "Ecce! homo sum." – I believe it is the correct thing to quote Latin, when come of age.

In the evening I stood champagne. The most killing stuff ever brewed. We were all ill though Cairnie was the only one to give outward & visible signs of an inward & physical distress. We had speeches and songs till 12 o'clock.

Is it incumbent on me to write something on this most auspicious event. What shall it be? A sermon? Scarcely. A funereal dirge? Decidley [sic] better.

> I had rather be an infant
> upon my mother's knee
> Than a 6 ft. man with a bearded chin
> of age & at liberty

CHORUS (strictly Greek)
> Tweedledum
> Tweedledee
> I had rather be a schoolboy
> full of hilarity
> Than a grave señor, come to man's estate
>   And nearer futurity
> Tweedledum
> Tweedledee.

Scarcely up to the mark this, either. Can it be the champagne that has so addled my pate? Happy thought! Let the champagne be my excuse. I will finish the dirge at a future date: the toga has scarcely got time-stained enough yet for moralizing. (8 July 1884)

Once again, the lack of activity at the *estancia* during winter bores Herbert. He complains of 'loafing about with nothing to do' (10 August 1884), of 'passing time as best I can' (1 September 1884), and, contrary to previous assertions of the quality of life at Los Yngleses, now claims that 'this is a miserable existence' (10 August 1884). When the shearing season arrives, he rejoices at being occupied again and embraces the normally unenviable task of all the associated administration with relish: 'I have got most of the office work on my shoulders, so thank heavens I have something to do at last' (8 October 1884).

Herbert's health was again causing him some concern, however, and after shearing had finished he journeyed to Buenos Aires, where he consulted a new doctor:

> Visited D^r. Colbourne in the morning. Pronounced me far too excited & deferred sounding my heart till the next morning. (8 December 1884)

> D^r. Colbourne saw me. Irregularity of the heart. Am to stop smoking as a first experiment. (9 December 1884)
> Had my second visit from D^r. Colbourne, in which his opinion was not so favourable. No wine now, and tincture of digitalis three times a day. (13 December 1884)

> D^r. Colbourne here again, and this time he noted a great improvement. (16 December 1884)

Happily, Herbert's heart complaint was evidently of a minor nature, for by New Year he 'played lawn tennis most of the day' (1 January 1885).

Early in 1885, shooting appears to have become the favoured leisure activity of the residents of Los Yngleses, and Herbert eagerly records some particularly bounteous expeditions, such as the following:

> In spite of last night's jollity all up with the sun & a great packing of guns & bottles went on till 8 a.m. when the volanta with Brown and the dogs started. We followed on horseback – 8 of us all told – and arrived at the Laguna Milan a little before the volanta. Till luncheon time it was very desultory shooting 22 ducks & a swan being the bag up to midday. After a hearty meal we all braced up for the grand battue.

We worked one narrow cañadon [creek] the whole afternoon with
brilliant success. [...] The following is the list of the gamebag
>
> 26 Canvass Backs
> 15 Teal
> 31 Brown Duck
> 5 Swan
> 1 Snipe
> 1 Plover
> 1 Nutria
> <u>1 Small</u> grebe
> <u>81 head</u>   (22 February 1885)

Another new hobby developed at the *estancia* a few months later – playing polo. Herbert participated enthusiastically in the sport, which was just beginning to reach the country that today produces many of its most able exponents:

> Had a game of polo with very great success. (28 June 1885)

> Had a very good game of polo today. We are all becoming great swells at it. (5 July 1885)
> Had a good game of polo today. Very hard fight. (12 July 1885)

On 31 May 1885, Thomas Gibson purchased La Tomasa, an *estancia* of some 6,072 hectares at Cacharí, close to the town of Azul. This property, named after the late daughter of its previous owner, would become another jewel in the crown of the Gibson empire. Herbert made his first visit to the ranch in August and recorded his observations in some detail:

> This is the new Estancia we have bought. 2¼ leagues in extent & well wooded with artificial plantations. The head station consists of 1 big dwelling house – brick – with vineyard 3 rooms. Another do. [ditto] with 7 rooms in which is situated the pulperia [general store]. Facing this is another brick range with accomodation [*sic*] for the peons. Behind this is a big brick galpon, a palomar [dovecot], & 3 sheds for fine rams & shearing. Also a sheep bath with mechanical chiquero [arrangement of gates and pens to control passage of sheep through dip]. Fruit trees abound on all sides, & there are 3 big potreros [fenced enclosures]. (6 August 1885)

He concludes that La Tomasa is 'altogether a good estancia' and adds, completely out of the blue, 'Here I expect to spend the next year' (6 August 1885). The last remark heralds the dawn of a significant new phase of Herbert's life story; in a few months' time, he would indeed move to La Tomasa, not as senior foreman, as he had been at Los Yngleses, but as manager in his own right, having been entrusted by his father with the administration and stocking up of the ranch. In fact, La Tomasa took up much more than twelve months of Herbert's life, being one of the properties at which he would reside for long spells in the following years.

Between August and his departure for La Tomasa at the beginning of December, Herbert continued to live at Los Yngleses, but was increasingly occupied with making plans for the new *estancia*. His diary from this period contains little worthy of note, aside from an amusing incident while travelling by *galera* (stagecoach) to Buenos Aires:

> Started in the galera. Fellow passengers were 2 priests, Cardosa's wife & mother in lawn [*sic*] & 3 men names unknown.
> Got stuck in a cañadon [creek] just before the arroyo de los perros [literally, 'stream of the dogs']. The 3 men got out & the ladies also, in a cart that happened to be crossing at the time. But the wary priests would not budge. Half an hour later, standing on the shore, we had the pleasure of seeing the galera tumble over with the priests inside. The latter scrambled through one of the windows wet & miserable. (28 September 1885)

On 2 December, Herbert said his goodbyes at Los Yngleses and set off for La Tomasa. Although the new ranch lay at a similar latitude, it was necessary to first travel north to Buenos Aires before catching the train south-west again to Cacharí station close to La Tomasa, as no railway lines crossed that part of the country from east to west. Although the distance as the crow flies between the two properties was still considerable, Herbert would often ride back and forth in the coming years, until his father asked him 'to discontinue these long rides' on the grounds of economy, since 'he thought it came cheaper to travel by train and galera, than using so much horseflesh'.[54]

With his departure from Los Yngleses, Herbert's apprenticeship had come to an end. In the four years since his arrival in Argentina, he had acquired a veritable wealth of knowledge: he had learnt the sheep-breeding business inside out; had gained numerous insights into dealing with the class of men who would now

---

54 Herbert Gibson to May Mackern, 31 May 1925.

respect him as Don Heriberto, their *patrón* (boss); and had acquired the sound grasp of Spanish, both written and spoken, essential to conduct business in Argentina. In summary, Herbert was now fully prepared to try his hand at running an *estancia*, but only time would prove if he was truly ready to rise to the manifold challenges that lay ahead.

CHAPTER 4

MANAGER

When Herbert took charge of La Tomasa in December 1885, he found an *estancia* of great promise, but which badly needed the attentions of a capable and vigorous manager. In a letter to his now-widowed sister May some forty years later, occasioned by her receiving La Tomasa as part of her patrimonial inheritance, Herbert described the history of the ranch and its state when acquired by the Gibsons:

> It is forty years ago, today, since my father bought the Tomasa from Don Manuel Babio through the agency of the land broker "Willie" White. […] The price was $40 per hectarea, the total area being 6072 hectareas. […]
>
> It was composed of three "suertes" or lots, each of ¾ of a square league. The "suerte" was the measure of land grant in use ever since Juan de Garay founded Buenos Aires in 1580. It measured 9000 "varas" by 3000 "varas", or Spanish yards of 33 English inches. Don Manuel Rozas [Juan Manuel de Rosas] had founded Azul in 1835; and after the Rebellion in the South of the Province in 1839 was quelled; and the standing army of Militia disbanded in 1842; Rozas granted to each soldier a "suerte" of land. […]
>
> Don Manuel Babio was a Spanish storekeeper, who, bit by bit, bought these "suertes" from the original owners or their heirs. […]
>
> The terms of the sale to my father provided that Babio should not deliver the land until Nov. 1885; to give him time to move out his livestock to land he owned in Trenque Lauquen.
>
> The name of the Tomasa was given by Babio to his estancia in memory of a favourite daughter called Tomasa, who had died. It had nothing to do with my father's name. Babio asked us not to change the name, and my father agreed.

> [...] There were 18 "puesteros", all with flocks on shares partly owned by themselves; which was one of the reasons that Babio had in asking for six months to give time to all these share shepherds to remove their sheep. The total number of sheep was 26,000 when I arrived; all very inferior cross-bred merinos. At Puesto Nº2, which is now the Cabaña Miramonte, the share shepherd was a French doctor of sorts, the only one in the whole Cachari district, called Planchon. [...]
>
> There were no fences, either boundary or divisionary. It was all open camp, and a mass of paja abounding in cuises, or wild guinea pigs. The number of wild cats (gatos pajeros) and foxes was prodigious. The most common grass or weed was a plant with a very wiry stem with a yellow flower, called "boton de oro" ["gold button"]. The wiry stem got between the claws of the sheep's hoofs and lamed them. It has almost disappeared.[55]

Herbert's first task at La Tomasa was to build up and improve the *estancia*'s stock, which he immediately set about doing by bringing a troop of some 7,000 sheep from Los Yngleses, soon to be followed by another 6,000 head, including one of the Gibsons' best Lincoln flocks.[56] Once the first drove had arrived, he began checking the sheep and allotting them to the various *puestos*:

> Worked the troop today, counting it & starting to divide into flocks. (21 December 1885)
>
> Finished the division into flocks today & despatched the various flocks to their puestos. (22 December 1885)

Herbert's diary entries from the first months of 1886 are generally short and concern routine *estancia* matters, suggesting that the responsibilities of management left little time for recording trivia or the extended musings to which he had been prone in the past. Highlights of a business nature included some successful ram sales, despite a visit from one 'ferocious customer [...] in a tall hat & a black coat, who got very vicious about the rams and went away in high dudgeon' (18 February 1886), and the preparation of some of the ranch's 'fine ewes' for an exhibition at the Palermo show ground in Buenos Aires (23 & 24 April 1886).

---

55 Herbert Gibson to May Mackern, 31 May 1925.
56 Herbert Gibson to May Mackern, 31 May 1925.

Herbert's trip to town for the exhibition also fulfilled another purpose, that of attending May's wedding to Dr George Mackern: 'At church where May got married to D[r.] Mackern. Afterwards wedding breakfast at Mackerns' in Calle Larga' (6 May 1886). The happy couple went to Montevideo on honeymoon and Herbert headed to Los Yngleses to make arrangements for a lavish party to mark the union:

> Began to make preparations for a grand baile [ball or dance] on the 12th of next month. (28 May 1886)
>
> Started my arrangements for baile. Writing invitations. (31 May 1886)

Most of the guests are those who live and work on Los Yngleses – the peons, *puesteros*, and their families – and the newly-weds themselves do not attend, presumably deterred by the arduous journey from their home in Buenos Aires to the *estancia*. The *baile* is to take place in the large *galpón*, or shed, the building that is the hub of operations during the shearing season and is used for storage of wool bales the rest of the year. Herbert works tirelessly in transforming this unpromising site into a venue suitable for the grandest of celebrations:

> Working at galpon today clearing away bales & making place ready. (4 June 1886)
>
> All day in the galpon putting up flags &c & making grand preparations. (9 June 1886)
>
> Working like a Trojan at the galpon which is now assuming a gorgeous appearance. (11 June 1886)

Herbert wasted little space in his diary describing the dance itself, but instead inserted into the volume an account (in Spanish) he published in the local newspaper, the *Patria* of Dolores. Two even more eloquent testimonies to the scale and success of the event have survived in letters by Herbert's brothers Ernest and John. Each of them wrote to their sister May describing the dance in all its magnificence:

> On the 11th inst. [*sic* – it actually took place on the 12th] John, Herbert & I gave a little dance to the "Yngleses" people, in honour of your

marriage. John has promised to write you details. Suffice it to say that it was an immense success. The big galpon was really well-decorated & lit (some of the decorations being surpassingly fine, & – besides lamps – the consumption of wax candles passing 300). One hundred & eight (108) couples were counted upon the floor at one time; & the total number of our people was estimated at from 300 to 400. The like has not been seen in the province! The people began to arrive about 5 p.m.; at 6 p.m. we sat down to dinner, & the basis being two oxen roasted whole, you can imagine the accessories in the way of roast suckling-pigs [6], turkeys [10], hams [5], chickens [50], plum-puddings [10], big cakes [10], "pastels" [1100], besides tinned & potted meats, pastry, confectionery, sweets, etc etc. Also champagne, french and carlon wine, brandy, anis, vermouth, caña, liqueurs & "lemonadas"; hot soup (about 80 gallons), coffee, tea, & chocolate. About 7 p.m. the dancing began, & went on till daybreak – fast & furious – when a few people began to leave; but rain coming on at 8 a.m., Herbert & I announced that the dance must go on, cut down the lasso which surmounted the trophy of arms (amidst furious "vivas" & applause), & sent out to slay another ox for breakfast. On went the dance till mid day, without break or cessation, & then we sat down to breakfast. – Somebody counted the survivors at the tables, & they were 102! – On rising, at 1 p.m., I called for the "despedida" or farewell dance, and I'm blamed if they did not keep it up till 3 p.m.![57]

Ernest has asked me to give you an account of the dance given here in your honour – but I have read his letter & he leaves me little to tell, – at least to tell in a letter – for I could talk about it for a couple of days. It was the most wonderful event I have seen yet at the shrine of Terphsicore [*sic* – Terpsichore, the Muse of song and dance].

To begin with we worked a couple of days at decorating the galpone – and with great success – it looked like a ball room & the floor was very good. – Flags round the walls – arrangements of blue and white (the Argentine colours) – the Argentine arms & an immense placard with 'Amistad y Progreso' [Friendship & Progress], – the father's photo at one end in an immense wreath & draperies & two carriage lamps – a photo of you and Eva at the other end with ditto ditto. – The immense beams were some of them beautifully done – Ernest had a great hit with his stands of arms, guns, revolvers, rifles, tennis

---

57 Ernest Gibson to May Mackern, 14 June 1886.

racquets, golf clubs, polo clubs, horns, whips, spurs &c. Hinchliff made a great success, & his beam, wreathed in festoons and formations of canes, & feathery foliage, took precedence to any decorations I had seen in churches. […]

The guests began to arrive about 4 o'clock & the whole estancia was alive with carriages, carts & horsemen & horsewomen all streaming in one direction. – We had a big bonfire to light the late ones. […]

We had a Master of Ceremonies & his word was law – we all obeyed him. – After dinner he asked me to play a waltz – and I started with one specially composed for the occasion, viz. 'The Yngleses Waltz' – (copies, 21/- each, to be had from me.) – […]

That brings me on to the subject of dancing. – The natives do dance beautifully & have a far greater variety of dances than we have. – They scorn squares, except one they danced & that only once. – Only four danced it & for grace & neat footing it was very fine. – We had slow waltzes, quick waltzes, polkas, mazurkas, & a great many native dances. – The girls waltz (some of them) beautifully and reverse very well – I even got one of them to do that quick running step which we do at home and she never made a faux pas. […]

How the natives last the way they do is a mystery. – I got completely exhausted at 4.30 a.m. – and had to go to knock off – but was at it again at 9 and kept at it till 3 p.m. – then slept for about 12 hours. – Ernest & Bertie [Herbert] lasted the whole time, & did not go to bed till the second night. For hosts they were incomparable & were 'viva'd' wherever they went. […]

We had one song that tickled me immensely. – A man sat down in the middle of the room with his guitar. Ernest, Bertie & I were put in front of him – and a crowd of 300 stood round us. – He sang a long impromptu song all about the guv'nor [Thomas Gibson], the great marriage, Gibson H$^{\underline{nos}}$ [Gibson Brothers] the Yngleses, Ernest & his deeds, the great dance the like of which had never been seen and never would be again & so on. […]

There was not a hitch in any thing, not even a fight. The arrangements and foresight (for it was a big contract) reflect great credit on Ernest & Bertie & those who helped them.[58]

---

58 John Gibson to May Mackern, 15 June 1886.

In the weeks following the party, Herbert spent some time in Buenos Aires, before returning to La Tomasa, accompanied by Ernest and a canine companion given to him by a member of his new brother-in-law's family: 'Brought a little bull terrier bitch pup wh. young Mackern gave me. Christen'd her "Tomasa"' (26 July 1886). A few days later, the two brothers set off on a tour of Gibson properties in the district of Bahía Blanca, a town in the far south of Buenos Aires Province. The only feature of Bahía Blanca that seems to have impressed Herbert is its pier, but he was kept entertained by Ernest's tales of a previous journey to the region:

> Bahia Blanca is any thing but picturesque. The streets are wide, houses on the whole good, but there is an endless sand storm and the desolation is greater by the want of trees. From Azul south there are scarcely any trees and their want makes the landscape blank. We passed the government house & post office, one of the oldest buildings in Bahia, with its front paved with cannonballs.
>
> In the afternoon we visited the port. Half an hour's drive in a hackney carraige [sic] through a flat plain, covered with sand & wanting in vegetation brought us to the handful of buildings clustered round the pier or mole. Here there is a station, the train going into the town: & a saladero. The pier made by the Ferro Carril del Sud Company is handsome: some 120 yds long, fifty out straight & seventy parallel to the shore, it carries a double pair of railway lines, & several moveable cranes. A ship of about 800 tons was unloading timber. The creek is wide but the dredged channel is narrow & marked with buoys. (2 August 1886)
>
> My brother Ernest pointed out to me the road he had taken in 1880 on horseback, when he rode out to visit the father's land on the far side of the Rio Negro, on which occasion he nearly lost his life. He showed me the little ranch where he spent the first night & wh. was sacked by the Indians 8 months later on, the men being killed & the women taken prisoners. This was only 3 leagues from Bahia Blanca! (3 August 1886)

After his travels, Herbert returned to La Tomasa and soon received news of his mother's death. Curiously, his diary records little more than the bare facts, enclosed within double black lines, and gives away little about the writer's emotions:

Went in to Azul with Smith last night. Saw him off this morning by the Bahia Blanca train & returned myself by the mid day train.

On arriving at the station I rec$^{d.}$ a telegram bearing the sad news of my poor mother's death. It had been cabled out this morning: she died last night.

Returned to the estancia & stopped all work. (1 September 1886)

One of Herbert's Cacharí acquaintances was also soon to meet his maker, in rather more dramatic circumstances: 'Heard too of the death of poor Electric Smith who was run over by a car, & refusing to have his leg amputated was carried off by gangrene' (6 October 1886).

For the next six months, Herbert continued his usual round of activities, basing himself at La Tomasa but making frequent trips to Buenos Aires, Los Yngleses, and other Gibson properties. A few of the more interesting entries from his diary are transcribed below:

At La Tomasa: Having heard at sundown that Anderson & others had left for a dance in the neighbourhood without asking permission, I went out myself at 9 p.m. or so & changed the padlocks of all the gates. (12 October 1886)

Anderson & B. Nuevo dismissed. The rest let off with a warning. My ruse had been successful & none of them had been able to enter the camp overnight. (13 October 1886)

Had a heavy hailstorm y'day some of the stones weighing 14 grammes! Did no damage. (18 October 1886)

Settled into a very severe tormenta [storm] growing worse towards night.
  Lost sheep in the night – 330 hd [head] from Pioli's flock. (20 October 1886)

Cholera made its appearance in Bs. As. [Buenos Aires] having been imported they say by the Italian steamer "Perseo" on the 3rd of the month. (9 November 1886)

The "Ministro de Gobierno" [Minister of Government] passed today at 7.30 a.m. in a special train for Azul, where he presides over the elections for governor. A row is anticipated. (4 December 1886)

Started early this morning in a carriage with George [George Gibson, Herbert's cousin] to visit the Russian colonies & the quarries.

About 14 miles from town we descended a valley, & crossing a small brook entered the little hamlet of Nieva [...]. There are 35 families in Nieva. The cottages are modest, mud walls with thatched roof but whitewashed and clean. At each cottage we saw a four wheeled waggon & a cutting machine. These colonists own one to four chacras [plots] of 150 acres a chacra. They bought them in 1876 when the colonies were founded, at about £40 each chacra. They are now worth over £400. The people are polite & tidy. They have a little church & a railed in God's acre.

A straight track of 5 miles brought us to the foot of the sierras (350 ft high) & we visited some of the quarries. They sink as deep as 48 to 50 ft, taking out three kinds of stone, one of which takes a polish like marble. These stones are all formed of Pampa clay & lime.

They also burn lime here.

Got back to Azul towards sundown. (16 December 1886)

A Señor Boréa here asking 500 sheep for inoculation from scab. He desires to bring forward his discovery (the result of 5 years' study & which he says will eradicate the disease by inoculation) by curing sheep in various estancias and then claiming the national recompense. Agreed to give him 500 to cure the cost of so doing being 7 cto. [*céntimos* – cents] p. animal. (15 February 1887)

At Los Yngleses: Saw by tonight's letters that Borea had been a regular fraud. He has absconded with 700 m/n [*moneda nacional* – units of national currency]! Experentia [*sic – experientia*] docet. (6 March 1887)

A very good game of polo, but came to an awkward termination. In following up the ball I received Garretts [*sic*] club, as he was doing a back stroke, full in the face between the eyes.

Got myself bandaged up & lolled about in an armchair the rest of the day. (20 March 1887)

Had a very good game of polo in which French, Enoch & Chilvers joined.

Went down to Juan Olasar's to have breakfast. Had 5 courses of fowl & very heavy wine. (27 March 1887)

> **In Buenos Aires:** George [Mackern] is up in Cordoba travelling with a faculty of doctors. (4 April 1887)

> Shifted my belongings to May's house, where I shall stay until George returns. (5 April 1887)

> Went with Willie Mackern to the Colon theatre in the evening where we saw an excellent zarzuela "Catalina" founded on the history of Pedro the Great of Russia, acted by the same company that I saw last year in the Nat. Theatre. (9 April 1887)

On 17 April 1887, Herbert embarked upon his first journey 'home' since arriving in Argentina five-and-a-half years earlier. The voyage itself was uneventful, the highlight, quite literally, being the view of Rio de Janeiro's impressive new lighthouse:

> See this evening the magnificent Rio Janeiro lighthouse with its three revolving lights, red, green & clear. The power of these is enormous & at a distance of 3 miles the rays of each light renders clear the very finest rope at the top most point of the mast. When exactly within the full blaze the eye tires itself looking at the light as if it were a sun. (24 April 1887)

After docking at Southampton on 13 May, Herbert spent a few days in London, where he visited, among other attractions, 'Buffalo Bill's entertainment' (16 May 1887). He then took the express to Edinburgh and remained in Scotland until early July, catching up with relatives, visiting old haunts, and, curiously, beginning to compile an English-Basque dictionary:

> Had a glorious day's golf with John [Herbert's brother] & a man called Thomson at Gullane. (19 May 1887)

> Rode with Eva [Herbert's sister] & spent the evening with the Matthews. (27 May 1887)

> Went out to Craiglockhart where we played tennis. (28 May 1887)

> Called upon the Hays & spent the evening at the Conservative Club. (1 June 1887)

Went down to N. Berwick to play golf. (10 June 1887)

Left early this morning with John for S. [St.] Fillans at the head of Loch Erne [*sic* – Earn] in Perthshire. Spent most of the day on the loch. (17 June 1887)

Drove with John & a fellow called Clark to Killin near Loch Tay and so on to Lochay where we were kindly attended by the fair Bessie Cameron, a great beauty of these parts. (19 June 1887)

Up [from North Berwick] to town [Edinburgh] again & got some of my dictionary done.
    N.B. I started to write an English-Basque dictionary on 18th of this month: it will take me about a year & will contain some 40,000 words. It is purely for my own use. (23 June 1887)

Went with Hope [Herbert's brother] to Greenock where we met MacAlister & so on to Hunter's Quay where we saw the famous "Thistle" the fastest yacht in this country & built to race the Americans.
    In evening, having returned to Edinburgh, called on St. John Day (author of "Hist. of Iron & Steel" &c) where we met Prof. Armstrong, M$^{r.}$ Brown the electrician, Melville the artist & Rev. Johnson a church luminary. (30 June 1887)

In the evening we went to see Sarah ~~Bernhardt~~ Berndhart [*sic* – he was right first time!], a magnificent actress. (8 July 1887)

On 10 July, Herbert sets out on a tour of England, starting with the Royal Agricultural Show in Newcastle, then on to Spalding to attend an exhibition of Lincoln sheep, and thence to Gloucester to visit Hempstead Court, the school now run by his old friend Harry Brereton. He then travels, via London, to Elmham, to visit his own *alma mater*, the Norfolk County School:

In morning to Elmham church where M$^{r.}$ Legge dispensed religion & evening up to the N.C.S. to chapel. Chapel [built in 1883; Herbert had left school at the end of 1880] very pretty building but green glass in windows spoils effect. M$^{r.}$ & M$^{rs.}$ Watson rec$^{d.}$ me very kindly. Did not stay to supper. Only one boy at school whom I remember – Overman. (24 July 1887)

Up to school at midday where I dined with Watson at the head table. Very funny sensation. Afterwards went over the school. Same old place.

In the evening we all went up to the school concert which was very good. School breaks up tomorrow. (25 July 1887)

While staying in Norfolk, Herbert travels to the Ely Show and also to Norwich to hear the Prime Minister, Lord Salisbury, speak 'very well' (27 July 1887). After briefly returning to Edinburgh, he departs again by train to Liverpool in the company of a friend named Thomson, from where they set sail to Spain to undertake a 'grand tour' of that country. Herbert describes their vessel, the Cunard S.S. *Morocco*, as a 'small boat and decidly [*sic* – decidedly] dirty' with only '20 passengers in all, including 3 ladies' (22 August 1887). Six days later, they reach Gibraltar, from where I shall let Herbert take up the narrative:

Awoke this morning to find ourselves lying off Gibraltar. Fine looking place. Enormous rock with small town. Landed in a felucca and went up to the Royal Hotel. Shortly afterwards I started in search of the tomb of Uncle John who died here in 1828. I eventually found what beyond doubt is the monumental slab, but the inscription is entirely defaced. (28 August 1887)

Started very early this morning in a steamer for Malaga. A most enjoyable trip of 7 hours. […]

Malaga is "de fiesta" at present. The feast commenced on the 19th & lasts until the 31st. This in commemoration of the 4th centenary of the entry of Isabel & Ferdinand into the city. (29 August 1887)

Went to a bullfight. […] 8 bulls killed. Very fine bullfight. (31 August 1887)

Left for Granada by the 1.15 train. Train crowded. Had to travel 3rd to Bobadillo. The pass through the Sierra Nevada was very fine. (1 September 1887)

Visited the Alhambra. Most wonderfully dainty palace. (2 September 1887)

Left at 5 a.m. by diligence for Jaen. Arrived at 2 p.m. The road is very picturesque. Saw the cathedral at Jaen. Took the train from there to Espelini and there caught the express (!) for Madrid. (4 September 1887)

Arrived at Madrid early this morning. Went to Hotel Continental, at the Puerta del Sol.
Visited the British Minister, M^r. St. Clair Ford, and mooned about the town all day. (5 September 1887)

Visited the Museo de Pinturas, the finest in the world. Some of the pictures magnificent.
Intended to go to Pamplona tonight, but we went to the wrong station, and so had to spend another night in Madrid. (6 September 1887)

Arrived at Pamplona at 1 p.m. this afternoon. (8 September 1887)

Took the 4.38 a.m. train to S. Sebastian. Exceedingly picturesque journey. Arrived at this watering place at 10.30 a.m.
Thomson made enquiries about steamers & eventually discovered that he would have to go overland.
Great crowd of French & Spanish visitors here: the Queen is staying at this place at present. (9 September 1887)

Thomson left at 11 a.m. this morning for London.
Saw the Queen embark on the "Destructor" en route for Bilbao.
Returned to Pamplona at 10 p.m. (10 September 1887)

After Thomson's departure, Herbert continues to tour northern Spain alone. Much of his time is spent meeting relatives of his Argentine acquaintances of Basque origin, most of whom are *puesteros* on the Gibson properties:

At midday Lucio Aizkorbe's brother – a peasant – called on me. (11 September 1887)

Off this morning early to Arrisa [perhaps Ariza] to see Lacunza's people. The village doctor happened to be going the same way so we joined company.

> Met a whole crowd of Lacunzas at the village, all full of enquiries. He has two brothers one José Felipe & the other Atanasio, the latter not very well off. [...] One of J. M. Lacunza's daughters wants to go out. His son Fernando Lacunza also very full of enquiries. In fact had a lot of questions put. (12 September 1887)
>
> Saw J. Olasar's mother & niece, gave them the letters &c, had a good breakfast & got back to Pamplona at 8 p.m. (22 September 1887)

At the end of September, he began his journey home, travelling by train from San Sebastián to Paris and thence on to England: 'Left S. Sebastian at 11 a.m. Travelled all night & arrived in Paris on Fri 30th at 5.30 a.m. left again at 8.20 a.m. & arrived at London at 5.30 p.m. Beastly weather the whole way' (29 & 30 September 1887). After a couple of days in London, he headed back to Edinburgh: 'Left for Scotland by the Flying Scotchman & got into Auld Reekie at 7 p.m. Pater met me on my arrival' (3 October 1887).

Despite having been away for almost six months, Herbert's break from Argentina was far from over. While in Edinburgh, he enjoyed a variety of entertainments and excursions, such as visiting the Forth railway bridge during its construction in the company of his brother Hope and another engineer, attending a recital by the child prodigy Hoffman, and taking dancing lessons:

> Joined Hope & Macalister on their way to the Forth Bridge. Went up to the top of one of the piers, over 300 ft, in a lift. Good view of the channel fleet. (10 October 1887)
>
> Aggie [Hope's wife] Hope and I went to the Hoffman pianoforte recital in the Music Hall. Hoffman, a child of 10 years, is a wonderful musician. (29 October 1887)
>
> Finished my dancing lessons with Atkinson. [...]
> In the evening, went to the MacGregors' where there was a big dance on. Came away about 1 a.m. (3 November 1887)

Herbert and his friend Jimmie Dowell then travelled to London for a week, where they spent much time in the company of two female acquaintances identified only as C and V. Herbert also took a trip to Brighton to visit his disabled brother: 'Went down to Brighton where I called on Dr. Scatliff & saw my brother Percie. He has grown a good deal, looks well, but has not any greater power of articulation than when I left in 1881. Only stayed a few hours & returned to town' (10 November 1887).

Shortly after Herbert and Jimmie Dowell have returned to Edinburgh, C and V come to visit them. Exactly where the girls stay is not clear, but Herbert repeatedly refers to it as 'the harem', sometimes abbreviating it to simply 'the h.'. Wherever this 'harem' was located, he was certainly a frequent visitor:

> Dropped into the harem for dinner where C. & V. received me with open arms. Had a very jolly evening. (28 November 1887)
> Went through to Glasgow. Called upon the James Millers, Miss Anne Taylor, the Robert Millers & Cousin Etta Robertson. Got back to the h. at 6.30 and had a very fine & large evening. (29 November 1887)
>
> In the evening passed a few hours at the h. (1 December 1887)
>
> Most of the day in the h. (3 December 1887)
>
> A lazy morning in the h. and left at 5.30 p.m. (7 December 1887)
>
> At the h. most of the day. (9 December 1887)
>
> Evening at the h. (10 December 1887)
>
> Spent most of today at the harem. (11 December 1887)
>
> Knocking about town & at the h. all today. (12 December 1887)
>
> At the h. most of the day. (13 December 1887)
>
> At the h. most of the day & went to the Dowells in the evening. (14 December 1887)

Finally, on 16 December, C and V went back to London and Herbert started to make preparations for his return to Argentina after New Year. One of his last engagements in Edinburgh was at the Freemasons' Hall, where he was inducted into the Masonic Order, becoming a member of St Mary's Lodge No. 1 (24 December 1887). En route to Southampton, Herbert spent a few days in London, staying at the Tavistock Hotel but spending much of his time with V, who seems to have lived in Park Walk:

> Met V. at 6 p.m. at the Holborn where we had dinner. Afterwards went to the Trocadero & then back to Park Walk.' (3 January 1888)
>
> Left Park Walk at 4 p.m. & returned to the Tavistock Hotel. Having asked several old Norfolcians to dinner, the first of them appeared, James. He was followed by the two Hickmans, Fletcher, & Girling. Had a very jovial dinner. (4 January 1888)
>
> Took V. to dine at the St. James & afterwards a box at the Pav. Supped at the Globe & then back to Park Walk. (7 January 1888)

Herbert and V appear to have become very close and she is deeply upset by his imminent departure for South America: 'At midnight V. sent for me. Went down & found her very much broken down. Left her again at 2 a.m.' (8 January 1888). The next day, Herbert leaves London early for Southampton to join his boat and V is never mentioned in the diaries again.

The voyage passes uneventfully, the highlight, as usual, being the stopover at Rio:

> Arrived today at Pernambuco after an 11 days steam from Lisbon. Nothing of very great interest on the road: we had 3 concerts, a debate & some athletic sports. We also started a bi-weekly newspaper of which Dr Wyatt Smith & myself were the editors. On the 21st we had a very close view of some waterspouts which are more interesting than pleasant. (27 January 1888)
>
> Arrived at Rio early & went ashore. [...] We first went out to the Botanic Gardens & in the afternoon we went up to Petropolis. We steamed across the Bay & there got into a train which took us through most gorgeous scenery, finally ascending a terrific gradiant [*sic*], the steam engine having a patent centre cog wheel which fits into corresponding slots in the rail & so literally climbs up.
>
> Away up in the hills, Petropolis is a delightful little town. (1 February 1888)

On reaching Buenos Aires, Herbert spent a couple of days in the city and then three weeks at Los Yngleses, before returning to La Tomasa.

In early April, he starts a fresh volume of his diaries with a significant revelation, namely that he has taken Argentine citizenship and, in keeping with his new nationality, will henceforth record his memoirs in Spanish:

> Al comenzar un nuevo tomo y principiar de nuevo con buenas resoluciones he tomado un paso que sea comendable ó sea indigno me parece debido. He dejado de ser Escoces y he adoptado una patria nueva. ¡Desde hoy soy Argentino! Y como tal considero que es mi deber usar la idioma de mi tierra.
>
> Y esta resolución no ha sido el proceder de una idea lijera. He tomado consejo, he pedido permiso á mi padre, y viendome trasladado á este mundo nuevo, con todos mis intereses y simpatias en ello, me he hecho Argentino.
>
> Habran muchos que condemnen esto mi acto. Que dirán que ha sido el entusiasmo loco y pruriente de un joven soñador. Sin contradecirles les diré con toda humilidad "Ponganse en mi lugar. Pesen bien los deberes de todo ser humano, y dejando como indigna toda cuestion de interes personal y de ganancia particular, juzgen por el base mas ancho del DEBER si hago bien ó mal.
>
> ¿Y por este dejaré de acordarme de la tierra donde nací? Cuando una mujer deja el hogar paterno para acompañar á la vida de su marido, se olvida de su madre? ¡Que vista tan corta! Que fallo tan iliberal!
>
> Y ultimamente registraré lo que siempre ha sido mi axioma de vida. "Péze bien la opinion de cada uno y después resuelva segun su mismo paracer." (3 April 1888)

[On starting a new volume and beginning afresh with good intentions, I have taken a step that may seem either to be commendable or shameful. I have ceased to be Scottish and have adopted a new country. From today I am Argentinian! And as such I consider it my duty to use the language of my land.

And this decision is not the product of a whim. I have taken advice, I have sought my father's permission, and given that I have transplanted myself to this new world with all my interests and sympathies, I have become Argentinian.

There will be many who condemn my decision. Who will say that it has been the mad enthusiasm and prurience of a young dreamer. Without wishing to contradict them, I say with all humility, "Put yourselves in my place. Weigh up well the duties of every human being, and leave aside as unworthy any issue of personal interest or individual gain, judge by the broadest notion of DUTY if what I have done is right or wrong.

And will I stop remembering the land of my birth? When a woman leaves her parents' home to accompany her husband, does she forget her mother? What shortsightedness! What an unreasonable error!

And finally I shall record what has always been the axiom of my life. "Weigh up well the opinions of everyone and then decide for yourself."]

At this point, Herbert began to spend much of his time at Los Yngleses, running the *estancia* while Ernest travelled back to Scotland to get married. In the meantime, the day-to-day management of La Tomasa was left in the hands of Herbert's trusted friend and employee 'Don Mauricio' Garrett. While at Los Yngleses, he started to take a full part in the life of the nearby port town of Ajó and was soon elected President of the local School Council, a position whose principal duties consisted of chairing meetings and presenting awards at prize-giving ceremonies.

In June, Herbert is distressed when one of the valuable rams the Gibsons had imported from Britain falls ill. Sadly, despite his best efforts to save the beast, it succumbs:

No salí hoy. El carnero "Prince" se enfermó esta mañana y pasé la mayor parte del dia atendiendolo. (8 June 1888)

[I did not go out today. The ram "Prince" became unwell this morning and I spent most of the day attending to him.]

Ayer en la mañana murio el carnero. Habiamos conseguido curarlo de su enfermedad original "cystitis" pero los esfuerzos que hizo, debidos probablemente a las medicinas que tuvimos que administrar, le causó una hemoragia que lo llevó en pocos momentos. (18 June 1888)

[Yesterday morning, the ram died. We had managed to cure his original illness, "cystitis", but the efforts he made, probably on account of the medicines we had to administer, caused a haemorrhage that carried him off in a few moments.]

In December 1888, Ernest and his bride Alice (née Donaldson) finally arrived at Los Yngleses, some six months after their wedding. Early in January 1889,

Herbert prepared a magnificent party to celebrate their marriage, of similar scale to the one thrown in honour of May and George Mackern after their wedding. Among the numerous supplies Herbert purchased for this spectacle were 30 turkeys, 80 chickens, wines, flags and fireworks (10-11 January 1889). The dance took place on 19 January and was attended by over 400 local people. Two weeks later Ernest and Alice hosted a picnic to reciprocate the kindness shown to them by the attendees. The latter was, however, a rather more select affair, the guests numbering around 70 members of what Herbert describes as the 'aristocracy' of the district (3 February 1889).

In August 1889, Los Yngleses was affected by an unusually severe fall of snow, which exacted a heavy toll on the livestock:

> Esta mañana ha amanecido todo el campo blanqueado con nieve. Ha caido nieve de anoche hasta las cuatro esta mañana. En todas partes hay una capa blanca de grosér de 3 a 6 pulgadas. (14 August 1889)

> [This morning the whole camp was white with snow. The snow fell from last night until four this morning. There is a white covering everywhere, between 3 and 6 inches deep.]

> Sali para los rincones para ver el dano que la nieve ha causado, mandando 2 peones á los otros costados de la estancia. Resulta la perdida total 821 lanares, 50 vacunos, 2 yeguarizos. (15 August 1889)

> [I went out to the corners [far-flung parts of the ranch] to see the damage caused by the snow, sending 2 peons to the other sides of the *estancia*. 821 sheep, 50 cattle, 2 horses are lost.]

In September, Herbert visits La Tomasa for the first time in several months and is disappointed with the condition of the *estancia* under Garrett's administration:

> A las seis de la mañana estuvimos en La Tomasa. Encuentro la estancia bastante mal, y me parece que Señor Mauricio tendrá que moverse con mas celeridad si quiere gobernar bien acá. (17 September 1889)

> [At six o'clock in the morning we reached La Tomasa. I find the *estancia* in quite a bad state, and it seems to me that Señor Mauricio will have to move with greater haste if he wants to manage it well.]

Iain Stewart

In spite of his qualms about the management of La Tomasa, Herbert seems content to let Garrett get on with the task and wastes little time in departing once again for Los Yngleses.

In November, Herbert takes a brief trip to Buenos Aires, where he attends to various business matters and witnesses an interesting spectacle in the Florida Gardens:

> En la noche fuimos al Jardin Florida donde trabaja una compañia de "variedades". La conclusion del programa es un experimento en "hipnotismo" en el cual una mujer está sometido á hipnotismo, o sea mesmerismo, y despues llevado á una jaula de leones africanos, muy feroces; despúes de producir un estado cateliptico en su cuerpo lo ponen arriba de dos sillas y los leones saltan por encima.
>
> Interesante sin duda – pero para mí horroroso y sin objeto; mas que demostrar al publico á que fines de riesgo pasaría un hombre para ganar unos pocos pesos. (20 November 1889)

[In the evening we went to the Florida Gardens, where a variety company was working. The conclusion of their programme is an experiment in hypnotism in which a woman is hypnotized, or mesmerized, and then taken to a cage of very ferocious African lions; once her body is in a cataleptic state, she is placed across two chairs and the lions jump over her.

Undoubtedly interesting, but in my opinion horrifying and pointless, other than as a public demonstration of the risks a man will take to earn a few *pesos*.]

Back at Los Yngleses, the arrival of 1890 is celebrated with an impromptu dance:

> Anoche á las diez sacamos la mesa y demas muebles de la sala y nos preparamos para un baile. Hacia un calor atroz pero esto poco nos importaba.
>
> A las doce en punto tocamos la campana en saludo al año nuevo, y cantamos "Auld Lang Syne". Despues hicimos entrar á las sirvientas y bailamos hasta --- quien sabe que horas. (1 January 1890)

[At ten o'clock last night, we removed the table and other furniture from the room and made preparations for a dance. It was atrociously hot, but that did not bother us much.

At the stroke of twelve we rang the bell to greet the New Year and sang "Auld Lang Syne". Afterwards, we brought in the maids and we danced until --- who knows when.]

A few days later, Ernest Gibson was in less jovial mood when, having been summoned to a meeting at the town hall in Ajó, he found that none of the local officials had turned up. He arrived at 3 pm, the hour of his appointment, and waited in vain all afternoon. It transpired that they had gone en masse to the races! Enraged, Ernest borrowed a sheet of paper, four nails and a hammer from the local storekeeper and firmly attached the following notice to the door of the municipal building:

ERNEST GIBSON

FROM 3 P.M.

TO 6.30 P.M.

JANUARY 12, 1890

'They may be able to remove the paper,' he announced with glee on returning the hammer to the storekeeper, 'but the nails...' (12 January 1890).

Around this time, Herbert made an attempt to revive his erstwhile literary ambitions and began work on a novel (21 January 1890). With characteristic speed, he completed a draft of some 430 pages, entitled 'And All for Love', in less than six months (10 July 1890), and went on to produce the final version in a further four weeks (8 August 1890). Unfortunately, Herbert's diaries contain no hint of the novel's content and the manuscript does not appear to have survived among his numerous papers. The only thing we can say with reasonable certainty is that the work was never printed or published.

During this period, we learn of Herbert's attachment to a rather enigmatic female acquaintance. Reminiscent of his earlier references to C and V, she is initially identified only as G. The first mention of G in the diary records that she is seriously unwell: 'Fuí a ver G. Está muy enferma. Fiebre tifoidea' ['I went to see G. She is very ill. Typhoid fever'] (20 February 1890). Whatever the nature of Herbert's relationship with G, it is sufficiently close for him to take charge of her care and move her from her present accommodation to a better house:

Sigue muy enferma G. La hicé llevar á otra casa. (21 February 1890)

[G continues to be very ill. I had her taken to another house.]

Con Matthew todo el dia: y de enfermero toda la noche. (22 February 1890)

[With Matthew all day: and was a nurse all night.]

G's condition starts to improve somewhat, just as Herbert himself falls ill. Surprisingly, it does not seem to have crossed his mind that he may have contracted the same infectious condition as his patient. Perhaps Herbert's complaint was indeed unrelated, as he certainly makes no mention of the intestinal symptoms characteristic of typhoid:

En cama. Influenza, fiebre, catarro, que sé yo. (1-4 March 1890)

[In bed. Flu, fever, catarrh, who knows what.]

Empiezo poder caminar pero no puedo salir de casa todavia. (5 March 1890)

[I'm beginning to be able to walk, but still can't leave the house.]

G is next mentioned on 24 March, when a little more about her identity is revealed: 'Visité a Eugenie (Georgette). Está mejor pero aun debil' ['I visited Eugenie (Georgette). She is better but still weak'] (24 March 1890). Thus we discover that G stood for Georgette, but she is now mysteriously transformed into Eugenie, occasionally abbreviated to E. To my mind, this raises a number of questions about her likely status. Assuming for the moment that Eugenie was her real name, what sort of woman is likely to have assumed an alias such as Georgette and for what reason? If it was an identity adopted for professional purposes, it seems likely that she may have been an actress or courtesan. Given Herbert's often-expressed penchant for theatrical entertainment of all kinds and his tendency to fall in love, albeit usually from a distance, with leading ladies, one might like to think that Eugenie's occupation was the former, although the latter seems more likely.

In early April, we learn a little more about Eugenie, namely that she comes from Switzerland and now intends to return home: 'Mañana Eugenie se embarca para Francia; á reformar y volver á su familia en la pequeña aldea en Suiza. Pobre Eugenie!' ['Eugenie embarks for France tomorrow, to reform and return to her family in the little Swiss village. Poor Eugenie!'] (4 April 1890). The next day, Herbert escorts her to the boat that will take her to a bigger vessel for the Atlantic crossing: 'Acompañé á E. hasta la Boca y la dejé abordo el pequeño vapor que la ha de conducir ál "La Plata", – y volví solo' ['I accompanied E. to La Boca and I left her aboard the small steamship which will take her to the "La Plata", – and I returned alone'] (5 April 1890). A note of wistfulness can be detected in Herbert's final words, I think, suggesting that he is truly sorry to see Eugenie go and hinting at the closeness of their relationship.

Shortly after Eugenie's departure, Herbert starts to make preparations to enter a selection of the Yngleses livestock into a major agricultural show in Buenos Aires. He sends seventeen sheep, one pig and a cow, but harbours reservations about the sheep's chances of success as they are suffering from scab. More impressive than the animals is the Yngleses stand, consisting of numerous wool samples exhibited on imposing structures. According to Herbert's description, the display consists of three units, the centrepiece a pentagonal tower some eight metres tall crowned with a glass globe containing a fleece from the Yngleses stud flock. More than fifty other fleeces are arranged around the five sides of the tower and there are also assorted photographs of the *estancia*. On either side of the central structure, there are two mushroom-shaped assemblies of around two metres in height and nine or ten in circumference, each holding ten fleeces. Herbert asserts, impartially of course, that no other stand in the exhibition bears comparison with that of Los Yngleses (28 April 1890).

Unfortunately, Herbert's worries about the condition of the sheep are not without foundation. Most are expelled for showing signs of scab and some rams are unclassified on account of only having nine months' wool on their backs instead of the required twelve. The exclusion of the rams riles Herbert and he feels that a gross injustice has been done:

> Lo que mas duele es que, en primer lugar no habia ovejas lincoln en toda la exposicion tan buenas como las nuestras y muy pocos carneros, y en segundo que (salvo unos miserables animales expuestos por Zeballos y Senillosa) éramos los unicos criadores argentinos que expusieron el verdadero producto de su estancia, siendo todos los demas importados. (3 May 1890)

> [What hurts the most is that, firstly, there were no Lincoln sheep and very few rams in the exhibition as good as ours, and, secondly, that (save for a few miserable animals displayed by Zeballos and Senillosa)

we were the only Argentine breeders who showed the authentic product of their *estancia*, all the rest being imported.]

He seems to derive little satisfaction or consolation from the fact that both the wool display and the pig took first prize in their respective categories (3 May 1890).

A few days later, Herbert is in better spirits and takes part in a polo match. The encounter, between teams representing Los Yngleses and 'The World', takes place at the prestigious Hurlingham club in the western outskirts of Buenos Aires. Hurlingham, founded around 1888 in imitation of the west London club of the same name, soon became one of the social centres of the British community, as well as a venue for polo, cricket, golf and horseracing. The result of the match is a resounding defeat for Herbert's Yngleses side, on account of their inferior ponies, but the post-game festivities more than make up for the loss:

> ¡Gran match de Polo!
> "Los Yngleses" v. "El Mundo".
> Representaron á Los Yngleses, Ernesto, yo, Furber, Matthew y Garrett. "El Mundo" encontró campeones en las personas de Ravenscroft, Libbock, England y los dos McClymonts.
>
> Jugamos en Hurlingham, pero era un juego muy disigual. Los cinco miserables petizos traidos de Ajó, cansados y desechos por el viaje, á penas caminaban. Entre tanto nuestros oponentes tenían quince caballos, mas grandes que los nuestros, y en magnifico estado.
>
> El resultado era sabido – 9 puntos á uno. Pero batimos valientemente como puede constar el muchachito que habia dejado de cascotear pajaros para mirar al juego y que nos sirvio de "una entusiasta y animada multitud de espectadores".
>
> Volvimos á la ciudad, sino llenos de gloria al menos llenos de alegria y excelente "whisky". (7 May 1890)

> [Great polo match!
> "Los Yngleses" v. "The World"
> Los Yngleses was represented by Ernest, myself, Furber, Matthew and Garrett. "The World" found champions in the persons of Ravenscroft, Libbock, England and the two McClymonts.
>
> We played at Hurlingham, but it was a very unequal game. The five miserable ponies brought from Ajó, tired and exhausted by the

journey, could barely walk. Our opponents, on the other hand, had fifteen horses, bigger than ours and in magnificent shape.

The result was a foregone conclusion – 9 goals to one. But we fought bravely, as could be confirmed by the little boy who stopped stoning birds to watch the game and who served as "an enthusiastic and animated crowd of spectators".

We returned to the city, if not filled with glory then at least filled with joy and excellent whisky.]

By the end of July 1890, Argentina was immersed once again in political turmoil. The first news of the outbreak of revolution reached Los Yngleses on the 27th, although it was two more days before Herbert learnt the full details. The rebellion had broken out in the early hours of the 26th and was led by Dr Leandro Alem, a firebrand opponent of President Miguel Juárez Celman, and a number of generals. The revolutionaries massed their forces near the centre of Buenos Aires, holding the Plaza Libertad and Palermo Park. The president fled the city, leaving the defences in the charge of his deputy, Carlos Pellegrini, and the famed General Roca. According to Herbert, there was talk that some 3,000 had been killed in just the opening days of the engagement, although the overall death toll is usually put at nearer 1,000. At first, the rebels enjoyed overwhelming superiority of numbers, but inexplicably hesitated to strike and claim victory. Their delay proved to be a fatal tactical error, since it allowed the government time to gather its forces. When battle commenced in earnest, the revolutionaries were quickly obliged to capitulate. The result, however, did nothing to strengthen the position of Juárez Celman and by 8 August he resigned in favour of Pellegrini. This development is hailed by Herbert: 'A las doce de la noche un telegrama de Ernesto – "Juarez Celman ha renunciado y ha sumido el mando Pellegrini" – ¡Viva! ¡Que buenas noticias!' ['At midnight a telegram from Ernest – "Juarez Celman has resigned and Pellegrini has assumed power" – Hurrah! What good news!'] (8 August 1890).

Out of the wreckage of the rebellion emerged the beginnings of one of the major forces in twentieth-century Argentine politics, the Unión Cívica Radical (Radical Civic Union). Leandro Alem, leader of the uprising, had been the driving force behind the Unión Cívica de la Juventud (Civic Union of the Youth), a group of young, middle-class intellectuals committed to democratic principles and opposed to the corrupt, cliquish administration of Juárez Celman. Prior to the revolution, the UCJ had become simply the Unión Cívica after entering into an opposition alliance with the far from youthful Bartolomé Mitre, a former national president whose power base lay in the Buenos Aires oligarchy. Although they shared similar aims, tension was present between Alem and Mitre from the start; Alem advocated revolution as the only way to achieve the UC's goals, whereas Mitre was committed to negotiation with members of the ruling group. Ultimately, this was to lead to a split within the Civic Union movement, Alem heading the Unión Cívica Radical (Radical Civic Union) and Mitre's faction becoming the Unión Cívica Nacional (National Civic Union). While the influence of the latter soon waned, the UCR established itself as a formidable political force under the leadership of future national president Hipólito Yrigoyen, who had inherited the leadership after Alem's suicide in 1896.

Shortly after the 1890 uprising and before the movement split, Herbert took his first step into the realm of Argentine politics by deciding to establish a local branch of the Unión Cívica in Ajó with his brother Ernest and friend Carlos Santa Coloma: 'Resolvimos (Ernesto, Sta Coloma y yo) instalar un Comité de la Union Cívica y empezamos cambiar cartas' ['We resolved (Ernest, Santa Coloma and I) to form a Committee of the Civic Union and we began to exchange letters'] (13 October 1890). Two other local landowners, Carrizo and Borde, joined the group and together they organized an inaugural demonstration. The *estancieros* turned up with large contingents of their men and the crowd soon exceeded 600. After an open-air rally of sorts, with food, music and toasts, they marched through the streets of Ajó, stopping for photographs in front of the church (1 November 1890).

By early 1891, the schism that would soon appear in the Unión Cívica nationally was foreshadowed by a division among its adherents in the Ajó area. The local problem stemmed from the fact that two branches of the UC were attempting to operate in the same region. One Señor Cueli attempted to negotiate a 'fusion' between the group founded by Herbert and company and the other committee led by Martín Campos. While Herbert was in favour of reconciliation between the two branches, he was not alone in objecting to Cueli's intervention: 'Todos muy indignados con el proceder "caciquioso" de Cueli. Queremos la fusion, si, pero hemos de iniciarla y lograrla voluntariamente y no por mandatos' ['Everyone is very indignant about Cueli's high-handed approach. Yes, we want fusion, but we must initiate it and achieve it voluntarily, not by decree'] (3 February 1890). Finally, after three days of meetings, the two sides reached agreement and appointed a single committee to represent them. While the solution was agreeable enough to Herbert in principle, he was unhappy with his role as joint secretary on the new committee, since he shared it with a man for whom he had little time: 'Personalmente no he de permanecer mucho tiempo en el comite pues me han nombrado secretario juntamente con Garcia y mi proximidad á ese caballero poco me agrada' ['Personally, I won't remain on the committee for long as I have been named secretary jointly with Garcia and proximity to that gentleman does not appeal to me much'] (5 February 1891). Thereby, Herbert's active involvement in the Unión Cívica came to a close.

Herbert's other public endeavour at this time, his Presidency of the Ajó School Council, also soon ended in disillusionment. He found himself frustrated by the bureaucracy of the national education authorities, which seems to have been compromising the ability of teachers to work effectively: 'La Direccion General de Educacion ha enredado de tal suerte el organismo docente de este partido que va costar mucha capacidad y mucha constancia para reformarlo' ['The Directorate General of Education has enmeshed the teaching profession of this district in such a way that it is going to take much ability and determination to remedy it'] (25 February 1891). Herbert himself, however, had no appetite for the task ahead and chose to relinquish his position: 'Hace algunos dias que mandé mi renuncia' ['A few days ago, I sent in my resignation'] (25 February 1891).

After the failure of the July 1890 revolution, the political situation in Argentina remained far from stable. On the same day that he wrote of his resignation as President of the School Council, Herbert recorded an attempt against the life of General Roca, one of the most senior figures of government: 'El dia diez y nueve á las ocho de la tarde atentarón asasinar á Roca, un joven de 15 años habiendolo pegado una bala que le hirió en el brazo. El 21 se declaró el pais en estado de sitio' ['At eight o'clock on the evening of the nineteenth, there was an attempt to assassinate Roca, a youth of 15 having fired a bullet that wounded him in the arm. On the twenty-first, the country was declared to be in a state of emergency'] (25 February 1891). Political and economic turbulence was very much the order of the day, and little improvement occurred during the following months. In July 1891, Herbert wrote despairingly of the turmoil: 'Las noticias politicas no son muy halagueños. Revolucion en Catamarca y Santiago; escisión en la Union Cívica – estafacion completa en el mercado, – ¡vaya un pais alegre!' ['The political news is not very encouraging. Revolution in Catamarca and Santiago; a split in the Civic Union – complete fraud in the markets – what a happy country!'] (2 July 1891). The atmosphere of financial instability had a tangible impact upon the Gibsons' business, for the company that acted as their export agent, Rodger Best & Co. of Liverpool and Buenos Aires, ceased trading:

A las seis de la tarde recibí telegrama de Hope anunciando telegrama del padre al efecto que la casa de Rodger Best y C^{ia} han suspendido pagos. Determiné ir enseguida á la ciudad y hice mis preparativos. (23 July 1891)

[At six in the afternoon, I received a telegram from Hope with details of a telegram from Father to the effect that Rodger Best & Co. have stopped payments. I resolved to go at once to the city and made my preparations.]

Estuve en lo de Best. Hay poca duda q^e se liquidan. Atribuyen la causa principalmente al Banco Ingles que ha cerrado sus puertas. Es muy sensible q^e la casa de Best concluya de esta manera, despues de haber sido una de las primeras para tres cuartos de un siglo. (25 July 1891)

[I was at Best's and there is little doubt that they are winding up. They attribute it principally to the fact that the Banco Inglés [English Bank] has closed its doors. It is very sad that the house of Best is to end in this way, having been one of the foremost for three quarters of a century.]

In January 1891, Herbert had taken charge of Linconia, another Gibson property, which lay just two and a half leagues from the Yngleses homestead. At this time, Linconia was not technically an *estancia* in its own right, but the '*cabaña*' of Los Yngleses; in other words, an outpost of the ranch inhabited by those responsible for its farther reaches: 'Me trasladé á la cabaña 'Linconia' á dos leguas y media de la estancia, donde voy á vivir para dos años adelantando nuestro interes en la parte norte de la estancia' ['I moved to the Linconia station, two and a half leagues from the ranch, where I shall live for two years, advancing our interests in the northern part of the *estancia*'] (2 January 1891). Linconia was named for the prized flocks of Lincoln sheep that had become the mainstay of the Gibsons' wool production. Despite the fine quality of these animals, it seems they attracted little attention from other Argentine breeders, as Herbert is disappointed to discover at an auction in March 1891. Having arrived with hopes of selling his stock at high prices, his aspirations are soon brought down to earth with a bump:

Remate de las ovejas! Nuevo desengaño.
Sueño:- Una asamblea inmensa, todos los estancieros principales de la Provincia, gran entusiasmo y al ver el precio de cada oveja pasar -----0000000 pesos un grito entusiasmado de admiracion.
Actualidad:- Un grupo de personas que parecen por la mayor parte cocheros y vendedores de diarios; se vende primero algunas plantas de jardin; luego un lote de campo; despues "unas ovejas del Señor

Gibson de raza ... ¿como decia V^d que era la raza, señor? ... ¡ah! es verdad! ... lincoln argentina ... vamos á ver caballeros, que oferta para este precioso lote de ovejas lincoln argentinos! Un movimiento de interes entre la gente que después desaparece en apatía general: un hombre á mi lado me pregunta si son capones: una oferta falsa, palpablemente evidentemente azoteamente falsa, de veinte pesos. Un largo rato sin mejoria en la oferta; el rematador se vuelva ronco; me parece que se enoja; luego me echará las culpas ... me escapo á la calle, me voy al club y escribo una carta á mi prima Catalina Gibson contandole las ultimas y mas graciosas cuentos de la estancia.

Volví al local del remate á las cinco y vendé todas las ovejas en el local y las otras que aun permanecen en Chascomus á Juan Lean en veinticinco pesos cada uno.

¡Ah, Heriberto; cuando aprenderas? (24 March 1891)

[The sheep auction! Another disappointment.

Dream:- A huge assembly, all the principal ranchers of the Province, great enthusiasm and, on seeing the price of each sheep pass -----0000000 *pesos*, an excited cheer of admiration.

Reality:- A group of people who mostly appeared to be coachmen and newspaper sellers; first, a few garden plants are sold; then a plot of land; afterwards "some of Mr Gibson's sheep of the ... breed, what breed of sheep did you say they are, sir? Oh, that's right! Argentine Lincolns ... let's see, gentlemen, what am I offered for this valuable lot of Argentine Lincolns?" A movement of interest among the gathering, which then fades into general apathy; a man at my side asks me if they are wethers; a false offer, palpably, evidently, blatantly false, of twenty *pesos*. A long spell without any improvement in the offer; the auctioneer becomes hoarse; it seems to me that he is losing his temper; then he will blame me ... I escape out into the street, I go to the club and write to my cousin Catalina Gibson telling her the latest funny stories about the *estancia*.

I returned to the auction site at five o'clock and sold all the sheep in the place and the others that remained in Chascomús to John Lean for twenty-five *pesos* each.

Oh, Herbert, when will you learn?]

A month later, Herbert reveals another side of his character when he stops the cab he is riding in to inspect the horses, horrified by the driver's cruel treatment of them. On alighting, he finds that the poor beasts are 'covered with wounds' and 'so thin that they could scarcely remain standing'. Enraged, he summons a policeman and demands that the driver be arrested and taken to the nearest station. Unsurprisingly, Herbert has to endure a torrent of insults from the coachman and sarcastic comments from bystanders, but has the pleasure of seeing the driver marched off into custody (2 April 1891). In his diary, he generalizes about the condition of Buenos Aires coach horses, stating that he has previously examined the horses of around fifty coaches in the square where they congregate daily without finding even one pair of healthy animals. He attributes their sad condition to the low price the drivers are permitted to charge – just one *peso* per hour, which was the equivalent of little more than a shilling.

Around this time, Herbert and his brothers began to discuss the idea of opening an office in Buenos Aires. The one previously founded by their uncle on his arrival in Argentina in 1819 had been closed in 1828 as part of the liquidation of the majority of the Gibsons' assets after his untimely death. Since that date, business that had to be transacted in the city, such as making arrangements for the exportation of wool and other *estancia* products, had been taken care of by Rodger Best & Co. as agents. With the demise of Best's in July 1891, plans to reincorporate the firm of Gibson Brothers acquired new urgency. By late August, the business was up and running with Herbert, Ernest, Hope and John as partners, the latter, a chartered accountant, having taken care of the requisite formalities.

During this period, Herbert became an active participant in the embryonic Argentine Rural Society. This organization gathered in many of the principal landowners and would go on to become a powerful influence in country life. Herbert regularly attended the Society's meetings and outings, and wrote occasional articles for its journal, *Anales de la Sociedad Rural* (*Annals of the Rural Society*). In 1892, at just twenty-nine years of age, he was elected Treasurer and would later rise to the office of Vice-President. Most importantly, he went on to be co-founder of the Society's Rural Show in 1894, a major event in the social calendar of Argentina's landowning classes that continues to prosper to this day.

Herbert's diary entries from the latter part of 1891 relate few events of major significance, but do include a couple of unhappy experiences. First, one which shows that roaming packs of wild dogs had once again become a major nuisance at Los Yngleses, despite their virtual extermination in earlier decades:

> Esta mañana amanecieron 7 carneros muertos por los perros del puerto otros 14 heridos. Va siendo cada vez peor esta plaga de perros. Entre los heridos habia "Tandilero", carnero vendido á Santamarina

y precioso animal. Debía haber marchado con la tropa mañana. (2 September 1891)

[This morning we woke up to find 7 rams killed and 14 injured by the dogs of the port. This plague of dogs is getting worse all the time. Among the injured was "Tandilero", the ram that has been sold to Santamarina, a valuable animal. It was due to have left with the troop tomorrow.]

Then, while travelling to Buenos Aires by train from Mar del Plata at the end of the month, Herbert witnesses a horrific incident:

A los pocos kilometros de Mar del Plata el tren pasó por encima de un hombre destrozando el craneo y brazo izquierdo. Sin duda había intención de suicidio pues el hombre estaba escondido en un alcantarillo y levantó la cabeza en el momento que pasaba el locomotor. Levantamos un certificado de los hechos en la estacion Carnet. (30 September 1891)

[A few kilometres out of Mar del Plata the train ran over a man, crushing his skull and left arm. Without doubt, he had intended to commit suicide, because he had been hiding in a drain and raised his head at the moment at which the engine was passing. We made a report of the event at Carnet station.]

At the end of the year, Herbert reveals that he has decided to reverse his decision of April 1888 to keep his diaries in Spanish. Although his command of the language was basically sound and he clearly possessed an extensive vocabulary, it seems that writing in his adopted tongue remained an effort and placed restrictions on his ability to express himself:

— Fin de 1891 —
Y fin de escribir mi diario en Castellano. Seguiré, mientras viva en la Republica Argentina, en hacer todo lo que pueda para mi pais adoptivo, pero pensaré siempre en ingles y hé de escribir mis pensamientos y vida en el idioma que me es mas natural emplear. Ya basta de esfuerzos que no me son simpaticos. Me figuro que hé pasado los años de sueños é imágenes, y hé despertado á la realidad de la lucha mundana. (31 December 1891)

[— End of 1891 —

And the end of writing my diary in Spanish. For as long as I live in the Argentine Republic, I shall continue to do everything I can for my adopted country, but I shall always think in English and I must record my thoughts and life in the language that comes most naturally to me. Enough of efforts that are not pleasing to me. I reckon that my years of dreaming and fantasy are in the past, and I have now woken up to the reality of the daily struggle.]

Thus ends the volume and with it this chapter. Now, at the age of twenty-eight, Herbert perceives that he has completed the transition from youth to fully-fledged maturity. He has gained competence in the craft of *estancia* management, having acquired skills and knowledge that will serve him well throughout the remainder of his days, has begun to make a name for himself in public life and become, in every sense, a man of the world. As will become evident in the following chapter, Herbert is about to launch into a phase of great intellectual activity that will consolidate his developing reputation as a significant individual in the life of Argentina and, in particular, of her British community.

Los Yngleses by Thomas Gibson (figure in doorway may be artist himself)

Wagon train carrying wool to the port of Ajó by Thomas Gibson

CHAPTER 5

MAN OF LETTERS, 1892-1911

As we have seen in preceding chapters, Herbert displayed his literary inclination from an early age and, as a youth, even harboured ambitions of a career in writing. Joining the family business and heading to Argentina seemed to put an end to this dream for a while, and for several years his efforts amounted to little more than the occasional contribution to *The Norfolcian*, his old school magazine. The first real sign of a revival in his activities came in 1890, with the drafting of 'And All for Love', his only attempt at the novelist's craft. By 1892, however, we start to see evidence that Herbert is set to turn his talent to more practical aims by combining his flair for the written word with his considerable knowledge of Argentina, particularly its rural aspect. During a sojourn in Great Britain that year, Herbert gave an address to the London Chamber of Commerce that was subsequently published as 'Farming in the Argentine as a Field for Capital and Labour' in both the *Chamber of Commerce Journal* and the *South American Journal*.[59] In this paper, he paints a detailed picture of the current state of farming in Argentina and its future prospects, with special emphasis on sheep-breeding, ending with a wholeheartedly optimistic forecast and an impassioned plea for foreign settlement:

> There are still many broad acres awaiting the colonist, who will find in them a safe investment for his modest capital, and a sure means of increasing his worldly belongings. [...] Despite the difficulties in which the Republic has been plunged for some time, sheep-farming was never more prosperous than it is to-day. [...] What we want is capital combined with labour. We do not want people to send us

---

59 'Farming in the Argentine as a Field for Capital and Labour', *Chamber of Commerce Journal*, 10 August 1892, 186-92. Reprinted in *South American Journal*, 3 September 1892, 257-61. A report on Herbert's London speech was carried in a special European news edition of *La Nación*, the leading Argentine daily (27 August 1892).

their money; we want them to bring it, and stay and live with us to look after it. [...] Great as are the troubles in which our country has immersed herself, she will surmount them; and her commerce is still but in its infancy. [60]

This article foreshadowed the appearance, less than a year later, of one of Herbert's most important works, a monograph on *The History and Present State of the Sheep-Breeding Industry in the Argentine Republic*. Close to 300 pages in length, this volume was published in Buenos Aires in 1893 and is dedicated by the author to his father, Thomas, 'one of the first pioneers of the Sheep-breeding Industry in the Argentine Republic'. In his introduction, Herbert describes the intended readership as both the 'prospective colonist who looks abroad from his over-crowded country in search of a new home where he may settle and progress' and the 'sheep-farmer already come to the country, with a view to assist him in the selection of his stock and in the manner of breeding them at a profit'.[61] Like Herbert's previous article, much of the advice is aimed squarely at the 'modest working capitalist' looking for a 'comfortable home' and a 'fair return for his labour and outlay' (*Sheep-Breeding*, p. 1). Well illustrated and with a range of maps and plans, the book seems to offer sufficient detailed information to serve as a comprehensive instruction manual for the novice farmer, yet still contains enough material of a more general, historical character to make rewarding reading for anyone with an interest in late nineteenth-century Argentina. Of greater import than my own opinions, however, are those that were advanced by contemporary expert reviewers. As the following extracts illustrate, Herbert's work was greeted by an overwhelmingly positive welcome, receiving favourable write-ups in a varied range of publications across the English-speaking world:

> ***Cork Constitution*, 20 September 1893:** "The History and Present State of the Sheep-breeding Industry in the Argentine Republic" is the title of a work, by Herbert Gibson, just published by Ravenscroft and Mills, Buenos Ayres. It will be found of great value to sheep farmers in that country, and to those who propose to engage in the industry, which the author regards as one of a solid nature and sure of continued existence. [...] The book is a most interesting one, and gives most important information on the special subject with which it deals.

---

60 *Chamber of Commerce Journal*, p. 192.
61 *The History and Present State of the Sheep-Breeding Industry in the Argentine Republic* (Buenos Aires: Ravenscroft and Mills, 1893), p. 1.

International Courier, **30 November 1893:** A handsome volume of three hundred pages by Mr. Herbert Gibson has recently been published, in which the history of the Sheep-Breeding industry in the Argentine has been very carefully and lucidly set forth.

Land and Water, **4 November 1893:** Mr. Herbert Gibson has done his colony good service in publishing this book. [...] We cordially recommend the book to colonists already in Argentina and those intending to make a start in the country, while the energetic young capitalist seeking a profitable investment, combined with a healthy life in a good climate, will do well to study Mr. Gibson's work before he finally makes up his mind.

The Speaker, **30 September 1893:** We have read the book with interest, and strongly recommend it to those who lack, as well as to those who have, faith in the future of Argentina.

Canterbury Times **(New Zealand), 30 November 1893:** The author, Mr. Herbert Gibson, is a son of Mr. Thomas Gibson, one of the pioneers of sheep-breeding in the Argentine; and while his work is not a mere guide to sheepfarming, or a handbook to the country, his practical knowledge of his subject stands forth in every page, and gives his writings the stamp of indisputable authority.

Manchester Guardian, **12 September 1893:** There is a great deal of technical information with reference to the diseases of sheep and their treatment, and with regard to poisonous weeds; and, finally, the question of sale is handled at considerable length, as also is the freezing of the carcases and the handling of wool. The work is excellently illustrated, and we are shown the machinery of the great establishments where the sheep are killed and frozen.

Vanity Fair, **11 January 1894:** Can any good thing come out of Nazareth? At all events, a most excellent book can be written and published in Buenos Ayres. In the mere matters of paper, printing, and binding "The History and Present State of the Sheep-Breeding Industry in the Argentine Republic" is everything to be desired. It is well and copiously illustrated, and furnished with maps and plans, and is, moreover, exceedingly well written.

Other reviewers, while praising the book itself, cast doubt over its robustly optimistic view of Argentina and highlighted the risks of investing in the country:

> ***The Field*, 14 October 1893:** The author of this well-written volume is the son of one of the first pioneers of the sheep-breeding industry in Argentina, to whose initiative much of its success is due. […] One of the most interesting chapters in the book is that on the selection, purchase, and administration of a sheep farm. We commend this to the reader who may be in search of details on the farming of the country. […] We do not know a better book of its class; it is unfortunate that country it relates to is infested at present by those most dangerous races of mankind, which are incapable of being governed.

> ***The Spectator*, 11 November 1893:** The Argentine Republic is not in good odour at the present moment with English capitalists, who are, perhaps, hardly in a humour to hear of its industries. It may be expected, however, when the lapse of a little more time has cooled their resentment, and enabled them not only to take a calmer view of the situation, but also to recognise the undeniable share of responsibility which their own recklessness incurred in the late financial disasters, that they will learn to distinguish between the plausible schemes of bogus speculations and the genuine enterprise offered by the two great industries which actually constitute the wealth and prosperity of the country. The solid progress of stock-raising and agriculture in the Argentine Republic deserves a more serious attention than it has yet attracted; and Mr. Herbert Gibson's account of it, in one of its aspects, that of sheep-farming, comes at a very opportune moment, if only to remind the English creditor that the Republic still depends upon other industries than that of floating bubble companies, or starting rotten banks. […] On the whole, his book, though treating often of much debatable matter, calls for very little adverse criticism, and the author may be fairly congratulated upon having accomplished a very useful and a much-needed work.

> ***Australasian Pastoralists' Review*, 16 October 1893:** With the recent publication of a history of Australian sheep-farming and stud flocks one must cordially welcome such an exhaustive work as Mr. Herbert Gibson's well-illustrated "History and Present State of the

Sheep-breeding Industry in the Argentine Republic" (Buenos Ayres: Ravenscroft and Mills, publishers, 1893), more especially when such a volume is ably written, brimful of interest, and above all, opportune. [...] Mr. Gibson is a staunch believer in Argentina, but when the impartial reader (if any reader can be called impartial) sums it all up, he will, we believe, give his verdict and declare in favour of Australia. Argentina is nearer to England than we are, and it has many advantages, and immense undeveloped resources, but it does not, and, doubtless, never will, possess our crowning advantage above and beyond all – of living under the law and liberty of the British flag. Besides, Australian sheep-breeding is far ahead, because more attention and pains have been taken and directed towards its perfection. Our classing is superior, and the sorting of our wool infinitely better. Even now revolution spreads its wings abroad in the promised land of South America, and, like firedamp, may break out at any moment when little expected.

However one judges Herbert's tome, one thing is certain: it established his reputation as a voice to be heeded on farming topics in Argentina. In the years following publication of *The History and Present State of the Sheep-Breeding Industry*, Herbert's status was further enhanced by his authorship of a series of works on related subjects. The first of these was an article describing the successful cultivation of alfalfa, or lucerne, in Argentina, published under the auspices of the Royal Agricultural Society of England.[62] This paper was printed alongside an equivalent study of the role of lucerne in English agriculture by another author, thus acquiring a comparative dimension that Herbert himself would sustain in two texts produced the next year.[63] Having made an offer to the Ministerio de Obras Públicas (Ministry of Public Works) in Buenos Aires to review different aspects of rural progress in Argentina and Great Britain, Herbert was commissioned to prepare two reports, one on the production of butter and cheese, and the other on the export of both live cattle and meat products.[64] Written in Spanish, these documents brought Herbert's considerable expertise to the attention of influential circles and may well have contributed to the escalation of his engagement in public affairs that soon followed.

---

62 'The Cultivation of Lucerne in Argentina', *Journal of the Royal Agricultural Society of England* (3rd series) 6 (1895), 675-684.

63 W. Fream, 'The Cultivation of Lucerne in England', *Journal of the Royal Agricultural Society of England* (3rd series) 6 (1895), 684-690.

64 *Informe sobre la producción de manteca y queso*; *Informe sobre la exportación de ganado en pié y de carne congelada y fresca en el Reino Unido* (La Plata: Talleres de Publicaciones del Museo, 1896).

By 1897, Herbert had become *Intendente* (Mayor) of the new town of General Lavalle, named after a hero of the post-independence era. Essentially an expanded version of the old port of Ajó, a sizeable portion of General Lavalle was built on land expropriated by the government during the 1880s from the original area of Los Yngleses. Given this history, it is not surprising that close links persisted between town and *estancia*. One of the most significant projects undertaken by Herbert as *Intendente* was to press the national government to dredge the bar, some four kilometres in width, which impeded navigation through the mouth of the Ajó river. The population of General Lavalle had now reached 2,000 and the town's importance as a centre for the local meat and fishing industries was burgeoning. While its port already handled a considerable quantity of shipping, a more easily navigable entrance was essential for its expansion to continue. On behalf of his community, Herbert produced a persuasive argument in favour of the dredging project, supported by statistical appendices and a petition signed by all the most prominent residents of the district.[65]

1899 marked a busy year of writing on agricultural topics for Herbert. One of his most significant contributions was a pamphlet in which he undertook a wide-ranging review of the different systems used in Argentina and Uruguay for cutting identifying marks into sheep's ears, together with a summary of the regulations in force in the United States, New Zealand and New South Wales.[66] The study was completed in preparation for an Argentine Rural Society conference on the same topic and as a first step towards establishing a single national standard for the identification of livestock. During this period, Herbert also contributed a series of three substantial, illustrated articles for the *Stockbreeder's Magazine*, a British publication. Describing cattle, horse and sheep-breeding practices in Argentina respectively, the articles, when taken together, offer a comprehensive overview of the country's livestock industry.[67]

Also in 1899, Herbert was appointed the delegate of the Argentine Republic to the International Commercial Congress in Philadelphia, USA. The Congress was hosted by the city's Commercial Museum, which enjoyed close links with Argentina, its collection having been founded on the donation of all that

---

65 *Provincia de Buenos Aires, Intendencia de General Lavalle: Petición y memoria elevada al Superior Gobierno de la Nación solicitando el dragado de la barra del Riacho de Ajó* (La Plata: Talleres de Publicaciones del Museo, 1897). On the other activities of the General Lavalle municipality during this period, see *Provincia de Buenos Aires, Intendencia de General Lavalle: Memoria, años 1897 y 1898* (Buenos Aires: Jacobo Peuser, 1899).

66 *Sistema de señales para el ganado ovino* (Buenos Aires: La Agricultura, 1899).

67 'Cattle Breeding in the Argentine', *Stockbreeder's Magazine*, April 1899, 54-63; 'Horse-breeding in the Argentine', *Stockbreeder's Magazine*, May 1899, 147-155; 'Sheep-breeding in the Argentine', *Stockbreeder's Magazine*, June 1899, 334-342.

country's products displayed at the 1893 Chicago International Exhibition. Following his return from the USA, Herbert presented a fifty-three-page report on the Congress to the Argentine Rural Society, in which he outlined some of the proceedings and made recommendations on how Argentina could improve its representation at future commercial events.[68] He laments, for instance, the fact that Argentina had failed, almost entirely, to promote its status as a producer of raw materials, such as cereals, meat, wool and wood, areas in which, Herbert claims, the country should have been the main rival to the British colonies (p. 17). He cites the size and prominence of the delegations sent by the 'Anglo-Saxon' colonies as evidence of the seriousness with which they viewed matters of trade and as the example to which others, especially Argentina, should aspire. Australia and New Zealand sent no fewer than 58 delegates to Philadelphia, Canada 37 and South Africa 10, many of whom were drawn from the highest ranks of public office, including ministers past and present.

Herbert's criticism of Argentina's official apathy towards the Congress pales into insignificance alongside his condemnation of the protectionist trade measures pursued by his nation's government. He strongly advocates free trade, despite the fact that few countries, with the exception of Great Britain, espoused such a policy at the time, and predicts dire consequences for Argentina if she continues to impose punitive tariffs on foreign goods. Herbert's opinion was nothing if not controversial and was roundly attacked in an assessment of his report published in the English-language *Review of the River Plate*. The anonymous article, which is by no means wholly supportive of the Argentine government's record either, suggests that Herbert's critique of Argentine protectionism is ill-conceived:

> Mr. Gibson is very emphatic as to our need for free trade. After enumerating the disadvantages under which this country labours as regards the development of home industries – the spare population, the want of coal and iron, the abundance of the fertile land, the woful [sic] lack of immigration – he goes on to say – "In the face of all these circumstances recourse is had to a protectionist system of political economy. The spirit of the most optimistic sinks, and his faith becomes despair, in view of a hallucination which is leading us to national suicide."
>
> The conclusion seems a little too extreme. The protectionist system of the United States, of which Mr. Gibson speaks as if it were

---

68 *Informe presentado á la Sociedad Rural Argentina por Heriberto Gibson, delegado de la Sociedad ante el Congreso Comercial Internacional de Filadelfia* (Buenos Aires: Jacobo Peuser, 1900).

well adapted to its present situation – which we take leave to doubt – was introduced at a time when the country was in somewhat a corresponding situation to that of Argentina at present. Its huge production of raw material, and its progress in manufactures, have been alike the creatures of protection. There is hardly a British colony, of those so well represented at the Congress, which has not adopted a similar system. It is a little misleading to speak of an immigration which does not come, when, as we have had occasion to point out, the immigration into this country compares favourably with all others save the United States. And it is a pity to speak of the fiscal policy of this country as if protectionism were its chief weakness. If we are eventually to fall by national suicide, it will be on account of maladministration of justice, and because of over-taxation and taxation foolishly applied, not necessarily protective in its character.[69]

Four weeks later, Herbert's lengthy rebuttal appeared in a letter to the editor, in the course of which he revealed his knowledge of economics through citation of John Stuart Mill and Thorold Rogers and demonstrated that the author of the review of his report had, in fact, misread or misunderstood aspects of his argument.[70] In response, the *Review*'s editor 'readily admit[ted]' one of Herbert's corrections and confessed that part of the original report had been read 'without due care'. However, on the core issue of free trade versus protectionism as the economic model that Argentina should follow, the editor refused 'to join issue with Mr. Gibson'.[71]

In 1903, Herbert would expound his views on economic matters more fully in a series of articles for the Dolores-based newspaper *La Patria*.[72] Perceiving that the nation stands at a vital juncture economically, Herbert offers a comprehensive analysis of its current circumstances and the competing views of its future fiscal direction. He claims no special qualifications for the task in hand and is at pains not to link his opinions to any political movement:

> El objeto del presente estudio es de recorrer á luces de un simple ciudadano el actual sistema económico del país en sus manifestaciones más importantes, analizar en breve sus efectos, y tratar de indicar las

---

69 'Mr. Herbert Gibson's Report', *Review of the River Plate*, 24 November 1900, p. 6.
70 'Protection', *Review of the River Plate*, 22 December 1900, pp. 6-8.
71 'Editorial Note', *Review of the River Plate*, 22 December 1900, p. 8.
72 'Reflexiones económicas', *La Patria* (Dolores), 11, 29, 30 August, 13, 15, 16 September, 28 October 1903.

mejoras de que es susceptible sin que medie el objeto de atraer ó substraer la opinión á ninguno de los partidos públicos que disputan la representación administrativa. (11 August 1903)

[The object of the present study is to evaluate from the viewpoint of a simple citizen the country's present economic system in its most important manifestations, to analyse briefly its effects, and to try to indicate the improvements to which it is susceptible, without the object of attracting opinion to, or detracting it from, any of the public parties which compete for administrative representation.]

Indeed, rather than jumping on the bandwagon of any existing political group, Herbert predicts that once people reach a better understanding of Argentina's economic condition the party political landscape will be transformed, with new alliances forming around agendas of solely economic issues:

En realidad, cree él que escribe, cuando se concocen mejor los puntos salientes de nuestra economía nacional se producirá un cambio radical en la formación de los asi titulados partidos políticos, y se levantarán nuevas agrupaciones de elementos diversos cuya bandera no será otra que un programa económico. (11 August 1903)

[In reality, the author believes that when the salient points of our national economy are better known there will be a radical change in the formation of the so-called political parties, and there will arise new groupings of diverse elements, whose standard will be nothing other than an economic programme.]

Although he makes no claim to be the exclusive agent of the people's economic enlightenment, and hence of a fundamental realignment of the political landscape, Herbert clearly considers that his articles will make a contribution to this process. Returning to one of the central themes of his report on the Philadelphia Congress, Herbert fiercely attacks Argentina's protectionist trade tariffs, which he sees as totally unsuited to the nation's circumstances:

En vano se busca en las faces de nuestra situación industrial una causa que autorice ó explique un sistema prohibicionista tan singularmente extremo. Tenemos una población reducida y un territorio de vasta extensión. Nuestra industria se limita á la cosecha de los frutos que produce esa tierra fertil que es la admiración de toda persona inteligente que la recorre. Carecemos de los elementos necesarios á las indústrias de artefactos, á decir el carbon, el hierro, el petroleo; ó si existen están aun en las entrañas de la tierra. No tenemos una población que se dedica por causas naturales á las manufacturas, ni tenemos la obra de mano en el pais para practicarlas. Las herramientas que empleamos las recibimos de Inglaterra, Estados Unidos, Alemania, Canada y Australia; las ropas que vestimos vienen todas de Europa — ¿A que una protección si no hay nada á proteger? ¿A que cerrar nuestras puertas á la entrada de los medios que son necesarios al edificio de la potencia nacional? (16 September 1903)

[One seeks in vain among the features of our industrial situation a cause that authorizes or explains such a singularly extreme protectionist system. We have a low population and a vast territory. Our industry is limited to the harvest of the fruits of that fertile land which is the admiration of every intelligent person who crosses it. We lack the necessary elements for manufacturing industries, that is to say coal, iron and oil; or if they do exist they are still in the depths of the earth. We do not have a population that is naturally inclined to manufacturing, nor do we have the workforce to practise it. We receive the tools we use from England, the United States, Germany, Canada and Australia; the clothes we wear all come from Europe – What is the point of protectionism if there is nothing to protect? Why close our ports to the means necessary for building national power?]

He shoots down the argument advanced by some that it was precisely because of protectionism that the United States had become a great industrial power and that Argentina should, therefore, follow the example set by its northern neighbour. Instead, he argues, the foundations of US prosperity lay in the innate characteristics of that country and its people and long predated the imposition of protective tariffs. Moreover, he predicts that the North American economy would have flourished just as well under a system of free trade:

Los que sostienen el sistema proteccionista como medida que fomenta á las industrias nacientes de un pais nuevo señalan á los Estados Unidos como evidencia irrefragable de la bondad de su doctrina. Echan en olvido que las industrias existieron primero que la protección que las ampara bajo las tarifas Dingley y MacKinlay. Existieron porque el pais posee el recurso inmenso de la materia prima; — hierro, carbon, cal, petróleo, etc; porque en su vasta población tiene un mercado de enorme consumo; y porque el genio industrial caracteriza notablemente á esa nacion. Separándose de la tarifa aduanera como medio de renta y mirándola únicamente como supuesto estímulo á la industria nacional, no han [sic – hay] en toda la manifestación productiva de aquel pais indicio alguno que permita dudar que bajo el sistema del mas libre cambio en su actividad comercial no hubiera alcanzado al mismo grado de importancia. (13 September 1903)

[Those who support the protectionist system as a means of fostering the emerging industries of a new country point to the United States as the irrefutable evidence of their doctrine's validity. They overlook the fact that the industries existed before receiving protection under the Dingley and MacKinlay tariffs. They existed because the country possesses an immense resource of primary material – iron, coal, lime, oil, etc.; because the country has, in its vast population, an enormous consumer market; and because that nation is notably characterized by its industrial tendency. Leaving aside the customs tariff as a means of revenue and viewing it solely as an alleged stimulus to national industry, there is no indication whatsoever in the productive example of that country which leaves room for doubt that under a system of the freest trade it would not have attained the same level of importance in its commercial activity.]

While Herbert devotes most space in his economic articles to his personal bugbear of protectionism, he also indicates the dangers to commerce of a debased currency, such as that circulating in Argentina around the time of writing. Although devaluation of the paper currency in respect to gold proves beneficial to producers (such as farmers), he argues, it is most certainly detrimental to traders, and the net impact on the nation's economy is negative:

La razón porque mientras subia el oro, ó mejor dicho mientras el papel moneda continuaba desvalorizándose, el productor que vive del fiado se verá favorecido no es de difícil explicación. El productor hacia sus compras al fiado á un precio de papel arreglado al tipo corriente de oro, y cuando venia á realizar su cosecha, también á un precio de papel arreglado al tipo corriente de oro, la diferencia de premios producida en el intérvalo por la suba de oro, hacia que la conversión representaba para él una amortización de su deuda. [...]

Por la misma razón que el productor lucraba del oro el comercio padecia. [...] Concedemos que el comerciante hizo sus operaciones y escalonaba sus precios arreglado á las fluctuaciones del papel desvalorizado. Concedemos que el importador compraba oro á plazos para equipar sus ventas á papel con sus obligaciones á oro. Concedemos sobre todo que el pais en conjunto perdia con la suba del metálico. No desvirtuan estas consideraciones á las bases de la proposición que la suba del oro favorecia al productor que contraia al fiado y á papel deudas á liquidarse con los frutos de la cosecha venidera. (28 October 1903)

[It is not difficult to explain the reason why the producer living on credit found himself at an advantage so long as gold rose, or more accurately while paper money continued to devalue. The producer made his purchases on credit at a paper price fixed to the current gold rate, and when he came to trade his harvest, also at a paper price fixed to the current gold rate, the difference in values produced in the interval by the rise of gold meant that the conversion served as an amortization of his debt. [...]

For the same reason that the producer feathered his nest on gold, business suffered. [...] We admit that the businessman carried out his operations and adjusted his prices according to the fluctuations of the devalued paper currency. We admit that the importer bought gold on instalments to balance his sales in paper currency with his obligations in gold. We admit above all else that the country as a whole lost with the rise of gold. These considerations do not detract from the basis of the proposition that the rise of gold favoured the producer who purchased on credit and in paper currency and repaid his debts with the fruits of the next harvest.]

I think we can detect in Herbert's views on economics a significant influence of the great thinkers of the Scottish Enlightenment, many of whose works he had probably encountered in his bibliophile youth. His resolute opposition to protectionism calls to mind Adam Smith's analysis of the 'unreasonableness' of most restraints placed upon the importation of goods from abroad.[73]

---

73 'To give the monopoly of the home-market to the produce of domestick industry, in any particular art or manufacture, is in some measure to direct private people in what manner they ought to employ their capitals, and must, in almost all cases, be either a useless or a hurtful regulation' (Adam Smith, *An Inquiry into the Nature and Causes of the Wealth of Nations*, Book IV, Chapter 2).

Interestingly, the one exception in which Smith allows that some form of trade restrictions may be legitimate is in retaliation to anti-competitive measures imposed by another nation; indeed, Herbert displayed an analogous, if not quite identical, position during the economic downturn in the years following the First World War, when he instigated a 'buy from those who buy from us' campaign in Argentina.[74]

Around the same time that he was expounding his economic theories in the pages of *La Patria*, Herbert was also becoming a regular speaker and writer on an eclectic range of political, historical and cultural topics. Towards the end of 1902, he gave a lecture to the English Literary Society of Buenos Aires on 'The Baconian Cypher in Shakepeare's Plays'. According to a report of the event carried in the *Buenos Aires Herald*, Herbert's talk rejected the view then being advanced by a Mrs Gallup from the United States that applying one of Francis Bacon's published word ciphers to the plays of Shakespeare 'revealed the most blood curdling results'.[75] While dismissal of Mrs Gallup's absurd contentions was uncontroversial, it seems that Herbert also rejected the more plausible claim that Bacon was in fact the author of some of the works traditionally attributed to Shakespeare. This provoked an outraged letter to the editor of the *Buenos Aires Herald* from a self-proclaimed Baconian writing under the pseudonym of 'Yorick'.[76] 'Yorick' opens by lamenting the fact that no time was allowed for questions at the conclusion of Herbert's lecture, claiming that 'one or two, at least, of those present, might have had something to say which would have removed the impression that the lecturer, in demolishing the absurdities of Mrs. Gallup, had established his case'. Then, having attempted to distance mainstream Baconians from the excesses of those of Mrs Gallup's persuasion, Yorick closes by asserting that the 'time will come when the claims of the Stratford player to the works that now bear his name will be regarded as one of the most astonishing frauds in the annals of literature'. If not exactly a major or highly original contribution to the Shakespeare versus Bacon polemic, it seems that Herbert's address to the English Literary Society at least succeeded in stirring up heated cultural debate in the salons of the British community of Buenos Aires.

---

74 'The case in which it may sometimes be a matter of deliberation how far it is proper to continue the free importation of certain foreign goods, is, when some foreign nation restrains by high duties or prohibitions the importation of some of our manufactures into their country. Revenge in this case naturally dictates retaliation, and that we should impose the like duties and prohibitions upon the importation of some or all of their manufactures into ours' (*Wealth of Nations*, Book IV, Chapter 2).

75 'The Baconian Cypher in Shakespeare's Plays', *Buenos Aires Herald*, 6 November 1902.

76 'Shakespeare v. Bacon', *Buenos Aires Herald*, 6 November 1902.

In June 1904, Herbert again addressed the English Literary Society, talking on the history of the Jesuit missions in Paraguay.[77] The meeting was presided over by Herbert's brother-in-law, Dr George Mackern, who, at the end of the lecture, invited contributions from the floor. Two members of the audience spoke, one making 'some pungent remarks regarding the Jesuits', the other defending the missions in Paraguay as 'socialistic communities, and most successful ones'. Thus, it would seem that quite a lively discussion ensued. The detractor of the Jesuits then challenged Herbert, whose talk had, on the whole, presented quite a positive view of the missions in Paraguay, to say 'how he [...] would like to live under Jesuit rule to-day'. Herbert retorted with a rhetorical question, asking the Jesuits' critic 'how he would like to have been an Indian in Paraguay 200 years ago', and so the meeting came to a close.

When Manuel Quintana was elected President of the Argentine Republic in 1904, he issued a plea to his fellow citizens to collaborate actively in the project of building a 'great nation' with a 'great destiny'. Herbert was quick to take up Quintana's rallying cry and penned an eloquent essay expounding the virtues of 'civic duty'.[78] He criticizes the 'spirit of indifference' endemic among the Argentine people and laments the fact that a 'community whose heritage is 715 millions of fertile acres, liberated of all serfdom, emancipated from the sullen traditions and inter state jealousies of the old world, endowed constitutionally with the most liberal charter, is forgetting the duty of the citizen to the State' (p. 1). Herbert rejects the pursuit of personal goals to the neglect of the common good and argues that all great nations encompass the 'recognition of the individual that he is a coefficient of the State', a view which, he claims, is the foundation of 'Christian political economy' (p. 1). Mindful of his readership, he lambasts the insularity of Argentina's British community and the attitude held by some of its members that 'public life is foul and their association with it will defile them' (p. 2). He deems this last sentiment the 'most inexcusable', since 'where things are foulest is where the cleanest men are required', believing that this is an 'unassailable plank in the Christian social platform' (p. 2). At the same time as exhorting members of the community to individual effort, Herbert remains aware of the need for more concerted action and calls for the formation of a Civic League to foment a sense of duty among the citizenry. As the 'man in the street and the labourer on the land are ignorant of the construction of the country's institutions', such an organization is needed 'to inform them, to build up as in the United States of America the primaries, leading therefrom to a

---

77 'English Literary Society. Lecture by Mr. Herbert Gibson', *Buenos Aires Herald*, 16 June 1904.

78 'Civic Duty', *Buenos Aires Scotch Church Magazine*, May 1905, pp. 1-3.

representative municipal regime, and thence in political order to the higher institutions of the Federation' (pp. 2-3).

Later in 1905, it would seem that moves were afoot in Argentina to ensure that Sundays were treated as a day of rest. A 'Sunday Rest Observance Association' had been founded, and Herbert addressed a meeting of members of the British community to argue in favour of its aims. Referring to the assertion of 'many travellers that the most characteristic trait in English life is the English Sunday', Herbert further claimed that a 'great majority of the thinking men of English origin' attributed the 'prosperity of that nation' to the tradition of the 'English Sunday' and went on to develop a strong argument for keeping the seventh day of the week for rest and religious observation. Leaving aside the puzzle as to why a Scotsman should hold up the *English* Sunday as the paragon to which all should aspire, when the Sabbath was almost certainly marked with greater reverence in the land of his birth, I think we can detect a note of dissonance between Herbert's present words and previous actions. According to entries in his diary dating from the years he spent learning the *estancia* business at Los Yngleses, a large part of young Herbert's typical Sunday was spent engaging in sporting activities, chiefly golf, polo or lawn tennis. In his speech, however, he states:

> I am told that it is dangerous to suggest any limitation of games on Sunday. Well, I have no quarrel with games. Life's a dull business and we all want what fun we can get out of it – kiddies and grown ups alike. But if Sunday is only to cease being a day of labour commercial to become a day of labour sportive, with the demands of high tension twentieth century sport [...] we are only going to take the boot off one foot to put it on the other. We don't work too hard here, we work too long. When we have our Sunday secured to us I believe that we are going to ask for our Saturday half-holiday too. That and the recognised holidays of the year are sufficient for the national playground, and we shall still have our Sunday to turn from the ground and understand life in its highest and most durable facets.[79]

So, while sports are recognized as an important form of recreation, Sunday is not a fitting day for play. Incidentally, if Herbert thought that the 'tension' of 'twentieth century sport' was high in 1905, one can only wonder what he would have made of the professionalism of today!

---

79 'Sunday Rest – Mr. Herbert Gibson's Address at Meeting held in Beranger Hall on Tuesday Night', *The Standard* (Buenos Aires), 3 September 1905.

At the end of May 1906, Herbert made a well received speech at a banquet to mark the wedding of King Alfonso XIII of Spain to Princess Victoria Eugenie (known as Ena) of Battenberg, a granddaughter of Queen Victoria.[80] Held in Prince George's Hall, a centre of the British community in Buenos Aires, the banquet brought together 'four hundred leading Spanish and British residents gathered round the festive board'.[81] In his speech, Herbert celebrated the union for its capacity to reinvigorate the historical links between the British and Spanish heritages:

> Las bodas que celebramos esta noche sellan por su hecho imborrable la unión sincera y estrecha entre los pueblos español y británico.
>
> Son pueblos que se deben mutuamente estima, como la han merecido á nombre de la civilización y el progreso al mundo entero. Han sido los españoles y los ingleses, cuatro siglos atrás, los "pioneers" atrevidos cuyas naves han surcado los mares desconocidos para abrir á la emigración europea nuevos horizontes para su marcha civilizadora. Animados por una rivalidad que honra, —porque la lucha digna obliga al respecto mutuo de las partes contendoras, han legado aquellos héroes de otrora á los pueblos europeos nuevas tierras para labrar y nuevos climas para fundar sus hogares tranquilos y dichosos.
>
> [The marriage we are celebrating tonight seals by its indelible fact the sincere and close union between the Spanish and British peoples.
>
> They are nations that owe each other mutual esteem, such as they deserve in the name of worldwide civilization and progress. The Spanish and the English were, four centuries ago, the daring pioneers whose ships cut through unknown seas to open new horizons to the civilizing march of European emigration. Inspired by a rivalry that was honourable, since worthy struggle obliges the contending parties to feel mutual respect, those heroes of yesteryear have bequeathed to the people of Europe new lands to work and new climes in which to establish their peaceful and happy homes.]

He also highlighted the importance of both the British and Spanish communities in the life of modern Argentina:

---

80 Princess Ena's parents were Princess Beatrice, Queen Victoria's youngest daughter, and Prince Henry of Battenberg.

81 'Commemoration of the Spanish Royal Wedding', *The Standard*, 31 May 1906.

En los tiempos modernos y en esta tierra cuyo progreso motiva con justicia la admiración de las naciones del viejo mundo, las colectividades española é inglesa han contribuido en primer renglón al desarrollo de las industrias rurales que constituyen por fin el eje de la potencia argentina.

[In modern times and in this country whose progress justly inspires the admiration of the nations of the old world, the Spanish and English communities have contributed in the first degree to the development of the rural industries that, in the end, form the core of Argentine power.]

Having then alluded to 'una nueva y franca era de acercamiento entre las razas que habitan las partes civilizadas del mundo' ['a new and frank era of rapprochement between the races that inhabit the civilized parts of the world'], Herbert closed his speech with toasts to the long life of King Alfonso in both Spanish and English: '¡Viva el Rey Alfonso!'; 'Long live King Alfonso!'.

Shortly after participating in the celebrations for the royal wedding, Herbert had occasion to pen a lengthy letter to the editor of *The Standard*, part of which constitutes a response to another correspondent who, under the nom de plume 'Britisher', had written questioning the motives of those in the British community who had applauded the marriage and expressing his own reluctance to join their ranks. This division of opinion within the English-speaking circles of Buenos Aires leads Herbert to a wider consideration of what we might term their lack of community spirit, particularly in regard to the reception given to newly arrived fellow countrymen. There is no British institution to assist newcomers nor, would it seem, is help forthcoming from their established compatriots:

> For many years past there has been a consciousness among the various circles of the British community that their closer union is necessary. In Canada there is a St. George's League, a St. Patrick's League, a St. Andrew's League, constituted to give a helping hand to the newly arrived Englishman, Irishman, or Scotchman. In this country there is nothing – nothing to help on the active factor; only philanthropical institutions to succour the maimed, the poor, and the destitute.
>
> The newcomer of British origin, good or bad, sturdy pioneer or beachcomer [*sic*], vigorous or derelict, drifts from office to office where a British name is on the doorplate in useless quest of a job awaiting him. The man in the office is busy, he doesn't want anyone

within the narrow sphere of his own influence, he knows that there is plenty of work – somewhere – but he isn't an immigration agent. He knows in his heart, if he has one, that the British shoulder pushes hardest and truest in the day's work – but he hasn't got time to help the newcomer along. The fellow shouldn't have come; or if he came he should have brought a letter of introduction; or if he did bring a letter of introduction he ought to have known that everybody brings letters of introduction, and anyway it was all a beastly nuisance.[82]

In an attempt to tackle the disunity that existed among the various constituents of the British community and to lend assistance to new incomers, Herbert goes on to propose the establishment of some sort of association:

If indeed there is to be a consolidation of the British community in Argentina, it must be for something more than junkettings. It may call itself a British Chamber of Commerce, or a British Argentine League, or what it will, but its programme will be an emasculated one if it does not comprehend some of the following purposes:
1. To assist respectable British immigrants to the Argentine to obtain suitable employment.
2. To provide the newly arrived British immigrant of the working classes with house and board for two days after his arrival, and help him to find an engagement.
3. To establish a register to bring employer and employee within knowledge of one another.
4. To inform British subjects at home and in the colonies, by means of publication and other methods of advertisement, on the conditions of the Argentine as a field for labour and capital.
5. To foment the international trade between the Argentine Republic and the British Empire.
6. To promote the friendly relations between Argentines and British, commercially, socially, and politically.
7. To assist the interests of British residents in the Argentine Republic, and especially of those settled in the National Territories.
8. Within the limits of the Argentine Constitution to forward by every accessible means the immigration of British capital,

---

82 'British Representation', letter to the Editor of *The Standard*, 10 June 1906.

labour, and commerce; to exercise vigilance over these interests radicated here, and to stimulate the trade between the two countries.

Herbert would again address the fragmentation of the English-speaking community a couple of years later when he delivered a lecture on 'British Disunity in the Argentine Republic' to the St. Andrew's Debating Society in Buenos Aires. Not only did the British prove more reluctant than other immigrant groups to assimilate fully into Argentine society, held back by the 'circumstance of their Protestant religion', Herbert argued, but its members were 'split up into groups and factions'.[83] He posed the question 'what was the matter with them all' and pointed out that the 'previous generation were united and pulled together for their collective good, but now the camp was split up and rival flags were fluttering'. For the good of the community, Herbert urged his audience 'to join up [their] ranks and work together' and further proposed the necessity of fostering in the United Kingdom a 'better knowledge' of Argentina. One way of achieving both aims, he suggested, was to form an Anglo-Argentine Chamber of Commerce in Buenos Aires, together with a 'sister Chamber' in London to promote the Republic there. Herbert would continue to campaign for the formation of a Chamber of Commerce over the following years and was a key figure in its eventual establishment in 1914. His brother Hope was elected the first chairman of the Chamber in Buenos Aires, a post he held by annual re-election until 1918.

At the same time as drawing attention to the weaknesses of Argentina's British community and proposing ways to further its consolidation, Herbert continued to speak and write on various topics. A lecture on the Argentine uprising of 1810 against Spanish colonialism, which led to the achievement of full independence six years later, revealed his profound interest in the history of his adopted land.[84] This aspect of Herbert's character is further reinforced by his knowledgeable review of Paul Groussac's biography of Santiago de Liniers, one of the last Viceroys of the River Plate and the representative of the Spanish crown in the region at the time of the English invasions of 1806 and 1807.[85] Herbert displayed equal enthusiasm for disseminating the appreciation of British culture, as an article on the history and traditions of Maundy

---

83 'British Disunity in the Argentine Republic', *The Standard*, 7 July 1908.

84 'The Revolution of 1810 and After' (a report on Herbert Gibson's lecture to the St Andrews Debating Society), *Buenos Aires Herald*, 31 July 1906.

85 'Santiago de Liniers – Count of Buenos Aires', *Buenos Aires Herald Weekly Edition*, 13 March 1908.

Thursday shows. In the latter, he exhibits his characteristic desire to treat others with generosity and respect by appealing to the reader to live up to the spirit of the day: 'the good Samaritan [...] can best celebrate his Maundy Thursday by remembering that, as of yore, the needy and the poor are still waiting at his gate'.[86]

To live an industrious, harmonious and beneficent life is the central message of a piece on 'The Duty of Happiness' written by Herbert for the *Buenos Aires Scotch Church Magazine*. He starts by challenging the view that the pattern of a person's life is determined by genetic or environmental factors:

> This is an age that comfortably blames temperament, heredity, and predisposition, for all its backslidings. A man knocks you down with a thick club and takes your watch; and you are invited to examine his genealogical tree to find an explanation of his conduct and a solace for your loss.[87]

While arguing that 'it is an easy excuse to make heredity responsible for faults and habits of no use to ourselves and distressful to our neighbours', Herbert acknowledges that 'nature' has a part to play in the formation of character, but that it is within the individual's 'power, by cultivation or neglect, to produce the development of some qualities and the atrophy of others'. The function of the human being, he proposes, is the 'trusteeship of a wonderful and precious life, and the execution of his duty'; the latter is deemed a 'matter of the gravest import to his family, to his tribe, to his nation, and above all to the Creator who entrusted him'. According to Herbert, one's primary duty is to be happy, and he sets out a 'programme' for fulfilling it. Living in harmony with nature is a good place to start:

> You must go to bed betimes and rise with the dawn. Through the night vigil Nature has cleansed herself of the marks of the toil and sorrow of the bypast day that is dead. She arises anew, her face turned to the east, and welcomes the childhood of a new day. As the light strengthens and the tall poplars cast their shadows athwart their upright shafts, all the world around you gladdens into happiness. [...] You too are filled with elation; yesterday's troubles and difficulties have all dwindled mysteriously into nothingness. No new thing has happened; you are neither richer nor poorer, greater nor smaller, but you are happy;

---

86 'Maundy Thursday', *Buenos Aires Herald*, 16 April 1908.
87 'The Duty of Happiness', *Buenos Aires Scotch Church Magazine*, April 1908.

– gloriously, contentedly happy; happy to belong to a world whose richness and fullness have become revealed to you.

Next, one must work hard at whatever one does, 'for idleness is death' and 'in honest well-done work lies one of the secrets of happiness'. The type of work is of little significance in comparison to the way it is carried out:

> The importance of the work, as the world measures it, matters much less for the happiness of the individual and the ultimate benefit of mankind than the efficiency and thoroughness and cheerfulness with which it is executed. The effort each day to do one's work a little better, to achieve another rung in the infinite ladder to perfection, not only leads to success but it produces immediate happiness; and the happiness of the worker irradiates, carrying new vigour and inspiration to others. Happiness being a duty, and attainable most frequently through work, it is a duty to work cheerfully as if the particular work of each one were the finest occupation in the world, and he the luckiest of individuals to have come by it.

Whether or not one entirely agrees that work is the easiest path to happiness, this message does have a certain, if rather simplistic, appeal. All one needs to do, according to Herbert, is follow the rhythms of nature and complete one's labours diligently and with a light heart – if only life were so easy!

Not all of Herbert's writings from this period were concerned with such lofty themes as those we have been considering. In a long letter published in the agricultural and pastoral section of the *Buenos Aires Herald*, he expounds upon 'The Value of Manure', airing his views in response to an earlier article in the same publication which had suggested that the Argentine landowner was 'wasting the riches of his virgin territory' and should 'acquire from the United States and Australasia a rudimentary knowledge of the science of farming', especially with regard to the spreading of manure as a fertilizer.[88] Herbert rejects this criticism of local practices, asserting that the collection and spreading of manure is appropriate in what he terms 'close farming', where food is brought 'to the beast instead of sending the beast to the food' and animals frequently spend long parts of the year in stalls, but that it is entirely unsuited to Argentine circumstances:

> In our great stock-breeding estancias nature is engaged the whole year round, replenishing her own fertility by the decay of vegetation and

---

88 'The Value of Manure', *Buenos Aires Herald*, 13 August 1908.

animal matter, the collection of humus by ants and other agents, by the manure supplied by the stock and by the chemical process through which the soil draws from the air the factors necessary to convert its mineral wealth into plant food. In relation to this vast automatic process of fertilization the little manure heap outside the shed is unworthy of mention.

Indeed, the manual spreading of manure is not only superfluous, but also uneconomical. Since only a few animals are kept indoors in Argentina during winter, the quantity of waste collected is small and, if it had to be moved any distance across the *estancia*, would not 'pay the cost of cartage'. Instead, Herbert recommends that it should be used by the gardener or 'spread to some little patch for domestic tillage'. Even in the case of agricultural, as opposed to cattle or sheep-raising, establishments, artificial fertilization by organic or chemical means does not find much favour with Herbert; rather, he suggests, the 'road to success lies by the way of better tillage and constant cultivation, rotation of crops and maintaining the balance of the calls on the soil'. In reply to an exaggerated claim in the earlier article that a manure heap is 'worth its weight in gold in the United States or Australasia', Herbert offers to sell his own paltry pile for a mere '$5, paper, a ton'!

Herbert's contribution to the manure debate signalled an earnest return to agricultural topics for the next couple of years: a lecture delivered in Azul proposing the establishment of a school of stock-raising and agriculture in that town;[89] a brief note on alfalfa-growing in the *Pastoralists' Review*;[90] a synopsis of the history of stock-breeding in Argentina in the *Buenos Aires Herald*;[91] a lengthy, two-part piece for the *Buenos Aires Herald* on water storage and conservation, written in response to a drought in the Pampa Central region;[92] and a report on the Argentine meat trade for *The Times*.[93] It does not seem necessary to delve into any of these works here, save to say that all demonstrate in one way or another Herbert's profound knowledge of Argentine rural affairs and his deep commit-

---

89 'Las escuelas prácticas de ganadería y agricultura', lecture to the Union Club of Azul, 11 October 1908.
90 'The Progress of Alfalfa-growing in the Argentine', *Pastoralists' Review*, 16 November 1908.
91 'Argentine Stock-Breeding Reviewed – Records of the Past: Possibilities of the Future', *Buenos Aires Herald*, 1 January 1909.
92 'Water Storage in the Pampa Central: Suggested Solution of a Present Day Problem', *Buenos Aires Herald*, October 1910.
93 'Argentine Meat and the "Beef Trust": View of an Estancia Owner', *The Times*, 7 April 1911.

ment to their continued progress. Indeed, I think it would be fair to call Herbert, on the basis of a broad survey of his writings on agricultural topics, a modernizer or even a visionary, for he tirelessly sought out and espoused new and better methods for the management of Argentina's rural economy. That in itself did not mark him out as unique among his peers, for many landowners (and politicians) were keen to import the latest techniques from abroad; Herbert, however, displayed a rare faculty of discrimination, always paying due regard to Argentina's particular circumstances, promoting only those ideas which were in accord with local conditions and discarding the rest, as exemplified by his rejection of manure-spreading as a pointless activity.

Having studied Herbert's writings up to the year 1911, we have, in a manner of speaking, come the full circle. We have seen how he began to tackle agricultural matters around 1892, then branched out into a diverse range of other topics – economic, literary, cultural and historical – before stepping up his output on rural themes again towards the end of the period under review. The fact that we have now reached the cut-off date for the present chapter does not mean that Herbert ceased to be a productive 'man of letters' at this point – indeed, many significant works lay ahead – but before examining these we should first consider some other aspects of his life and activities.

CHAPTER 6

HUSBAND AND FATHER

Prior to 1895, Herbert had few dealings of a romantic nature with the opposite sex, save for his rather enigmatic relationships with Eugenie and V, referred to briefly in Chapter 4. Some time around the middle of 1894, however, he fell head over heels in love, although the object of his affections, a twenty-six-year-old widow by the name of Madeleine Jessie Paice, was a little slow to reciprocate. Madeleine was the daughter of a Church of England vicar, the Rev. W J Savell. Her first husband, George Leonard Paice of Wallington, Surrey, had died in 1889 in his thirty-fourth year. It seems that she had travelled to Argentina some time after her husband's sudden and untimely demise, on account of having connections there. For a long spell, she lived at La Casuarina, the *estancia* of George and Katie Gibson, Herbert's cousin and his wife. The exact nature of Madeleine's association with the Gibsons is a little unclear, her status apparently lying somewhere between that of a helpful friend and employee. In a letter of April 1895, Herbert wrote to Madeleine:

> You have made the Casuarina a pretty home for them, you have taught Katie how to make the best of camp life and shown her how to make a house pretty with nothing but a pair of clever hands […], you have taken charge of her two unruly boys and made them loveable honest little fellows.[94]

This makes Madeleine sound like a sort of housekeeper-cum-governess, but at the same time she seems to have been treated more or less as an equal by members of the extended Gibson family.

Herbert and Madeleine first met while she was visiting Los Yngleses; Herbert, by all accounts, was smitten at first sight, but his natural shyness left him tongue-tied and prevented him from making any but the most clumsy approach. For

---
94 Herbert Gibson to Madeleine Paice, 19 April 1895.

her part, Madeleine probably had no inkling of his true feelings at first. Even by early 1895, their relationship had not progressed beyond extreme formality, although Herbert missed no opportunity to show his beloved little kindnesses. In January, he addressed a wordy (and frankly rather pretentious) letter to 'Dear Mrs. Paice' describing some repairs he had arranged to have made to her rifle, which ended up amounting almost to the construction of a new piece, and apologizing for his own gaucheness:

> Your rifle has had such a doing! – The gunsmith had scarcely finished the reparation of the loading mechanism when he discovered that the barrel was all his fancy had not painted it; so he proceeded to renew it. But thereupon he fell foul of the stock and nothing would please him but to leap into the breach "in a manner of speaking" and complete an article that already bore the stamp of his handicraft. You may possibly not recognise the weapon in its rejuvenated state, – but I fear that the cooing turtle dove will still trace the same unerring individualism in its execution.
>
> If I have been more clumsy than the gunsmith in explaining the metamorphosis I owe you pardon. I have exchanged an old lamp for a new one, and I have apologised lamely as I know not what reminiscences I may have thoughtlessly destroyed. The same "wretched spite" which changed all the pleasant things I would have said down at the Yngleses into stupid commonplaces dogs me again and makes me turn my phrases awkwardly. I suppose I owe to the eternal unfitness of things my lack of expression on the first occasion that I desire to possess it.[95]

About a month later, Madeleine wrote to 'Dear Mr. Gibson' thanking him for the surprise gift of some art supplies:

> Two days ago I received some cadmium yellows, & lovely sable brushes with the stamp of "Gibson Hermanos" on the box; so I knew who the sender was, & hasten to write & thank you for them, & tell you how very much I appreciated your kindness.[96]

Quite how their relationship developed in the course of the next couple of weeks remains a mystery, but by the beginning of March all trace of reserve had

---

95 Herbert Gibson to Madeleine Paice, 19 January 1895.
96 Madeleine Paice to Herbert Gibson, 16 February 1895.

vanished and Herbert addressed an emotional outpouring to his 'dear Sweetheart':

> I have seen nothing but your face all day and my memory flies back every minute to the Casuarina avenue and gate. Is it all true, dear heart? Last night I awakened and thought for a cruel moment that I had only dreamt it; and then, when I knew it had all really happened I lived again through every breath of that short sweet walk to the gate, and I think that I must have again fallen adreaming, for the grey dawn crept through the window while I still held you in my arms. [...] As I write this I have your dear face before me and it wears the same kind smile that used to encourage me when I dully blundered over everything I desired to say, fearful that you should discover what lay at my heart and be angry at my presumption.
>
> Dear dear sweetheart of mine, why should I have only found out that you cared for me the moment before I was called to bid you good bye! And yet there is a sweetness in the thought that I longed for you when I deemed it hopeless that I should ever win you, that I heard you speak of others with a sinking despondent soul, it was not jealousy, dearest; I had no right to be jealous but only to be miserable, – and that between then and now there has dropped the soft spreading veil of your love.[97]

And so Herbert continued in similar vein for a further two pages!

Over the next few months, Herbert would compose many long, romantic letters to Maddie, as he soon started to call her. After a slow start, their relationship progressed rapidly; from a letter written by Herbert on 4 March, we learn that they were already engaged and that he had undertaken the formality of writing to her father. While many of his words of love should remain private, the following passage sums up Herbert's mood more than adequately:

> I am going to marry a very sweet gentlewoman, and I am very proud of having won her and so shall all those "admiring relatives and friends" be when they know her. And when that happens I think they will say that the heart followed the head, – tho' like most wiseacres they will know nothing about it, nor will we tell them. – As for your final sage reflection that I might 'afterwards regret it', I will only deign to take notice of such a suggestion when you can look me in the eyes

---

97 Herbert Gibson to Madeleine Paice, 2 March 1895.

and say that you really believe I could. My brothers may have married into wealthy families, – I am not so sure that you will hurl those wealthy families at my head when you know more about them 'boath'; – and my other relations may marry Hottentots, Peruvian princesses or Kaffirs with rings through their noses for all I care; but I want to marry you dear sweetheart. I can picture to myself taking you home to my father, and seeing him look approvingly at you and tell you that you have beautiful eyes, – whereat I shall not be the least jealous. He will be very proud of you darling when he knows you. He has been urging me to marry for the last ten years; but I knew that I should find my other half, the twin of happiness, if only I waited for you; and I knew that I had found her the first time I met you.[98]

In the same letter, Herbert tells Maddie that he wishes to buy her a ring and asks that she send him a 'tiny piece of thread so that [he] may know what size to get'.

For reasons that are not entirely clear, but may have been connected to Maddie's status as a widow or the fact that news of their betrothal had not yet reached her own family in England, the happy couple decided to keep their situation secret for a while. This led to all sorts of subterfuge, such as Herbert disguising his handwriting on the envelopes he addressed to Maddie at La Casuarina, using a different script each time he wrote lest George and Katie Gibson should become suspicious as to why their houseguest was receiving frequent letters from the same correspondent. Of his many friends and relations, Herbert confided only in his brother Hope, for he was his most trusted associate. On Easter Sunday 1895, Hope wrote to Maddie expressing his pleasure at the news:

> My dear Madeline [sic],
> Herbert has at last given me permission to write to you about the great news which must be kept secret for a while. But I do feel glad that I may now tell you how heartily happy I am that you and he have won each other. [...] I am very proud of my new sister-that-is-to-be and I feel sure that everyone of us will join in bidding you the heartiest of welcomes.[99]

Hope went on to give Herbert a glowing personal 'reference':

---

98 Herbert Gibson to Madeleine Paice, 4 March 1895.
99 Hope Gibson to Madeleine Paice, Easter Sunday, 1895.

> Herbert is a lucky fellow in winning such a sweet wife. And you too, Madeline [*sic*], are lucky in getting one of the best men who ever walked this earth. I know he is my brother and that it may not be good taste for one to say so much, but it is because I know him so well that I can honestly say that Herbert is the best specimen of a thorough gentleman I have ever met. How clever he is you already know, and you can guess to what a position he may rise in this world if he is spared. But you cannot yet know how genuine, good, and kind he is. And you will never know (for he will not tell you) the amount of happiness he has quietly caused – happiness created with a great deal of weary anxiety on his part and borne without a single grumble or complaint. Perhaps it is because he is what he is that he is so popular and such a favourite.

He also reflected on Herbert's standing in Buenos Aires and the bright future that was predicted for him:

> Although you have not had time to become very well known in Buenos Aires, Herbert has done so and I have often heard it said that one day – years hence – he would marry a great Argentine heiress and go in for a most exclusive field of politics and sheep and public reforms and all sorts of things, and end up by sucking maté and wearing bombachos[100] and chiripá[101]. I know you would not let him do the latter, but I know he will have a very sweet companion to assist him in all aspirations in the former.

Indeed, while Herbert probably never adopted the full gaucho dress code, he was later pictured wearing distinctly rural garb in photographs taken at the various Gibson *estancias*. As for the forecast of a distinguished public career, we have already seen evidence of its early development in Chapter 5 and will witness its full bloom in later sections.

While the letters Herbert wrote to Maddie between March and June 1895 are concerned primarily with pledging his undying devotion, they also provide the author with the opportunity to tell his future bride more about himself and his family. In one, he expands at length upon the decision he had made some years previously to take Argentine citizenship:

---

100   Baggy trousers, gathered in at the ankle, traditionally worn by the gaucho.
101   The loose, folded cloth worn around the gaucho's waist and tucked between his legs, a comfortable and practical garment for life on horseback.

There is a matter my sweetheart upon which I desire to write to you before more time has passed, for fear lest you upbraid me for my silence on it. – Ever so many years ago, when you were quite a child, I studied out a problem after my own lights, and with the consent and approval of my father, I became an Argentine citizen. I had at that time, dear love, only one life to consider, and that I held in too light esteem to hesitate where I thought my duty lay so clearly before me. I have been much criticised for what I have done, and I have never undertaken my defense until now, my dearest judge, my fair Portia, I come before you. [...] I am not going to weary you with a discourse on a creed possibly more tenable upon theoretic grounds than on practical ones, but I know, my darling, to what sympathetic response I appeal when I ask you to believe that my action was wholly blameless of personal ambition. The same interpretation of man's mission has led me to assist in a manner, more signalised by the lack of others who think as I do, in the affairs of this country; and I have already been honoured by an invitation to accept a deputyship, and later a portfolio in the Provincial Cabinet. These I have rejected because the time was immature. But I may be called some day to take up in another manner the pledge I have given to the country, and though as a mere unit here I might avoid the call, I do not think I can and I do not think you will ask me to. [...] You may perhaps hear some strange stories about me, – I have lately accepted the charge of a battalion of Ajó guards and those nearest to me will laugh loudest at me. [...] This is no longer an age of glove and rapier, but nations are still human; and some day – though I pray God to avert it, – I may be called to redeem a pledge which is no longer mine but yours.[102]

Not surprisingly, another topic that takes up considerable space in Herbert's correspondence is the arrangements for their forthcoming marriage. In early May, he wrote to Madeleine from on board the RMSS (Royal Mail Steam Ship) *Thames*, the vessel that was carrying him back to Britain, addressing the letter to the RMSS *Nile*, the ship on which she was travelling a week or so behind, and proposed an Edinburgh wedding:

You may perhaps be aware that my father resides in Edinburgh in a big house. The residents of Edinburgh are Christians and have

---

102 Herbert Gibson to Madeleine Paice, 20 March 1895.

churches convenient for marriages upon occasion. Do you see any particular just cause or impediment why you should not spend a few days in Edinburgh and be married to me there? All your family could be housed there comfortably I'm sure.[103]

In his next letter, Herbert seems to spring a surprise on Madeleine, one that we might speculate she would not have found wholly agreeable. After suggesting that after their wedding they spend time visiting both his old haunts and her friends around Britain, he goes on to state that 'there is one thing that puts the curb on my dreams of our wanderings together' and proceeds to explain:

Like my brothers I am really going home to live with and take care of my father. That was the understanding before I went down to the Casuarina to tell a dear princess that I wanted to make her my queen. Now that the father has got a new daughter, and one whom I know he will love very much when he sees her, he will look to us being with him almost all the time.[104]

While we cannot be certain that Herbert and Madeleine had not discussed this arrangement previously, one gets the distinct impression that the topic is being broached for the first time. He then enumerates the various reasons why the duty of caring for old Thomas must fall upon their shoulders:

If sister Eva remains at home of course we can get away from now and then, but even her presence is not sufficient for the father as she has her children and her friends whom she allows to absorb her time, and not knowing anything of South America she is not really a <u>companion</u> to him. The absence or presence of the Mackerns in England makes no difference. May who is poor girl a nervous subject always insists upon taking charge of the house she lives in to the no small discomfort of the inhabitants, and her health being bad, it does not suit her to do so. Mackern with his overbearing character is not a persona grata in my father's house; the dad knows him very well I think. So if they chance to go to Edinburgh it is on the shortest of visits.

The care of the pater therefore will devolve upon us, darling; and though we may be at times very desirous of spending a month or two away, we shall have to accommodate those trips to circumstance. In

---

103 Herbert Gibson to Madeleine Paice, 4 May 1895.
104 Herbert Gibson to Madeleine Paice, 10 May 1895.

summer the father generally goes to North Berwick which is really a very pretty place by the sea and where you can have as much or as little society as you please. In Edinburgh you will be very happy too, and I think we shall soon form a circle of friends after our own manner of thinking.

Quite what Madeleine thought of such restrictions on newly wedded life we can only guess. As far as we can tell, the couple abided by this plan for a time, although it was not to be so long until business took Herbert back to Argentina.

Returning to the wedding arrangements, the ceremony was set for 6 July in Edinburgh. In his letter to Maddie describing the plans that have been made, Herbert confirms that she, her parents, her sisters and some of Herbert's female relatives are all to stay at 1 Eglinton Crescent, the Gibson residence. As the house will then be full, brother John must lodge with friends and Herbert quips that he will himself have to 'sleep on the fourth step of Sir Walter Scott's Monument'.[105] It seems that the Gibson family had very much taken control of the wedding, even to the point of deciding what contributions Maddie's parents would be 'allowed' to make:

> Your pa is to be allowed to stand the phiz at the reception, & to provide the carriage that conducts you (my bonnie sweetheart) to the Cathedral. [...] What else? – Well, your pa (he is going to be a victim!) would do well to clear the decks at No. 1 by taking all the family out to lunch before the wedding, as that meal cannot be taken in Eglinton Crescent owing to the preparations for the reception après.

In the same letter, Herbert beseeches Madeleine to make a list of the items she would like to receive as wedding presents, as some have already begun to arrive and acquaintances are enquiring what they should contribute. Gifts received to date included a yellow satin cushion, a cigar cabinet that 'opens up and looks like a miniature doctor's washing stand' and 'four big beaten silver salt cellars with spoons'. Ever practical, Herbert ironically describes the cushion as 'useful in the land of fiery mustangs' and suggests trying to swap it through the pages of *Exchange and Mart* 'for a bull terrier or a second hand lawn mower'. Similarly, he proposes exchanging the cigar cabinet 'for a cloth bound copy of the Pilgrim's Progress or a brass padlock for the front garden gate', but the salt cellars are a 'lovely gift' that 'will do for other things, sugar bowls for after dinner coffee, holders for entremets'. While much of this is no

---

105 Herbert Gibson to Madeleine Paice, 26 June 1895.

doubt meant in jest, it reflects a genuine concern about the usefulness of their wedding bounty; in a later note, Herbert tells Madeleine that so many people have given cigarette boxes that 'you and I can set up a tobacconist's shop when we go to the Argentine'.[106]

The final preparation for the marriage that we hear of in Herbert's letters concerns his purchase of Maddie's wedding ring and demonstrates the romantic inclination he shows throughout their correspondence:

> The strongest rendering of the word <u>ever</u> that I know is the Spanish <u>siempre</u> [always]. And when I went up to town to order the little gold band that is to be the sign of our union before the world I told the smith to engrave the word <u>siempre</u> inside it.[107]

Unfortunately, we know little of the wedding itself or of the early years of Herbert and Maddie's married life, for no diaries or correspondence from this period appear to have survived. Ten months after the marriage, their first child, a girl, arrived stillborn (17 May 1896). The following year, their eldest son, Meredith Herbert (known as Chris), was born (12 October 1897), followed by Clement Herbert (23 August 1900), Gerald Herbert (7 September 1902) and Cosmo Livingstone Herbert (6 September 1904). Four days after Gerald's birth, Maddie wrote from North Berwick, where she was staying, to Herbert in Buenos Aires with details of the new arrival:

> My dearest Bert,
> Here I am trying to write you a little note in bed to let you know that I am getting on famously & now you will want to know all about it. Well on Sunday afternoon 7th Hope & Aggie came up to see me. I had been feeling wretchedly ill all day but it was not till after they had left that I discovered what was happening. Dr Matheson came at once – matters came to a crisis very rapidly & just before midnight another little Herbert Gibson was born. Throughout I had a very sharp time as the head presented differently from the usual order of things & Dr Matheson says had it been a first child instruments would have been necessary. Aggie was so kind & with me the whole time until morning as the after pains were very severe. Little Bertie is a big rollicking baby & makes use of his small lungs to a great extent. […] As I lie here I often wonder if the door won't open & you sweetheart come

---

106 Herbert Gibson to Madeleine Paice, 2 July 1895.
107 Herbert Gibson to Madeleine Paice, 27 June 1895.

in & sit down & read to me as you used to do when Chris was born (you didn't spoil me so much when Clem made his appearance) but I know it can't be. [108]

It becomes clear that after two sons the couple had been hoping for a daughter and Maddie is concerned that Herbert will be upset:
> Are you very disappointed that 'he' is not a 'she'? I was at first but am reconciled now, in fact when the end of the weary waiting came I felt I didn't care which it was so long as I got it over.

We next catch up with Herbert and Maddie in 1906, when he was in Argentina and she was staying at her parents' home in Croydon, Surrey. Herbert had been making a tour of the Gibson *estancias* during a time of drought and finally returned to La Tomasa with his 'face burned by the dry sun and peeling like blistered paint on a scalding iron roof'.[109] During his absence, which seems to have been lengthy, perhaps including a spell in Britain, La Tomasa has fallen into a state of disrepair under the (mis)management of one Fitzherbert and his assistant, Douglas Mills. Herbert tells Maddie that he has brought in a new manager, Graham, who has held the post previously, and that they have just completed an inspection of the west side of the ranch, finding a 'procession of scab, and disrepaired fences and dissolute management'. He reflects bitterly on the failings of the previous incumbents and describes the full consequences of their incompetence:

> Fitzherbert is already strolling about, a gentleman at large. He has handed over the tattered reins of his misrule to Graham in hot haste. Douglas Mills has handed in his resignation and goes too to-morrow. He "recognises that he could not get on with Mr. Graham" and does his little damned best to leave us stranded, on the eve of shearing, with no one but Graham and a raw nice young lad (Mr. Waugh – a gentleman) in the place. Let him go! I accepted his resignation in these words – "You couldn't get on with Mr. Runnacles whom I esteem as the most competent man I ever had in Ajó. You can't get on with Mr. Graham whom I am forced to call in, to save a disastrous situation. You have only got on once, and that was during the period the Tomasa was falling to pieces. You are of course leaving the ship at a time when you might have been of real use. But you can go: an unwilling horse is worse than no horse at all." [...]

---

108   Madeleine Gibson to Herbert Gibson, 11 September 1902.
109   Herbert Gibson to Madeleine Gibson, 8 October 1906.

> Everything, everything here is gone to pigs and whistles. The stock is scabby, neglected, boxed; fences on the ground; bulls and stallions mere shadows of thinness; the cabaña patio become the gambling hell of every Cachari and Pardo loafer; from top to bottom (bar the <u>estancia</u> side of the railway) the place stinks of the rot of criminal neglect.

Despite the amount of work needing to be done to bring La Tomasa back up to standard, Herbert is far from depressed; in fact, he relishes the challenge ahead: 'My soul is singing; here is a battle to fight and a goal at the end of it, a good old muddle and a stout heart to straighten it'. In a continuation of the same letter, dated 9 October, he tells Maddie that he has been 'working sheep' from 'sun up to sunset' and is 'as tired as a plough horse', but at least Fitzherbert and Mills have gone. He finds time, however, to answer an inquiry Maddie has made in a previous missive about finding work in Argentina for an acquaintance. Herbert's reply suggests that circumstances in the country are not exactly propitious, although his negativity owes more to the failings of the individual concerned:

> I am afraid sweetest that this is the last country for a man of 28 years to seek his fortune in. I shall do what I can, and am already cudgelling my brains; but my intimate conviction is that for a man of that time of life, with no recognised vocation, without Spanish, with expensive habits (as compared to the parsimonious Italian, German etc.) the Argentine is the very worst field. Men of ability and application succeed everywhere, and what has he been doing all these years to be cast up at high water mark, a piece of flotsam, "anxious and willing and of ability" and yet appealing for work and without qualifications for any! I am going to turn everything over in my mind before I write, but I fear that in the end I must be frank to avoid disappointment.

By early 1908, Herbert, Maddie and their children were all in residence at La Tomasa. Herbert spent most of his days engaged in the routine matters of *estancia* business, but took the occasional break with his family, such as a trip to the western city of Córdoba in February of that year. In October, he made his first visit to Los Yngleses since December 1903, an absence partly occasioned by the time he had spent in England, but more especially by a feud that had developed between him and his brother Ernest after their father's death. The exact origins of the fraternal dispute are not clear, but it seems likely that it was connected with the settlement of their father's estate, in which Herbert played a pre-eminent role. Over several years, Herbert, in consultation with lawyers and his siblings, drafted and redrafted proposals as to how Thomas's property should be apportioned among his heirs, but found that it was almost impossible to produce a scheme of division that satisfied all parties. In the meantime, he filled the unenviable role of administrator of the *Sucesión* (estate), having to juggle the conflicting demands of his father's assorted heirs whilst ensuring that the *estancias* continued to deliver them a respectable income. Brothers Ernest and John appear to have been the most difficult to please, and the input of sister May's husband, Dr George Mackern, was frequently problematic. Throughout this period, Ernest and his family continued to reside at Los Yngleses, which would eventually become their part of the inheritance.

During his visit of 1908, Herbert caught up with several old acquaintances among the staff at Los Yngleses, but his diary makes no mention of his brother or family, who may have been absent at the time (22 October 1908). The next day, however, while staying at a hotel in nearby Dolores, Herbert saw Ernest having dinner and approached his table 'and spoke to him wishing to make bygones be bygones and express [his] regret for anything [he] had either done or said to hurt him' (23 October 1908). Ernest was obviously in no mood to forgive and forget and Herbert's account of the episode concludes: 'he however ignored me and I withdrew – sorry for him rather than for myself' (23 October 1908). Sadly, the brothers were to remain unreconciled, although friendly relations between their families were quickly re-established following Ernest's death in 1919.

In November 1908, Herbert and family departed from La Tomasa to begin the long journey back to Great Britain, for the time had come for Chris to start prep school at Gore Court, Sittingbourne, Kent. The intention was that Maddie and the children would remain in England, while Herbert travelled regularly between Britain and Argentina. They rented a house called Fir Hill at Droxford in Hampshire's Meon Valley. Herbert described their new home as 'unpretentious', although it stood in some '8 acres of land the ground running down to the edge of the Meon stream' (22 December 1908). Before Chris left to start school at the end of January, the family spent much of their time in London, where Maddie was unfortunate enough to have her jewels stolen from their lodgings (3 January 1909).

Chris's departure for school passed off uneventfully, with none of the tears that might have been expected from a small boy separated from his parents for the first time. Herbert records:

> At 4.20 p.m. we saw dear Chris off from Victoria Station for his school at Sittingbourne. Other 25 boys or so went. Chris comported himself like a man, said good-bye bravely and waved his hat gallantly from the carriage window as the train moved out. (26 January 1909)

Just a few days later, however, Chris's pluck had dissipated and he wrote to his parents complaining that he was ill and unhappy. Like the deeply caring father he undoubtedly was,[110] Herbert immediately travelled to Sittingbourne, where he found Chris a little better, his ailments attributed to the combination of homesickness and having taken a cold bath (1 February 1909). By the time his father departed, Chris was 'brighter' and Herbert seems hopeful that 'the worst of his experience in this first venture into the "alone" [is] over' (1 February 1909).

A few days later, Herbert left Southampton aboard the RMSP (Royal Mail Steam Packet) *Avon*, bound for Buenos Aires, where, for the next five months, he engaged in his usual round of business activities. Perhaps the highlight of this period was the trip he made to inspect Gibson lands at San Rafael in the province of Mendoza. A highly descriptive travelogue is included in his diary, the literary quality of which is ably demonstrated by the following brief appreciation of the Mendoza landscape:

> I like this country. I like its cerulean sky and the eternal repose of its hills, its soft valleys, its little springs and streamlets, the potentiality of it and the repose of it. Here are none of the thorny shrubs of the Pampa Central, and if the grass is scant – in such a rainless zone – it is, even as a pastoral country, preferable to Dos Chañares & Sta Clementina [locations of other Gibson properties]. (5 April 1909)

Life cannot have been easy for Herbert at this time, separated from his young family for the first period of any length, continually immersed in matters relating to his position as administrator of the *Sucesión*, and, moreover, suffering

---

110 Herbert's compassionate approach to parenting is underlined in a letter to Maddie written some three months later. After expressing his happiness that Chris had returned home from his first term at Gore Court 'unchanged' by the experience, he wrote: 'This is the reward, darling, of love – of what some kind friends have called "spoiling and mismanagement" and laughed at – and what has been the training of the wisest mumsie in the world. Chris came to us when we wanted him badly, and you most of all. Instead of "systems" and "proper management" and "bringing a child up to know his proper place" we surrounded him with love and the result is that his darling mumsie will be his darling mumsie as long as he lives, that he will look upon his daddie as his pal all his life, and that all the finest fibres in his being will be kept well strung and sweet' (2 May 1909).

from moderate financial hardship. In April, he sent Maddie £300 to help cover her expenses, including the purchase of a car, but revealed in a letter that he had required to take a loan to do so: 'I am having to borrow a bit from the Bank to send you this £300 but I don't want to keep you waiting for your motor darling.'[111] He proceeded to enumerate the reasons for his situation:

> This current year's revenue is not going to be good – I don't mean that anything calamitous has happened but simply (i) there has been practically no sale of rams owing to over supply and lack of demand; and only a poor sale of bulls and stallions (ii) our principal products, wool, skins, capons, sheep are all very cheap this year. [...] The P. [Pampa] Central estancias are paying nothing and I shall be well pleased if they ever cover expenses; however they will soon be shut down now and cease to occasion us loss.

Another issue that concerned Herbert was Chris's ongoing unhappiness at prep school. During the Easter vacation, Maddie wrote to inform him that the situation had become so serious that she had resolved to remove Chris from Gore Court and send him instead to Oakfield School at Rugby, where a trusted acquaintance, Mr Hoffman, was one of the masters. Describing Chris's state of mind, Maddie observed:

> Chris has been utterly wretched with the thought that his holiday is nearly over & that he is to go back to Gore Court. The whole thought is spoiling his happiness & the other morning he broke down completely at the idea and asked me if it were possible to go somewhere else.[112]

After consulting Mr Hoffman, who opined that Gore Court was a 'very rough school to make a beginning in' and suggested that it was a place where boys were 'knocked about & hardened for public school' and far from the 'second home' a preparatory school should be, Maddie had no hesitation in enrolling Chris at Oakfield. On hearing the news, Chris's 'delight knew no bounds' and he solemnly promised his mother to try to do well.

In July, Herbert returned to Maddie and the children in England, having taken precautions to ensure that there would be 'no opportunity [...] for unnecessary expenditure' at the *estancias* during his absence (18 April 1909). On the

---

111   Herbert Gibson to Madeleine Gibson, 18 April 1909.
112   Madeleine Gibson to Herbert Gibson, 25 April 1909.

homeward voyage, during a stopover at Rio de Janeiro, he met up with old acquaintances Sir William and Lady Haggard, whose son Rudolf had recently gone out to Argentina for a spell and was currently employed at La Tomasa. Sir William Haggard's brother was none other than Henry Rider Haggard, the renowned author of many classic tales of adventure, including *King Solomon's Mines*, *Allan Quatermain* and *Montezuma's Daughter*, as well as works on agriculture and country life, such as *Rural England* and *Rural Denmark and Its Lessons*. Prior to setting sail, Herbert had been asked to represent a 'commission' of leading Argentine landowners who wished to invite Rider Haggard to visit their country with a view to writing about its rural industries. Accordingly, while in Rio, Herbert asked Sir William Haggard to write a letter of introduction to his brother. This facilitated the arrangement of a meeting, which eventually took place on 25 September and is described in detail by Herbert in the pages of his diary:

> By 3.26 p.m. train from L'pool St. to Ditchingham, Norfolk. A motor car met me and drove me to Ditchingham House where M$^{r.}$ Rider Haggard came to the door to welcome me.
>
> With a family resemblance to Sir William he is perhaps taller, and more loosely built, his frame suggesting considerable physical strength. He wears a full tho' not thick beard and his features are rough hewn, his face full of character, eyes keen and intelligent. His daughter Angela was there, and presently M$^{rs.}$ Haggard arrived having been on a motor tour in the west. She is a handsome pleasant woman, fond of sport and an outdoor life. With her was a son-in-law, a doctor whose name I never learned, a well read and pleasant man. A lady who I think is M$^{r.}$ Haggard's secretary completed the party.
>
> After dinner we went to the study – a long room with a great arched lattice window looking out on the garden – and had a long conversation on the subject of my visit. Mr. Haggard treated me with great frankness, and expressed his willingness to visit the Argentine Republic and to write a book upon its agricultural resources and rural economy. He estimated that the time required for the voyage, the visit, and the literary work, would withdraw him from his other literary undertakings and affairs for a period more or less of one year; and having regard to his reasonable compensation for a mission of this nature and duration he regarded it proper to indicate the sum of £3000 as a reasonable honorarium. We thereupon agreed that I should telegraph this, with further and less important details, to B. Aires. (25 September 1909)

Business having been attended to, Herbert spent much of the next day touring the Haggards' estate. The contents of the house, however, seem to have been the most impressive feature:

> Ditchingham House without being striking in its external appearance exhibits within at every turn the love for archeological [*sic*] research and the literary tastes of the owner. With the reliquia of the Egyptian, Greek, Mexican and homeland histories are mixed the weapons and the ornaments of ruder peoples. The rooms are all furnished and many of them panelled in oak; the atmosphere is one of past ages, and the style that of a country home as it might be two centuries ago yet still remains comfortable and pleasing. (26 September 1909)

Unfortunately, Rider Haggard was never to write on matters Argentine. On 8 October, Herbert received a telegram from Buenos Aires rejecting the distinguished author's fee as being 'in excess of what the Com^n [Commission] is prepared to pay' (8 October 1909). This left Herbert in the awkward position of having to inform Rider Haggard of a decision with which he did not himself agree, opining in his diary that '£3000 on a work by him is better spent money than £300 on a work by an agricultural professor [...] whom no one reads and no papers report' (8 October 1909).

Going back to the first days of Herbert's homecoming, his vessel had docked on 31 July 1909 at Southampton, where he was met by Maddie, Chris and Clem. After driving to Droxford in Maddie's new car – described by Herbert as a 'fine Beeston Humber' – he was reunited with his younger sons Gerald and Cosmo. The very next day, they drove from Fir Hill to visit Faccombe Manor, a 'pleasantly situated house standing about 900 ft. above sea level' in northwest Hampshire (1 August 1909). The reason for their excursion was that Maddie was proposing to rent the grand manor as the family's next English base. A couple of weeks later, Herbert called on the owner of the house in his London hotel and arranged the details of the lease, with a view to taking up residence in November.

Also in August, Herbert, Maddie and Chris travelled to London to see the final England-Australia test at the Oval. Unremarkable in itself, the trip was to have tragic consequences for one much-loved member of the family:

> Returned home by the 5.30 p.m. train and were met by Clem and Paco [the dog]. Alas! as we were returning poor Paco, startled by some boys at the bridge, ran under the horse's heels and the wheel of the trap passed over his head. Picked him up, unconscious, taking him home

and got up a man from the kennels who did what he could. (10 August 1909)

Sadly, the next day Herbert records: 'Paco died this morning having never recovered consciousness' (11 August 1909).

The remainder of Herbert's time in England passed uneventfully, save for leaving Fir Hill for the last time and setting up home at Faccombe on 22 November. Throughout his absence from Argentina, he continued to keep a watchful eye on business matters and one of his regular activities was to attend board meetings of the Maroma Estancia Company in London. This company administered the Paraguayan properties that were originally purchased by Thomas Gibson, one of which was a ranch called Maroma, hence the firm's name. The lands were located in the south west of the country, in the inhospitable zone known as the Chaco, infested by Indians, jaguars and numerous pests of the insect variety. In a volume published in 1934, Herbert's eldest son, Chris, described this territory in the following terms:

> Geographically and climatically speaking it is utterly different to Eastern Paraguay. From the river-steamer you look out on two distinct countries separated physically by but a ribbon of water, poles apart in nature. The undulating, hilly red soil of Paraguay, which will "grow anything" gives place to the vast, flat, marshy, silt-covered expanse of the Chaco, clad in forest, palm, scrub and long, coarse grasses. As you penetrate westwards it rises very gradually towards the foothills of the Andes, ten inches per mile. The handsome hardwood trees – quebracho, lapacho, palo santo or holy wood – are replaced by a more stunted, scrubby growth.[113]

Despite the forbidding aspect of much of the Chaco, the strip of land immediately bordering the River Paraguay made fine grazing land; according to Chris Gibson, when missionaries first introduced cattle to the area, it was found that they 'thrived and multiplied like fleas', despite the many 'natural drawbacks' to which they were exposed (p. 33). Later, when speculators began to move into the region, the government sold off vast tracts at rock-bottom prices. Thus it came about that Thomas Gibson, driven by his ravenous appetite for real estate, bought thousands of acres that he had never even visited. As Chris Gibson noted, purchasing land unseen was a risky business with many potential pitfalls:

---

113   Meredith H. Gibson, *Gran Chaco Calling: A Chronicle of Sport and Travel in Paraguay and the Chaco* (London: Witherby, 1934), pp. 33-34.

> In most cases they didn't know what they were buying. The glamour of owning several thousand acres at the expense of a few pounds sterling was quite sufficient lure. No internal survey had been made; and, indeed, even in the riparian zone of the Rio Paraguay, where exploitation is making slow progress, lawsuits over title-deeds and boundary lines are the order of the day. Buying "blind" off the map can be a snare and a burden. (p. 35)

Chris's view was informed by bitter personal experience; legal disputes involving their Paraguayan properties dogged the Gibsons until well into the twentieth century.

Herbert set sail for Buenos Aires once again in May 1910, the voyage being unremarkable save for a 'fine view' of Halley's Comet:

> This evening at 8 p.m. we had a fine view of Halley's comet, almost due west. The nucleus, which was very luminous and presented an irregular crescent shape about ¼ the area of the moon, was about 12° from the horizon and the broad tail swept up towards the zenith and seemingly 30° in length, though as it gradually became less visible without indicating any termination, it was impossible to estimate its total length. (21 May 1910)

Less than two months after his return to South America, Herbert found it necessary to venture to Maroma for the first time. His trip to Paraguay was occasioned by litigation raised against the Gibsons, contesting their ownership of one of the lots of land that had been bought 'off the map'. Herbert's account of the month-long expedition takes up some thirty-two pages of his diary; a much 'abridged' version, including most of the highlights, follows:

> Sailed today [from Buenos Aires] at 10 a.m. in S.S. "Asuncion" for Paraguay. Hope came to see me off. (28 July 1910)

> The scenery is monotonous – a river varying from one and a half to two miles in width, its low level shore on either side being fringed with trees. (29 July 1910)

> At Corrientes at 4 a.m., sailing again at 7 a.m. Corrientes is an imposing town, but it was too early for me to see much of it. Shortly afterwards we passed the confluence of the Paraná with the Paraguay,

which forms here an immense lake. [...] Up this [the River Paraguay] we proceeded with the densely wooded shore of the Chaco on the right bank, and the somewhat more sparsely treed banks of Paraguay on the left bank. Later on a bend of the river brought us in sight of Humaitá whose ruined and denuded church remains as a monument to the stubborn defence of this point by the Paraguayans during the war against the triple alliance of Brazil, Argentina and Uruguay. [...] The river becomes more picturesque and vegetation more luxuriant. One sees now numerous alligators or "yacarés" of varying sizes up to 8 ft, sunning themselves on the river shores. (1 August 1910)

The streets of Asunción are abominably paved. The houses are principally of the old fashioned Spanish colonial type with tiled roofs. There are more women than men in the streets, and they appear to do most of the work. Clad in cotton garments, their black hair hanging in two thick plaits down their back, sometimes a leaf cigar in their mouths, they carry all their load on their heads – baskets containing fruit, or linen, water jars, food or other wares for sale. Their complexion is olive, and all except the more-or-less well-to-do go barefoot. Guaraní is the prevailing language and one seldom hears Spanish spoken in the streets, but the deficiency of the Guaraní vocabulary is such that many Spanish words are used conveying the impression to the passer-by that the conversation is in pigeon Spanish. [...] Orange trees prevail everywhere, their fruit now hanging golden from the deep green leaved branches. Amongst flowers the most genial at present is the rose, but there is evident everywhere a love for colour and perfume. These people are flower growers. (2 August 1910)

At 7 a.m. we left this morning in the private carriage of Mr Lawton [manager of the Central Paraguayan Railway] on a trip arranged by Dr Soler [the Gibsons' Paraguayan lawyer]. The party consisted of Dr Soler and the Chief of Police, a Sr Usser, M^r and M$^{rs.}$ Lawton, Baron de Bildt [the Swedish ambassador to Paraguay, whom Herbert had met on a transatlantic crossing the previous year], M. Guiard the Secretary of the Fr. [French] legation in the Argentine, Mr de Chastillon and myself. [...] The railway runs through charming scenery, the valley in which the Lake Ipacaray is situated being soon reached. [...] At 11 a.m. we reached our destination, Sapucay, the village where the Railway "talleres" [workshops] are situated. Here a National Deputy [member of parliament] a Señor Villalba (who proved to be a poet in the Guaraní tongue) invited us to attend the municipal elections where there were a great number of Paraguayan peasants gathered. The village was en fête and we were treated to some Guaraní songs accompanied by guitars and fiddles. (7 August 1910)

Disquieting news of the Chaco Indians arrives. A detachment of soldiers has been sent to Loma Puná in connexion with a supposed theft of cattle and horses. The general opinion is that the Indians will rise and that neither life nor property will be safe if the Paraguayans give them cause for resentment. This indeed they have already done for last month, under the pretext that an Indian tolderia [village] at Carayá Vuelta had been stealing cattle (but in reality whose women folk had been tampered with by the young Sierras, owners of the place) a Paraguayan squad of soldiers crossed the River, fell upon the Indians, and ruthlessly shot down 22 men women and children. (13 August 1910)

Our road [to Maroma] lay through an endless palm-grove, the land being flat and seemingly low and subject to floods. The whole ground at this part near the river coast is one mass of "tacuarús" or anthills, standing some 2 to 3 ft high, and measuring from 3 to 4 ft in diameter. These mounds are very hard so that the wheel of the carriage makes no impression on them, and it was necessary to drive with the greatest care to avoid capsizing. [...]

At noon we reached the cattle yards of the "Corralito" paddock, distant some 23 miles inland from the River Paraguay. Here we found the Loma Puná peones [workers from the *estancia* of that name] engaged in working and branding the cattle, accompanied by some 10 soldiers who though nominally in pursuit of the marauding Indians are really engaged in assisting the cattle work and perhaps protecting the peons who are in mortal terror of the Indian people.

The heat has now become very great. Our peon deserted us at Corralito, being himself a deserter from the Army, and in fear that the soldiers would arrest him. We continued our journey and presently our peon emerged from a wood and rejoined us. [...] At a distance of say 35 miles from the River Paraguay we reached the Maroma fence, and crossing the Riacho Negro creek, which is now only 2 ft deep, we arrived at Maroma steading.

The steading presents a good and well ordered appearance, the buildings being all of palm post and mud with palm-tile roofs some of them covered with corrugated iron to collect the rain water. [...]

The heat still continues very great, the thermometer registering 95° Fahr in the office verandah. After dinner I attended Divine Service held by Mr Turner [a visiting missionary] in the quaint little Church. [...] The service was conducted in "Lengua" [an indigenous language], a lesson being read by an Indian named Manuel who has accompanied Mr Turner from the Mission, and who also gave a short address. The language is full of pleasing cadence, and the hymns which were (judging from the music) "Abide with me" and "There is a happy land" were accompanied by a harmonium played by M^rs. Saunderson [wife of another missionary]. Only some 6 Indian women and 5 Indian men, with a child or two, were present. Later on we had evensong in English at which the English people attended.

The Indian women are naked save for a deerhide apron which is wound round their loins and reaches down to a little below the knee. They wear a comb in their hair on one side of the head and sometimes a head band with a feather or two. The lobes of their ears have large blocks of wood that distend them to an abnormal size. Round their necks they wear strings of beads and on their wrists and ankles they have circlets made of feather plumes, said to be to protect them from snakebites. The men are also naked but wear a loin cloth, and their ornamentations are similar to those of the women. A number of Indians of both sexes came to see me and look at me. I shook hands with them and conversed as far as we could for they know only a few words in Spanish and less still in English. (14 August 1910)

Today Mr Turner lunched with us and told us of the new god set up within the last 2 or 3 years by the Lengua Indians. This god is a "voice" which they claim to hear, and which tells them that the Chaco is theirs, and that they may kill and take the cattle for their own use. One or two have even seen the person of the "voice" whom they describe as a man very short in stature, all clothed in black, with a black hat having a pointed cope. His face too is dark and terrible to behold, and he has a long black beard. He is not like an Indian or a white man, but is a being different to both. Mr Turner is trying to laugh them out of this very inconvenient superstition, but it seems to have taken a strong hold of them. (16 August 1910)

After touring the Maroma *estancia* and pronouncing it to be 'good grass land' stocked with cattle in 'fairly good condition and [...] well framed with enormous horns' (16 August 1910), Herbert returned to Asunción by steamer. As well as consulting Dr Soler about legal matters, he found time to visit a longstanding British resident:

> Called upon D$^\text{r}$ Stewart who is 80 years of age and has been in Paraguay since 1857. He came here originally as a medical officer of the British Government and went through the whole of the Paraguayan war in the exercise of his profession. (26 August 1910)

Dr Stewart, a well known and respected figure in Paraguayan society, regaled Herbert with tales of bygone days, reflecting on the bloody tyranny of the father and son dictators Carlos Antonio and Francisco Solano López. At the end of the visit, Herbert was left lamenting that he could not spend more time in Dr Stewart's company, 'hearing other tales of the strange and dreadful scenes he had witnessed' (26 August 1910). Two days later, he headed back to Buenos Aires.

For the next few weeks, it was business as usual for Herbert, his time divided between the Gibson Brothers' office in Buenos Aires and *estancia* visits. By mid October, he made final preparations for his next trip to Britain, only for his departure to be delayed by an outbreak of cholera aboard the vessel on which he intended to travel. Instead, he booked his passage on the *Highland Laddie*, which sailed directly from La Plata to London. This boat was, however, of a much inferior standard to the Royal Mail vessels Herbert customarily took and most of the passengers were drawn from lower echelons of society than his usual companions:

> The accommodation and style of this steamer compares, at best, to that of the 2$^\text{nd}$ class by a Royal Mail liner. The passengers, amongst whom are a number of Jews, are of the tradespeople or foreman class. Their greatest concession to "company manners" is to wear a collar at dinner, and on the two or three occasions when they have danced on the quarter deck in the evening the gentlemen find it more comfortable to dispense with their coats and waistcoats. Of four ladies with maiden names on board three travel without relatives or companions, speak broken English, and it would perhaps be as indiscreet as unnecessary to enquire by what means they earn a livelihood. The food is abundant but all except the plainest dishes are unpalatable and the material such as desert [*sic*] is of the cheapest

description. We have long since run out of mineral waters, soda etc., and stronger liquids such as gin, rum etc. were depleted before we had crossed the line. Fortunately, as I am the only passenger on board who drinks claret, there is probably enough to see me there. The discipline on board is slack, and I notice that the stewards and stewardess are allowed to participate in the daily "sweep" on the ship's run. There is a doctor on board but he was only visible for the first three days (when I noticed that he had the dirtiest hands I had ever seen) since when he has been confined to his cabin but whether for D.T.'s or another affliction I am unable to say. We have had "sports" of sorts on board, but I find the days very long and the company very dull – to my kidney. The Captain (Mr Bell) is a good honest Scotch soul; so also is the chief engineer, Mr Robertson. The want of electric fans in the cabins is felt during the hot nights in the tropics. (8–13 November 1910)

Herbert's evident distaste for his fellow passengers is unexpected of a man who habitually treated others, regardless of their station, with a decent measure of respect. Perhaps his slide into uncharacteristic snobbery is best attributed to frustration occasioned by the sheer tedium of the voyage and the comparatively insalubrious conditions aboard ship.

After landing at Weymouth and taking the train to Newbury, the nearest town of any size to Faccombe Manor, Herbert was met at the station by the chauffeur whom Maddie had employed in his absence. After quickly unpacking at Faccombe, he travelled to Rugby, where Maddie was visiting their two eldest boys at Oakfield. Next, they went on to Folkestone to visit Gerald at his school, Praetoria House. Cosmo would soon follow Gerald to the sea air of Folkestone, but, on account of being a 'fragile child', was sent to live with a couple called the Rodericks and not to Praetoria House (24 January 1911).

Herbert's stay in England, which was to last around five months, was taken up with the usual round of family activities and the occasional bit of business. 'Highlights' included the kitchen maid contracting blood poisoning after running a 'needle into her hand' (5 January 1911), a family visit to the dentist, during which Gerald 'had gas and two big teeth were removed' (13 January 1911), a trip to see a football match between Exeter and Coventry (18 February 1911), and a visit to Warwick Castle (20 February 1911). Herbert was much impressed by the latter, admiring the castle's 'imposing' grounds, which he declared to be 'full of beauty', and the collection of fine art within. He was particularly 'struck' by one work by a Spanish painter, probably Murillo, showing a soldier with the words 'Acqui estoy sin temor, y por la muerte no hay pavor' ['Here I am without fear, and there is no terror of death'] (20 February 1911). A couple of days later, Herbert entertained a 'party of giants' at Faccombe, his guests being a Mr Hervey who was '6' 6" high', his sister Peggie who was 6 feet tall, and a 6 foot 4 inch brother-in-law (22 February 1911). Other incidents singled out for attention in his diary include his notion to set out a golf course at Netherton Bottom on the Faccombe estate, only to decide that it would be 'impossible to form putting greens' due to the amount of moss (6 March 1911), and his induction into the Masonic Union of Oddfellows (14 March 1911). After a trip to London, he expressed annoyance at a 'not pleasant' meeting he had just had with his brother John over the business of the Maroma Estancia Company (10 March 1911).[114] Chris was a further source of worry at this time, having left Oakfield and started at Eton, where he was doing badly. Matters were sufficiently serious to require Herbert and Maddie to visit the school after receiving a cautionary letter from Mr Hill, the boy's housemaster (24 March 1911).

At the end of April, Herbert began the return voyage to Argentina, reaching Buenos Aires on 19 May. By then, disagreements over the management of his late father's estate had reached new levels of acrimony and, on 5 June, Herbert resigned his position as administrator. In other respects, Herbert's business activities continued much as before, although his appointment to a directorship of the Standard Insurance Company can be seen as the first sign of an interest in affairs beyond the confines of the Gibson 'empire'.

By early October, Herbert once again prepared to return to Britain. The voyage on the RMSP *Avon* was made memorable by the presence on board of the famous Polish pianist and composer (and later Prime Minister of his homeland) Ignacy Paderewski, who entertained his fellow passengers on the ship's rickety piano as they crossed the Atlantic (28 October 1911). Sandwiched in the pages of Herbert's diary is a faded sepia snapshot of the great musician on shore at Madeira, showing a dapper, middle-aged man in a pale tropical suit, cane in hand, with a boater-style hat perched atop his shock of hair. On reaching Lisbon, Herbert received a letter from Hope with news that their brother Ernest had suffered an unfortunate mishap while staying in Scotland, having had a 'faint or a swoon' and fallen on to an open fire, with the result that he 'was most severely burnt on the back and the arm' (1 November 1911). Ernest's condition was considered 'grave' and he was 'confined to bed, with a trained nurse and doctor in constant attendance' (1 November 1911). A further letter from his sister May told him that her husband, George Mackern, was in an 'acute state of

---

114 All was not well with Maroma and at the next board meeting (11 April 1911), the decision was taken to liquidate the company.

break-up the most severe of his various disorders being that of arterio-sclerosis' (1 November 1911).

One of Herbert's first thoughts on reaching England was to visit Chris at Eton, where he found that his eldest son had 'grown out of all knowledge' and seemed as tall as his father when wearing the College's 'top hat and long coat' uniform (5 November 1911). A few days later, Herbert travelled to Folkestone, where the 'youngsters', Gerald and Cosmo, greeted him with 'great glee' (11 November 1911). Herbert spent the next few weeks catching up with acquaintances at Faccombe and in London, fending off a 'most tiresome' bout of toothache, which led to his face becoming 'swollen beyond recognition' and having to be 'lanced' by a dentist (13-16 November 1911), taking a French lesson at a Berlitz school (25 November 1911), and visiting an 'oculist' to have new glasses prescribed (14 December 1911). Christmas Eve was overshadowed by a health scare involving Chris, the doctor at first suspecting appendicitis, but by Christmas Day he was pronounced 'all right again'. On 27 December, the whole family, including Hester, their maid, departed from Victoria Station en route to a three-week holiday in Switzerland. Shortly after this jolly family break, Herbert returned to Buenos Aires.

By this time, Herbert was spending more and more time in England, his stays in Argentina generally of shorter duration than before. This situation influenced his decision to turn down the opportunity of becoming a national deputy (equivalent to a Member of Parliament in the UK), having been invited to stand for election by one Dr Udaondo, a politically active friend (2 March 1912). Herbert may well have had additional reasons for refusing to become a candidate; since his flirtation with the Civic Union movement in the early 1890s, he had become somewhat disillusioned with party politics and steadfastly remained above the morass during his time as mayor of General Lavalle. Furthermore, with his finances continuing in a delicate condition and the settlement of his father's estate still pending, and with it the future of all the Gibson interests in Argentina, he probably felt unable to take on so demanding a role in the public arena.

Just before commencing his next voyage to England, Herbert received news of the death of his brother-in-law Dr George Mackern (2 May 1912). His health had been failing for some time and, following an abscess on the lung some months earlier, had appeared 'fragile in the extreme' at the time of Herbert's last visit to the Mackerns' Eastbourne home (25 January 1912). While not unexpected, therefore, George's demise gave Herbert cause for concern, for his sister May was prone to bouts of depression and he feared how she would cope with widowhood. On reaching England, Herbert wasted little time in calling on May, who was now lodging in London, and was disturbed by both her condition and, in particular, the attitude of her daughters:

> She looked normal, but the girls told me it was absolutely impossible to live with her, and the situation is a most perplexing one, for with all my knowledge of May's disorder I cannot but think her daughters are unnaturally callous and selfish. (5 June 1912)

A few days later, Herbert returned for a long talk with May, after which she seemed 'resolved to make a bid for getting back her self control' (10 June 1912).

One high point of Herbert's latest homecoming was a shooting trip to Scotland with eldest son Chris (9-17 August 1912). The pair stayed at an estate in the Glenshee area that had been rented for the grouse season by family friends. As well as a few days of excellent shooting, they motored to nearby Blairgowrie for a game of golf at the famous course there (14 August 1912).

By early October, Herbert was becoming increasingly worried about May's condition. On one occasion, he found her 'in a very bad state of physical health, and still worse as regards her mental state' (3 October 1912). No longer fit to be cared for by her nurse, May was placed in a doctor's home in Bournemouth. There she made remarkably good progress and, although she remained 'fragile' physically, Herbert soon declared her to be 'in a better mental state than I have known her for years' (22 November 1912).

Around the same time, there was another health scare in the family, this time involving Herbert's third son, Gerald. His school, Praetoria House, reported that he had not been 'fit for a long time' and called in their physician, Dr Percy Lewis, to examine him (16 November 1911). Dr Lewis carried out an analysis of Gerald's blood and, rather dramatically, declared it to contain 'alarming quantities of micro-organisms', recommending that the poor boy be taken to a specialist for treatment. Herbert and Maddie, however, sought the opinion of their own doctor first, who, after further blood tests, decided that all that was wrong with Gerald was a touch of anaemia, owing to the fact that he had 'outgrown his strength', and pronounced that he needed 'feeding up' (26 November 1911).

Early in the new year, Herbert headed back to Argentina accompanied by Maddie and their two eldest boys, Chris and Clem. The journey passed routinely, save for a couple of events. First, the family visited the Queen's Palace at Cintra during a stopover in Portugal, an imposing edifice of Moorish architecture (15 January 1913). Herbert, however, was more impressed by the several flocks of black sheep he observed en route to the palace! Less happily, they received news of the shipwreck of the *Veronese*, the vessel upon which Turnbull, a partner in the firm of Gibson Brothers, and his family were travelling out to Buenos Aires. The ship had run on to rocks off the coast of Portugal and rescue attempts had been frustrated by the 'boisterous state of the sea' (17 January 1913). Herbert pronounced himself 'deeply grieved' at the news (17 January 1913), a sentiment he reiterated when, on reaching Pernambuco, he learned that Turnbull's eldest son and only daughter had perished (25 January 1913).

Herbert and family spent a delightful couple of months at the Tomasa and Linconia *estancias*, but all too soon the time came for Maddie, Chris and Clem to return to England. After seeing them aboard ship, a rather melancholy Herbert reflected: 'So ends a most pleasant and happy family visit to the Argentine, and I turn now sorrowfully to a long lonely residence here to give my time to business' (11 April 1913). The next few months were dedicated mostly to routine activities, interrupted only by another trip to Paraguay. By early September, however, Herbert was back at Faccombe and reunited with his loved ones. Notable events during his first few weeks at home included a visit with Chris to the South Kensington Museum to see the Piltdown skull (16 September 1913), the destruction of the keeper's cottage at Faccombe after poachers set fire to the thatched roof (20 September 1913), and Clem joining his elder brother at Eton (24 September 1913).

Herbert was delighted on hearing that his eldest son had won the Eton Recruits Shooting Cup, an achievement he described as a 'feather in [Chris's] cap' (11 October 1913), his pride on this occasion contrasting sharply with the frustration expressed after a meeting in London with his rather indolent nephew, Theo Mackern. Herbert seemed to feel a sort of paternal responsibility for the young man after the death of his father and in light of the delicate state of May's health, but found nothing admirable in his character:

> Lunched Theo Mackern at the Argentine Club and had a chat with him about his future. He is a very disappointing lad, and seemingly doing no good at Cambridge. He does not want to take up medicine, but confesses to feel no vocation for anything. (22 October 1913)

Whenever he was at home, Herbert indulged his longstanding passion for theatrical and musical entertainments, regularly attending performances in London. At the end of November, he was present at a memorable show by the Scottish singer and comedian Harry Lauder:

> In the evening to hear Harry Lauder at the Palace Theatre. I had never heard him sing before and I realize the true cause of his popularity; his voice is good and pure and his fun is good honest clean fun, neither vulgar nor artificial. He is the 'people' at their best expressing the feelings and humour of the people as they themselves wish to see it expressed. (29 November 1913)

A week before leaving for a second family holiday in Switzerland, Herbert and Maddie travelled to Windsor to attend Chris's confirmation, along with around 190 other boys, at a ceremony in the Eton Chapel presided over by Bishop Gore of Oxford (13 December 1913). A short time after their return from Switzerland, Herbert gave a lecture about Argentina to an impressively large audience in London:

> This evening Maddie and I dined as the guests of the Royal Colonial Institute at the Metropole Hotel, and at which about 100 people were present, Sir Bevan Edwards being in the Chair. After dinner we repaired to the large lecture hall where to an audience of about 500 people including a great many ladies I gave an address, with lantern slides, on the Argentine. I spoke for one hour & ten minutes, and seemingly made a success. A great number of people I knew were there. May had come up with the children from Eastbourne. Afterwards we all repaired to the Trocadero [...] & had supper. (10 February 1914)

Only three days later, Herbert began the journey back to Buenos Aires, where he found Hope hospitalized with phlebitis (7-8 March 1914). More worryingly, it seemed that Hope had endured a 'long period of generally low condition', which had culminated in tuberculosis (14 March 1914). His doctor's prescription was a spell in the dry mountain air of the Córdoba hills.

In mid July, while much of the southern part of Buenos Aires Province lay submerged under flood waters, Herbert had an eventful trip to the Linconia ranch. Unable to complete the journey by the usual means of rail and horse, he was forced to travel much of the way by launch. The 'voyage' back to town ten days later was no less difficult, involving both a horse-drawn boat and raft! While having to rely on such transport arrangements was no doubt an inconvenience to Herbert and left him suffering from a 'chill on the liver or kidneys' (22 July 1914), his discomfort was quickly forgotten on hearing the devastating news that reached Buenos Aires just after his return: 'A war cloud has suddenly gathered in Europe. Following up a peremptory ultimatum Austria has declared war on Servia [Serbia]. Russia has mobilized. Germany has sent her an ultimatum' (28 July 1914).

Although Herbert immediately grasped the seriousness of the situation, even as perceptive a man as he could scarcely have realized the impact that the emerging crisis would end up having on both his own life and on those of his nearest and dearest. For Herbert, like the rest of his generation, the outbreak of war heralded the end of an era; whatever troubles he had faced down in the past were about to be eclipsed by the shadow of the most terrible conflict the world had ever known.

CHAPTER 7

COMMISSIONER

While Herbert was quick to appreciate the gravity of the circumstances in which his homeland was immersed,[115] the outbreak of war had relatively little impact on his daily existence for quite some time. Indeed, for the remainder of 1914 and much of the following year, he was concerned more with the ongoing arguments over the division of his father's estate. Brother John seems to have been the source of no end of trouble, bombarding Herbert with unfriendly letters, some of which contained 'unjust and indeed dishonourable propositions' and caused the 'greatest distress' to the recipient (20 September 1914). Even after John signed his consent, in February 1915, to the division of Thomas's estate according to the scheme agreed between the other heirs, the matter evidently continued to rankle him, and it was several months before he eventually let it rest. Having travelled out to Buenos Aires from London for face-to-face discussions with Herbert and Hope, John subjected his brothers to protracted expositions of his views, such as that described in the following entry from Herbert's diary:

> John called at the office to talk about certain division matters. It is the first time I have spoken to him since Oct 1912. He talked – and talked – and talked, from 10 o'clock to 1 p.m. All that was material to the meeting could have been dispatched in ten minutes: in fact all he came about <u>was</u> settled in that time. He has not improved. (9 June 1915)

When, more than a month later, John finally abandoned his objections and returned home, Herbert's relief was palpable:

---

115   Reflecting on recent developments on the last day of the year, Herbert wrote: 'Thus ends the most eventful and tragic year of my generation. The great nations of Europe are at each others throats, and the flower of humanity is in the trenches waging the most appalling war of the world's history' (31 December 1914).

> John has accepted the position and pulled up the pegs. All his criticisms are ended. He sails tomorrow. He is a sharper and a much more versed business man than me, but truth and honour have been on my side. (15 July 1915)

For the time being, it remained possible for Herbert to travel quite freely to and from Argentina, in spite of attempts by the German navy to isolate Britain. As he observed during one voyage, however, extra precautions were taken aboard ship in case of attack:

> The crew were mustered on the boat deck and instructed as to manning the boats in case of need. The boats were all swung free on the davits, and made ready for use, their oars, masts and sails being stowed handy, and water, light, oil and provisions put on each. These preparations are in prevision of the German submarine "blockade" of the British Isles, which though on the whole abortive, has been the cause of the loss of some steamers torpedoed without much consideration either for the class of steamer, or safety of the passengers.
> I packed all my most valuable papers in my dispatch box, and tried on the life belt in my cabin. […]
> No lights were shown on board at nightfall. I retired to my cabin and half undressed, putting the remainder of my clothes handy. Having made these preparations in case of being torpedoed through the night, I fell asleep and slept soundly. (13 March 1915)

Although Herbert's life continued more or less as normal, he decided to seek readmission to British citizenship on patriotic grounds, both as a mark of solidarity with the land of his birth in her hour of need and to be eligible for some, as yet undefined, role in her war efforts. After a considerable delay, his application was granted:

> Today, having at long last received my certificate of readmission to British citizenship, took the oath of allegiance before Mr. Long, a Commissioner for oaths, in Bath. It is now 25 years and seven months odd since I became a naturalized Argentine citizen. (19 February 1915)

By early 1915, Herbert's thoughts had begun to turn to how the conflict might affect his sons, especially Chris, whose eighteenth birthday was drawing near. The proper course of action, it was resolved, would be for Chris to undertake officer training on leaving Eton. This he duly did, not at Sandhurst as originally anticipated but at the Woolwich Royal Military Academy, from where he would eventually pass out in November 1916.

Although events on the continent were ever-present in the background, Herbert's diary entries for 1915 and most of 1916 contain only occasional specific references to the war, such as a description of the effects of a bomb dropped by a Zeppelin on to a quiet corner of London:

> Chris and I went to Queen Square off Theobald Street today to see the effects of a Zeppelin bomb there. The square is a peaceful backwater, a few old trees and shrubs in the centre surrounded by an iron railing, and the houses facing being tenements of the most modest description, including a Hospital for Children suffering from diseases of the hip, another for the Epileptic & Paralytic, another for cripples and a fourth for Italians. Nor is there anywhere near any building or industry of importance that could have served for a target. Into this harmless and impoverished quarter the Zeppelin had dropped its bomb that had blown out a huge crater in the centre among the trees, and shattered the windows and window frames of the houses, and chipped out portions of the masonry. A more useless mischievous and ruthless act of savagery it would be difficult to conceive. (17 September 1915)

At the beginning of November, Herbert started to take 'motor driving' lessons (2 November 1915), and before the month was out he had purchased a 'Studebaker 15/20 h.p. 1915 touring car' for the not inconsiderable sum of £240 (29 November 1915). Just how well he took to driving is open to some doubt, however, for his preference was for Chris to act as chauffeur whenever possible. In later years, it appears that he hired a driver more often than not.

Around this time, Herbert began to grow tired of his peripatetic existence between Britain and Argentina and he yearned for a permanent base. Faccombe Manor was his preferred choice of home, but sadly this desire was not to be realized. For reasons that are not entirely clear, but may well have had to do with Herbert's delicate financial position, he was unable to renew the lease. He felt the blow sorely, recording that 'it is a daily battle with self to submit to the failure in my dream that Faccombe might be, at last, my HOME' (16 January 1916). Once again, therefore, the family had to uproot themselves, deciding to relocate to Eastbourne. There Herbert took a 'special liking' to one property (25 January 1916), only to discover that the rent was beyond his means, and instead leased a house named Grange Corner for the months of April, May and

June (28 January 1916). In the meantime, he returned to Argentina and Maddie resided in their London flat at Montagu Mansions. When their tenure of Grange Corner ended, they moved to another Eastbourne residence, Compton Hurst. Not long after setting up home there, Herbert fell foul of the local authorities for contravening blackout regulations: 'Attended a summons today to the Town Hall for having exposed too much light from a window and was fined ten shillings' (18 August 1916).

While in Argentina during early 1916, Herbert made his first contribution to the war effort. Having been called to an interview with the British ambassador, Sir Reginald Tower, Herbert was asked to purchase wool on behalf of Her Majesty's Government (5 April 1916). Although he hesitated briefly in responding to this request, for the commission meant that he would have to remain in South America for a little longer than he had intended, Herbert's sense of duty dictated that he must accept. Even so, he was able to set sail for home just over a month later. One unfortunate incident ensured that it was a voyage he would remember for some time:

> I am heartbroken!
> This morning I put on a clean pair of white pants and as usual put my signet ring in the pocket while I shaved and washed. Then, when I came to continue dressing I found the pants were unmendably out of repair, and without thought I took them off and hurled them through the port hole – and with them my ring. (24 May 1916)

Perhaps Herbert got his just deserts for littering the high seas, but one can only sympathize with his sense of loss, especially since this was the second ring of sentimental value that he had 'mislaid' irretrievably:

> One, the first, I lost at Linconia on the 7th July 1900. This, the second, is too now gone. When I am rejoined to my dear wife I will ask her once again to give me a ring, once again to have "siempre" inscribed inside it, and this one shall not leave my finger until death has made it lifeless. (24 May 1916)

Once back in England, much of Herbert's thoughts were occupied by Chris and Clem. While he feared for Chris's future on account of the likelihood that he would soon be joining the war, Clem was on his father's mind for more pleasurable reasons, as he was proving to be outstandingly adept at cricket. An exceptional right-arm fast medium bowler, he 'bowled like a demon taking 7 wickets for 18 runs' for Eton in a match against the Woolwich Military Academy, in whose team his elder brother was playing (14 June 1916), and, a few weeks later, took 5 for 31 against Harrow (4 July 1916).[116]

Herbert's apprehension for what might lie in store for his eldest son is most clearly indicated in his diary entry of 12 October 1916: 'This is the birthday of my dear son Chris who is 19 years old today. May God grant that his next birthday may find him still well and strong and spared to me!' His concern for Chris's safety was well founded, for just over a month later he completed his studies at the Woolwich Royal Military Academy and thus moved a step closer to active service. Indeed, only two days after the passing out parade in front of the Duke of Connaught, Chris was ordered to report for duty:

> Chris, who came home yesterday, has got his posting orders to be at Southampton on the 1st Dec. to leave for France. No reference to his application to be attached to the Flying Corps. Went up to town to see Charlie Murray at the W.O. [War Office …]. He is taking the matter up, and will use his influence to get Chris attached to the R.F.C. [Royal Flying Corps]. (23 November 1916)

The very next day, whether as a result of Herbert's intervention or not, Chris received notice that his departure was to be postponed. Instead of heading straight to France, he went to the Larkhill Royal Artillery Practice Camp on 2 December, where, according to his father, he must 'remain for 10–14 days and then proceed to France, if, before then, he has not been attached to the Royal Flying Corps' (2 December 1916). Concerned at the lack of news about Chris's application to join the RFC, Herbert travelled again to London to raise the issue at the War Office:

> To the W.O. where I learned that Murray had left town for the north of England and would not be back before the 16th. Went on to Adastral

---

116 Clem would go on to captain Eton in 1918 and 1919. He later played for Cambridge University (1920-21), made 26 appearances in county cricket for Sussex, toured Australia and New Zealand with the MCC (1922-23), and represented Argentina (1926-38). Probably the highlights of his distinguished career were starring in a 'Gentlemen of England' XI against Australia at Eastbourne in 1921, taking 6 wickets for just 64 runs in the second innings and clean bowling the winning ball for the home side, and captaining a South American selection on their tour of England in 1932. His final first-class match was for the MCC in 1939. There can be little doubt that living in Argentina prevented Clem from scaling greater heights, perhaps even playing for England; 'had he been able to continue regular first-class cricket', his obituary in the 1977 edition of Wisden noted, 'he would probably have taken a high place' (p. 1041).

> House, and there presented myself to Major Armes, whose name Murray had mentioned to me in his letter of 11 days ago as the friend whose assistance he was using in Chris' case. Armes a very good sort. He told me that Murray had made no mention of the subject at all to him! He then had all the lists in Adastral House revised, but there was no mention of Chris' name there. He then telephoned to the War Office, but neither was there any record of Chris' application. Armes said he must now enquire at Woolwich, and as that would take a little time, would wire or 'phone me the result to Eastbourne. (6 December 1916)

No doubt somewhat disillusioned, Herbert returned home. Later that evening, he received a telephone call from Armes reporting that the authorities at Woolwich had decided not to submit Chris's application to the RFC 'as it was thought that he was overweight' (6 December 1916). Incensed, Herbert attacked the conduct of the academy's commander:

> So having invited a cadet to put in an application, the adjutant there thought fit to judge its merits himself (he could have done that at any moment without an application at all) and hold the application up, and leave the unfortunate candidate in ignorance. (6 December 1916)

Major Armes could do nothing more than suggest that Chris should try again. The next day, however, Chris received new orders to embark on 12 December. In a last-ditch attempt to delay his departure, Chris and Herbert headed to Adastral House, only for Armes to inform them that it was too late in the day to arrange for a transfer to the Flying Corps. Chris's sole remaining hope, according to the major, was to reapply from France, although this stood only a 'thin chance' of success (8 December 1916). Herbert's diary records both his son's distress and his own anger at the whole episode:

> This was a cruel moment for Chris. The tears came into his eyes, and my heart bled for my poor boy. But he showed great pluck, and in a moment was himself again.
>
> There are two men who have 'let him and me down'. These are the Adjutant Simpson at Woolwich who usurped the functions of the authorities at Adastral House by sitting on Chris' application; and C. Murray who had made much protest, – and done nothing. (8 December 1916)

Chris's departure to war was, understandably, an emotional occasion. Herbert accompanied his son from Eastbourne to Waterloo station, where Chris met up with other servicemen destined for France. From there, they headed to the coast:

> The special "embarkation" train left for Southampton at 11.50 a.m. and with it my dearly loved son who turns his young face to the grim experience of war. He went bravely "his flags flying" and his chin up. May God preserve you dear Chris from all the perils of war and bring you safely back to your father and mother! (12 December 1916)

Clearly, this was a trying time for the parents of any young soldier and Maddie suffered badly. For more than a week after Chris's departure, she remained mostly 'confined to her room' (14 December 1916), 'very poorly' (17 December 1916) and 'low spirited' (20 December 1916). Certainly, she was plagued by a nasty cough, but it is plain that the true cause of her malaise lay elsewhere. Soon, the first letters from Chris arrived, from which he appears to have been in good spirits, despite already having had a taste of danger:

> Chris finds his surroundings cheerful and optimistic. He has already been doing observation work on the front line, and a shell burst within 15 yds of him "nothing else to raise the wind" he adds cheerfully. God keep the dear boy safe! (23 December 1916)

By mid January, Herbert had learned more about the conditions Chris was experiencing:

> He has been in gun action practically since he arrived at the front on the 14th. For the past 10 days he seems to have been in a small sand bagged hole with four signallers, the target of incessant machine guns and others of heavier calibre, the place swarming with rats and in a sea of mud and water. He writes "If it weren't for the rats I could sit in that small inferno of machine gun bullets and crumps and pipsqueaks and whizz-bangs and feel quite cheery." (13 January 1917)

It troubled Herbert that he still had no news of exactly where in France Chris was located, presumably because such information was classified. On 22 January, however, this gap in his knowledge was filled:

> To town and did various oddments […]. I lunched Dr. Watts, who is the doctor of Chris' battery and is home on leave, at the Piccadilly. He gave me news of Chris, and above all told me where he was located: 2½ miles south of Ypres, by the side of a lake called Dickiebush at the north end of our salient. (22 January 1917)

The significance of this 'intelligence' soon becomes clear: Herbert was hatching a plan to get himself to France to be close to his son. At over fifty-two years of age, he was ineligible for military service, so instead offered his skills to the Church Army, applying to become a Superintendent of Huts on the Western Front (15 February 1917). During wartime, the Church Army, an organization similar to the Salvation Army but affiliated to the Anglican Church, provided and operated facilities behind the front lines for the rest and recreation of troops. Their premises, known as 'huts' in spite of the fact that some were quite sizeable buildings, were a much-needed haven from the conditions of the trenches.

Although Herbert's application to join the Church Army was successful, he had an anxious wait of more than two months before he was able to set foot in France. To prepare for his departure, he took some French conversation lessons and was inoculated against typhoid. In the meantime, Chris remained at the front, was 'slightly gassed in an artillery attack by the Germans' (7 April 1917) and had to cope with a 'painful experience with a brother officer who got shell shock and gas, and became nerve shattered' (22 March 1917). According to Herbert, Chris had to forcibly restrain his disturbed colleague, ending up with his hands 'full of the bites inflicted on him by the poor fellow' (22 March 1917).

On 21 April, Herbert finally left Eastbourne en route to France, taking up his duties there two days later with the rank of Commissioner. Initially assigned responsibility for the Church Army huts in the area occupied by the 2nd Army, his range was subsequently extended to include the territory held by the 5th Army. Some of the huts he supervised lay as little as two miles from enemy lines and were damaged frequently by artillery shells or bombs dropped from the air. Throughout his time at the front, Herbert kept a journal, separate from his main diary, which forms an important record of the day-to-day running of the huts and of the courageous efforts of his fellow Church Army volunteers to bring respite to the troops.

Characteristically, Herbert wasted no time in settling in to his new responsibilities and was soon engaged in a hectic round of visits to the huts under his charge. Based in the vicinity of the town of St Omer, he toured the region in an old Ford van. By 3 May, he had been reunited with Chris, and father and son shared a meal together at the latter's Battery Mess. Although Herbert plays down the risks of life so close to the front, the hazards confronting the Church Army workers were considerable. On one occasion, he tells of a visit to a hut near to which a shell had recently exploded, sending shrapnel into part of the building, 'killing one man, severely (or fatally) wounding another and inflicting wounds of greater or less severity on seven others' (5 May 1917).

Amenities at the huts varied considerably. Some offered little more than basic canteen facilities, while others contained reading and writing rooms, fully appointed chapels, and, in the case of one under Herbert's jurisdiction, quite an elaborate theatre complete with 'benches, stage and stage scenery, two pianos, electric light, walls decorated with handsome coloured pictures etc.' (7 May 1917). Some were staffed by Church Army volunteers or employees and seldom closed their doors; others were run by the troops themselves and opened only when men could be spared. Probably the most cherished item of furniture in any hut was its piano, around which battle-weary soldiers could gather for a singsong.

Reading Herbert's wartime journal today is a curious experience, for its focus on the Church Army huts conveys the impression that life at the front was actually a quite civilized affair; while we are more accustomed to hearing about the terrible casualties and appalling conditions in the trenches, Herbert writes of matters such as the interior of one hut being decorated with 'pale green distemper' (9 May 1917), of another being built in a 'chalet' style, 'surrounded by flower beds and tastefully bordered paths' (10 May 1917), and of his own efforts to ensure that the troops' demand for lemonade in warm weather was met. The notion of a rather genteel existence, albeit one lived in the shadow of death and destruction, extends to Herbert's dealings with Chris. On several occasions they are able to meet to take tea together or to dine at local hotels (9 May, 10 June, 13 June, 22 June 1917), and even manage to fit in a day trip to Dunkirk (2 June 1917).

An unsavoury incident involving one of the Church Army volunteers serves as a timely reminder of the realities of life in a war zone. Mr Mason, the superintendent in charge of the hut known as Jesus Farm, fell under suspicion for having visited the 'various wagon lines and unit camps' in the vicinity and for having 'made a map expressing certain local details' (25 May 1917). Fearing espionage, the authorities approached Herbert to check Mason's references. In an effort to 'protect the general interest of the Church Army and the confidence it enjoys', he resolved that it would be best for Mason to return home, only for the latter to express 'unwillingness to leave without "vindicating" himself' (25 May 1917). To allow Mason the opportunity of answering the allegation against him, Herbert took him before the Assistant Provost Marshal of the Division, who, having listened to his explanation, confiscated his map and instructed Herbert to remove him from the locale forthwith. Consequently, Mason was repatriated to England that very afternoon.

At the end of July, Chris fell ill, the membrane of his sinuses severely inflamed from the secondary effects of gas. According to Herbert, his temperature rose to 103° and, on 1 August, he was withdrawn from the front lines. No longer able to keep up to date with his beloved son's progress, Herbert immersed himself in the daily business of a Church Army Commissioner. With his prime motivation for being in France diminished, it was opportune that on 6 September he received a letter from Owen H Smith of the Ministry of Munitions asking him to engage in 'some very important business work in New York'. Herbert did not hesitate to reply in the affirmative, requesting only that he be permitted to continue in post until the end of the month in order to wind up his Church Army affairs and hand over to his replacement. Smith, however, responded that his services were required as soon as possible. Consequently, after a hurried farewell tour of the huts under his charge, Herbert sailed for Folkestone on 15 September.

At their first meeting in London, Owen Smith outlined two alternative ways in which Herbert could help the war effort: the first option was to go to the United States in connection with purchasing food; the other was to return to Argentina as Commissioner for the Royal Commission on Wheat Supplies (17 September 1917). Two days later, Smith brought news that the Royal Commission, chaired by the Earl of Crawford and Balcarres, definitely wished him to represent them in Argentina. Later that same afternoon, Herbert met with members of the Commission and accepted the role on offer, receiving instructions 'to control the buying of cereals for the Allies, and as far as possible to control the whole Argentine cereal production' (19 September 1917). The next month passed in a flurry of Royal Commission meetings in preparation for departure to South America. During this period, Chris arrived back in England, still suffering from the effects of gas and requiring minor surgery to correct the problem. Herbert recorded details of his condition:

> He was looking fairly well, but his colour is not good, he has frequent headaches, and pain behind the eyes. Evidently until the operation is performed of drawing the tooth and piercing the antrum to drain off the abscess, he will continue to have poison in his system. (28 September 1917)

In late October, Herbert set sail from Liverpool for Buenos Aires. On arrival, he quickly established his office as Wheat Commissioner in the Royal Mail's new building, the Edificio Británico. Only two days after landing, he already describes himself as 'well into harness' and 'tremendously busy' (24 November 1917). Despite the undoubted pressures of work, he still found time to engage in his erstwhile social pursuits. At the beginning of December, for example, he attended a St Andrew's Society luncheon, the guest speaker being Sir Ernest Shackleton. That evening, Herbert entertained the renowned polar explorer to dinner at the Jockey Club and thereafter 'spent a long evening in Shackleton's rooms' (1 December 1917). For the next few days, Herbert was caught in a whirl of official engagements of the highest level. First, he travelled to Montevideo to discuss the possibility of buying the Uruguayan wheat surplus, meeting with the Minister of Industry and Commerce, the Minister of Foreign Affairs and the head of the national bank (3 December 1917). The next day, he was back in Buenos Aires, conversing with a senior government minister. On 6 December, he attended the Casa Rosada, Argentina's presidential palace, for discussions with President Yrigoyen himself. Sir Reginald Tower, the British ambassador, was also present. There was little about the head of state that impressed Herbert:

> Don Hipolito Yrigoyen, the Pres. of the Republic, is a man about 62 yrs of age distinctly Basque in type, his hair short and close all over his head, eyes rather small, features plebeian, and strong physique. He dresses very indifferently, and has none of the social ease of one who is used to move in high places, but is courteous and not ungracious in his manners. His two ministers sat at the interview like boys in the presence of a head master. (6 December 1917)

At the meeting, Herbert offered to purchase 1½ million tons of Argentine wheat on behalf of the Allies for between $10 and $12.50 per 100 kilos. President Yrigoyen replied that he would need time to discuss the matter with his ministers and it was arranged that Herbert should return the following afternoon. The next day, the President proposed increasing the minimum and maximum prices to be paid to $12.50 and $15 respectively, and raised the amount of wheat to be purchased to 2½ million tons. Herbert countered by suggesting that all the wheat should be purchased at the new minimum price, which President Yrigoyen deemed a 'reasonable postulation' despite the opposition of one of his ministers (7 December 1917). Notwithstanding the President's apparent agreement, negotiations over matters of detail dragged on into early 1918 and it was not until mid January that a deal was finally reached. The terms of the so-called 'Wheat Convention' were described by Herbert thus:

> The Argentine Government opens a credit of one hundred million dollars to Gt. Britain and a like sum to France, and these Allied Powers with the concurrence of Italy agree to purchase two and a half million tons of cereals by the 1st Novbr., subject to minimum and maximum prices which have been agreed. (14 January 1918)

Trading under the terms of the 'Wheat Convention' was highly beneficial to the Argentine economy; not only did it assure a steady, substantial income for the nation's cereal producers, but the government could also anticipate a return from eventual repayment of the credit extended. Almost four years into the war, the Allies' finances were stretched to breaking point and Herbert had to supplement the loan from the government with others, totalling some four million dollars, from banks. The full extent of Herbert's considerable fiscal responsibilities is underlined in his report of a visit to the Banco de la Nación to set up banking arrangements: 'I shall have the immense credit of twenty millions sterling opened to my sole signature, and, when the French Govt. authorizes their minister, a like sum for account of that country' (30 January 1918).

It seems that raising money was becoming something of a speciality for Herbert, for around the same time as he was negotiating credit from the government and banks he launched an appeal for £1,000 to finance an 'Argentine hut' for use by the Church Army on the Italian front. He published a notice describing the work of the huts in all the English language newspapers, and both the *Buenos Aires Herald* and *Review of the River Plate* urged the public to contribute through supportive editorials. The appeal was a great success and the required sum was reached in less than two weeks.

As befitted a man in his role, Herbert was acutely aware of the need to spend scarce resources wisely during wartime. In addition to exercising prudence in his purchases of wheat, this led him to criticize what he considered the waste of taxpayers' money on Sir Ernest Shackleton's trip to South America. The explorer's lengthy stay – in excess of two months' duration – included much apparently frivolous entertaining as well as lecture engagements, all funded by the British government. At the beginning of February, Herbert was among the guests at one 'sumptuous dinner' and his account of the event develops into a sharp critique of Shackleton's tour: 'All Shackleton's expenses are pd. by the British Government, and tho' I have a great liking and admiration for Shackleton, I cannot but feel he is spending public money to no useful purpose' (2 February 1918). After listing the minor local dignitaries present at that evening's gathering, Herbert continues his attack, describing such affairs as 'mere social junkettings with a considerable element of the "pretty girl" in the picture'. He then adds that 'this is not propaganda or any other useful thing but a squandering of public money, and I think that Shackleton is being misled'. It was characteristic of Herbert's ability to always see the best in others, especially those that he held in some esteem, that he perceived Shackleton as innocent of blame. Such was his conviction that the great man was a victim of the circus that surrounded him that Herbert resolved 'to "take all the risks" and speak to him' (2 February 1918). Unfortunately for us, his diary contains no record of this conversation or its outcomes, if indeed it ever took place.

The early months of 1918 were truly a hectic time for Herbert. His days were occupied with endless rounds of meetings, arranging the purchase of as much wheat as he could lay hands on. Reflecting on the fact that he had bought no less than 210,000 tons of wheat in the preceding six days, Herbert quipped: 'I suppose I am buying more than any single man ever did even in the biblical days of Joseph' (16 March 1918). A month later, he summarized his purchases since the Wheat Convention had come into force on 1 February:

```
2,165,000   t. [tons] wheat
  149,500   "  oats
   62,200   "  maize
   27,400   "  linseed
2,404,100   (20 April 1918)
```

Organizing transport for such vast quantities of cereals proved to be quite a headache, especially during February when railway strikes were threatened. Other difficulties that Herbert had to surmount included an acrimonious dispute over the cost of the jute bags into which the cereals were packed and suppliers who attempted to provide inferior quality wheat. The latter led to a rift between Herbert and Mr Brancker, the local manager of Sanday's, one of the shipping agents. Enraged by Brancker's failure to inspect wheat before shipping it, Herbert accused him of 'neglect of duty' and demanded that he 'withdraw from the management of the firm and return to England' (5 May 1918). Presumably, Brancker complied, but this was not the end of the matter. During a visit to London later in the year, Herbert had to attend a 'long and most unpleasant meeting' with the two Mr Sandays, father and son, at which they severely criticized his conduct towards Brancker:

> The Sandays took the line that in asking Brancker to return home I had insulted their firm, that he had done nothing censurable, that it was all intrigue and jealousy and I myself an "amateur" had been misled and did not understand. (3 September 1918)

By this time, however, Herbert had discovered that Brancker had been undermining his authority since well before their disagreement:

> Brancker had written to Sanday's criticizing me even from the earliest days and shewing clearly that far from proposing to help me he wanted to produce the impression that I had made a muddle of things and caused ill feeling in Argentine circles. (3 September 1918)

The meeting ended without a satisfactory resolution, but Herbert's role in the affair was exonerated by Lord Crawford, chairman of the Wheat Commission, and 'other impartial men', who formed the view that Brancker had 'been little better than a traitor' and that 'in the general dealings of Messrs Sanday & Co. there is not much trust' (3 September 1918).

Returning to late May, Herbert was distracted from his usual tasks for a week by the presence of a high-level British diplomatic mission in Buenos Aires. The visiting party, led by Sir Maurice de Bunsen in the capacity of Special Ambassador and including representatives of the Army, Navy and Foreign Office, was feted upon arrival by a 'great crowd' and the entire city was 'be-flagged' (31 May 1918). The major purpose of the mission was to promote the Allied cause and encourage South American governments to align themselves unequivocally with it. However, despite the distinction of the delegates, they were, in Herbert's view at least, a rather inept bunch who made their case in unimpressive fashion. Only one member stood out as capable: 'James Grant M.P. is a strong man: the rest no qualifications' (5 June 1918). After a few days of hectic wining and dining, Herbert seems relieved when the mission leaves for its next stop, Paraguay, and he can return to business as usual.

Although his work as Commissioner kept him more than fully occupied and its responsibilities weighed heavily upon him, family matters were never far from Herbert's mind. Concern for his sons' welfare abounds throughout his diary entries from this period. Chris made a reasonable recovery from his gas-related illness and was sent back to the front at Arras. Clem, meanwhile, had to endure his own spell of poor health. Having suffered from a grumbling appendix for some three years, an operation finally became necessary and turned out to be a 'long and delicate one as the small bowel was found to be adhered to the appendix' (13 February 1918). As if that were not enough, no sooner had he recovered fully from surgery than he was struck down by a bout of jaundice. By June, however, news from both brothers was a source of pride for Herbert: Chris had received his promotion to First Lieutenant and Clem had been chosen to captain the Public Schools side at a forthcoming match at Lords (20 June 1918).

In July, Herbert returned home for the first time since becoming Wheat Commissioner. As he set sail from Buenos Aires, he was encouraged by news suggesting that the Allies had 'driven the first great blow of the gathering tide that is going to bring a peace of justice and right' (20 July 1918). His mood became even more upbeat on reaching Britain, where he enjoyed the 'jolliest homecoming' after being met by Maddie, Clem and Gerald. Even better, they brought news that Chris was safely ensconced in a military hospital at Brighton, suffering from 'nothing more serious than a wrist badly wrenched' and a 'septic foot' caused by spending '6 days and nights' in wet clothes (26 August 1918). For the next four months, Herbert spent much time in London attending meetings connected with Wheat Commission business. Among other places, his appointments took him to the Admiralty, Treasury, Ministry of Shipping and Foreign Office; at the latter, he had an 'interview and very interesting conversation with Lord Robert Cecil', whom he described as a 'man of striking intellectuality and [...] quite familiar with Argentine affairs' (6 September 1918). One meeting at the beginning of October, however, took an unwelcome turn when Herbert suddenly became 'really very ill' (1 October 1918). After 'violent vomiting in the lavatory', he was left 'unable to walk without fits of ague and faintness' and could only return to his London flat with the help of a nurse and taxi. For the next few days, he suffered from acute sickness and diarrhoea attributed to 'ptomaine poisoning', which also left him with 'great sores' on his chin (5 October 1918). Fortunately, both Herbert and Chris had recovered sufficiently from their maladies to mark the latter's twenty-first birthday, and spent a pleasant family day at home in Eastbourne:

> Chris is 21 years old today. Maddie and I gave him two pearl studs costing £65, and a cheque for £50. His Aunt Ethel gave him a beautiful thin half-hunter gold watch and evening Albert platinum chain. His Aunt Kitty gave him a gold penknife. Miss Roberts a pretty money wallet. Molly an onyx ashtray. Gerald a silver pocket flask. All "très bon" as Chris remarked. We dined in the evening at the Grand Hotel, just the three of us, and had a most excellent dinner, and afterwards spent a couple of hours in the ballroom. (12 October 1918)

Two days later, Herbert was able to return to work at the London office of the Wheat Commission and dine with its chairman, Lord Crawford, at his private residence. At this meeting, Crawford invited Herbert to become a full member of the Commission and indicated his intention to apply for a Royal Warrant to confirm the appointment. Although it was now clear that the war was drawing to a close, efforts to maintain the Allies' wheat supply continued apace. At a meeting between representatives of the Commission and Treasury officials, it was decided to approach the Argentine government to seek a fresh loan, this time for the vast sum of $250,000,000 (24 October 1918). The credit was to be apportioned between the Allies thus: 40% each to Great Britain and France, and 20% to Italy. In order to oversee negotiations in Buenos Aires, Herbert had to abandon plans for a trip to the United States and make arrangements to return to Argentina sooner than he had anticipated. Around the same time, Herbert was offered a seat on the Buenos Aires board of Liebigs', the London-based meat products company.[117] The position carried an emolument of £750 per annum, a sum that would have meant much to Herbert and his family in a period of financial uncertainty, but he considered that it would be inappropriate to accept so long as he continued in government service. Thus, with great regret, he declined the invitation.

On the morning of 11 November, Herbert took the 8.20 am train from Eastbourne to London, as he did regularly, scarcely expecting the momentous events he was about to witness:

> At 10.30 a.m. the news was known that the Armistice had been signed. Slowly at first, but swelling every minute, the London people began to display their rejoicings. Flags of all sizes were carried by people, motor trollies and taxi cabs crowded with men in khaki and girls, even elderly people thronged the streets with cheers and bursts of greeting to each other. (11 November 1918)

To his credit, Herbert tried to continue with business as usual, but it became impossible to do so:

> Lord Crawford had arranged a meeting at the House of Commons with Mr Baldwin, the Parliamentary Secretary to the Treasury, and Sir George Saltmarsh at 3.30 p.m. to discuss the question of Argentine purchases. But the ceremony at St. Margaret's Chapel where both Upper and Lower House attended Divine Service at 3.15 p.m. and the general unsettlement of everything caused by a London 'en fête' made it impossible. So Sir George Saltmarsh and I called at the Treasury

---

117 Liebig Extract of Meat Company was established in December 1865 and started manufacturing beef extract at a plant at Fray Bentos in western Uruguay. In 1899, they launched Oxo as a cheaper alternative. From 1873, Liebigs' also produced corned beef under the Fray Bentos label.

to fix a meeting for tomorrow, and I caught the 5.20 train home to Eastbourne.

This 'day of gladness' was, however, to have a 'sad ending'. On reaching home, Herbert was informed by Maddie that Geoff Gunther, Clem's best friend from his Eton schooldays, had fallen in action just a week earlier.

The following day, Herbert returned to London to attend his meeting at the Treasury, after which he received some significant news of a personal nature:

> Shortly before lunch Lord Crawford asked me into his room to tell me that it was the desire of the Food ministry to submit my name to the Prime Minister for the honour of knighthood in the O.B.E. That my services had been invaluable and he would like me to think over the matter and reply later.[118] (12 November 1918)

Although Herbert seemed hesitant at first, Maddie convinced him that it was his duty to accept the knighthood on the curious grounds that it would serve as a 'stimulus to the boys' (12 November 1918). And so, in January 1919, the honour was confirmed, prompting Herbert into reflective mood:

> Such are the vicissitudes of life! When the war broke out I was an Argentine citizen. When it ends I am a British subject and a K.B.E. The thought uppermost in my mind is that this would have pleased my dear father. (9 January 1919)

Leaving its personal import to one side, the award was significant for another reason. Few British citizens ordinarily resident outwith their homeland or her Empire received such honours, and certainly not when they had previously relinquished British citizenship. As had been, and would continue to be, the case in so many of his spheres of activity, Herbert once again had achieved uncommon distinction.

In December 1918, Herbert returned to Buenos Aires to resume his work as Wheat Commissioner. Throughout the voyage, he was troubled by an ankle injury received in mid November; although it appeared initially to be nothing more serious than a graze to the ankle bone, the wound became infected and

---

118   The Order of the British Empire was instituted in 1917 with both military and civilian divisions. Awards are divided into five classes: Knight or Dame Grand Cross of the Order of the British Empire (GBE), Knight or Dame Commander (KBE/DBE), Officer (OBE), and Member (MBE). Herbert was awarded the KBE.

was 'inclined to suppurate', necessitating daily dressing by the ship's doctor (15 December 1918). On docking at Rio de Janeiro, the vessel was held for two hours for inspection by the port authorities as it had been blamed for bringing an epidemic of influenza to the city on its previous voyage (26 December 1918). When he reached Buenos Aires, Herbert received a telegram from Maddie to tell him that Chris had, somewhat unexpectedly, become engaged to one Dorothy Bruce. Dorothy hailed from Canada, where her father, Major W D Bruce, had served with the North West Mounted Police. She had come to England during the war to accompany her brother, Stanton, who was an officer in the 2nd Lincolnshire Regiment.[119]

Herbert's workload as Wheat Commissioner eased somewhat with the end of the conflict. There can be little doubt that the efforts of the previous couple of years had taken their toll on his usually abundant energy, but Herbert found little relief in the slacker pace of the post-war era. On the contrary, his mood was rather downcast for much of 1919 as he became increasingly disenchanted with conditions in Argentina. The country was going through a difficult time, especially insofar as labour relations were concerned, and the socio-economic outlook was bleak. Just days after Herbert's return to Buenos Aires in January 1919, an anarchist-led strike broke out that quickly escalated into an abortive revolution, the so-called *Semana Trágica* (Tragic Week). Initially nothing more than a local dispute at a metalworking factory in the outskirts of the city, the strike spread after clashes between pickets and police. Violence perpetrated by both anarchist elements and their right-wing opponents of the *Liga Patriótica* (Patriotic League) threatened to degenerate into something close to civil war, as Herbert's account suggests:

> The strike has become a Maximalist revolution in miniature. There has been shooting in the streets. All the shops are closed. [...] There is a general feeling of suspense. No newspapers were in circulation today. (10 January 1919)

> The military have been called in. There is still a good deal of shooting going on. It is said that 400 were killed last night. (11 January 1919)

By the evening of 11 January, however, the worst of the disruption ended after President Yrigoyen's Minister of the Interior reached a negotiated settlement with the strikers. Two days later, Herbert noted that the 'unrest has not wholly

---

[119] After distinguishing himself in the war and winning the Military Cross, Stanton Bruce remained in the army, later serving in Malaya and rising to the rank of colonel.

disappeared but conditions have again become normal' (13 January 1919). Casualty estimates from the whole unfortunate episode vary, but some put the death toll at close to 1,000.

During the first half of 1919, Herbert became increasingly sceptical of Argentina's prospects. He described himself as 'much depressed by the outlook in this country' (28 February 1919) and talked of an 'impending agricultural crisis' as demand for Argentine exports dropped with the arrival of peace in Europe (3 March 1919). By June, social instability was rampant and a new bout of labour unrest had broken out:

> Taxis and cabs on strike today and rumours of a general strike and even of a mob rising. No papers have been published since the 29th May, the typesetters and other printers having gone out on strike, refusing to print the advertisements of boycotted concerns. (11 June 1919)

Little wonder, then, that Herbert felt 'rather dispirited in these days' and was 'wearying to get home' (9 July 1919). There were, however, a couple of bright spots on his otherwise cloudy horizon. First, there was news of a great triumph on the cricket field for Clem in the annual Eton versus Harrow match:

> On the morning of the 14th I got the fol. telegram from Maddie "Splendid victory for Eton at Lords. Clem brilliant. Chaired round the field and presented to the King". (17 July 1919)

The fact that Herbert highlighted this episode in his diary by enclosing it within a border indicates its significance to him. He went on to reflect proudly that it represented the fruition of the 'extraordinary gift, if one might so call it, for cricket' that Clem had displayed from an early age, and constituted the realization of the 'blue ribband' (17 July 1919).

Soon after learning of Clem's triumph, Herbert's spirits were again lifted by the celebrations held in Buenos Aires to commemorate the Allied victory. The first event was a grand luncheon at the Palermo park:

> With Hope in our "Sunday clothes" and tall hats to Palermo where a great function to celebrate the Allied victory. A luncheon of 1000 covers in the big Restaurant [...]. Sir Reginald [Tower, the British ambassador] replied for the Allied ministers with a very good speech, which

I had translated for him into Spanish, and somewhat contributed to. Then a parade of returned soldiers of all the Allied Nations, the British turning out about 350 strong and making much the best show. All were decorated with commemorative medals. (27 July 1919)

There was a show the same evening at the Colón theatre, at which a 'big house' sung national anthems and witnessed the performance of an '"Allied" programme'. A few days later, the Colón was once again the venue for a victory ball 'at which Argentine society was on exhibition in its best clothes' (4 August 1919). This event was of lesser appeal to Herbert, given the absence of a dance partner, and he stayed for just an hour before retiring to bed. By then, his thoughts were turning to his imminent departure for England and an eagerly anticipated reunion with Maddie and family.

Herbert's voyage home was routine, save for a brief stopover in Montevideo where he called upon the President of the Republic, Dr Baltasar Brum, who received him 'very kindly' (8 August 1919). The two men had become acquainted in the course of Herbert's work as Wheat Commissioner and seemed to have developed a cordial, and quite familiar, relationship. Towards the end of the journey, he began to feel unwell, his symptoms including a '"furry" tongue and a disconsolate "Little Mary"', the latter being a quaint Herbert euphemism for intestinal trouble (25 August 1919). He remained '"off colour", without appetite, a more or less foul tongue, and a feeling of discomfort in [his] intestines' (30 August 1919) for a month, before finally deciding to consult his doctor in England:

> Not yet feeling right since my stomach upset this day last month, having had no appetite and almost a nausea for food, diverse pains in my intestines etc. I went to see Dr Milligan today who thoroughly examined me. He found no symptom of organic disorder but a "disturbed" inside, caused probably by late meals in Argentina, too much desk work and insufficient out-of-doors exercise, and prescribed a tonic for my liver and three weeks away from work and plenty of open air. (24 September 1919)

Despite his complaints, Herbert had been well enough to attend Chris's wedding to Dorothy Bruce, which took place on 9 September at the Gibsons' parish church in Eastbourne. The Rev. Morris, the vicar from Faccombe who had become a close family friend, was imported to conduct the service. Following a brief reception at Compton Hurst, the newly-weds headed to London in a 'shower of horseshoe confetti' and with an 'old satin shoe' tethered to the rear axle of their car.

Although he was now at home with his family around him, Herbert continued in quite low spirits and was frequently unwell. The social unease that followed the war disheartened him and was uncomfortably reminiscent of that which he had witnessed recently in Argentina:

> Today there began a general strike of the railwaymen on all the railways in the United Kingdom. Transport completely suspended. This is little short of a revolutionary attempt on the part of the "Syndicalists" to strangle the vital energies of the Nation and enforce an ultra communist Regime. (27 September 1919)

A month later, Herbert received news from Buenos Aires that his estranged brother, Ernest, had died of bronchial pneumonia. While this event apparently had little emotional impact on Herbert, it is reasonable to suppose that he felt some sense of loss. Moreover, the fact that his sister May was 'much distressed' by the news caused concern, given her generally fragile disposition (27 October 1919).

At the beginning of November 1919, Herbert began the return voyage to Argentina. His mood was much lighter than it had been of late, as he was returning surrounded by loved ones. Accompanying him were Maddie, Gerald and Cosmo, as well as Chris and Dorothy. Of Herbert's immediate family, only Clem was missing, for a month earlier he had gone up to Clare College, Cambridge to start an undergraduate career that would, predictably enough, be notable for many achievements on the cricket field. The party packed so much luggage, 38 pieces to be exact, that a 'motor lorry' was required to ferry it from Eastbourne to Southampton docks (1 November 1919).

While Herbert would once again resume work as Wheat Commissioner on reaching Buenos Aires, and would continue to serve until 1921, the post occupied less and less of his time, leaving him free to return to previous activities, such as the day-to-day management of Gibson Brothers, and to develop additional business interests. In that sense, the dawn of the 1920s marked the conclusion of another phase of Herbert's life, that which spanned the Great War, and the beginning of a new one, replete with fresh challenges.

CHAPTER 8

THE TURBULENT TWENTIES

The first months of 1920 passed happily for Herbert. Surrounded by most of his family and with Wheat Commission business taking up much less of his energies than before, he was once again able to devote time to his beloved *estancias*, especially La Tomasa and a nearby property called Bellavista. The latter had become a particularly significant place in his life since he decided to build a 'cottage' there as an Argentine base for him and his wife (24 February 1919). By the early part of 1920, the new house was ready to be occupied, and Herbert and Maddie spent pleasant hours applying the finishing touches to make it into a home and planning their garden. In the meantime, Chris and Dorothy had taken up residence at La Tomasa and seemed to be relishing life there, while Gerald was learning the *estancia* business at another property, Los Ynglesitos.

In May, Herbert, Maddie and Cosmo returned to England where, on 8 June, Herbert received his knighthood from King George V at Buckingham Palace:

> I attended by command an Investiture at Buckingham Palace and received from the King the accolade and insignia of the Order of the British Empire. Maddie and I with Miss Roberts [Cosmo's governess] motored to the Palace, where I left her in the Quadrangle and was ushered in to a reception room where already many were assembled. We were divided into groups according to the decorations we were to receive, the total number of people, including five ladies, being more than a hundred, including a majority to receive the C.B.E. Then we marched out in single file; I among the first who were the KBE's. I found myself behind Philip Gibbs the journalist and in front of Harry Goschen. We walked, one at a time, up a carpeted alleyway to a raised dais where the king stood; here, when it was my turn, I knelt on the left knee, received the accolade on both shoulders, the ribbon put round my neck, the star pinned to my breast, and then rising I bowed, the King

shook hands with me expressing his pleasure to make my acquaintance, I bowed again, – and so passed on to the Quadrangle where I rejoined Maddie; – and Miss Roberts who had succeeded in getting in. (8 June 1920)

Shortly after Herbert's investiture, Maddie's health began to cause concern, as first she became rather lame and then developed phlebitis and varicose ulcers in the lower part of one leg, a common complaint among middle-aged women of stouter build. In October, Herbert and Maddie made the decision to give up their lease on Compton Hurst the following summer and began the search for a new residence in England. Otherwise, the remainder of 1920 passed in largely uneventful fashion.

Early 1921 found Herbert back in Buenos Aires and Maddie en route to join him. Her steamer arrived in Montevideo on 21 January where Herbert met her and pronounced that she was 'looking much thinner and wonderfully well' (21 January 1921). On the return crossing to Buenos Aires, Herbert had the bad luck to slip on the ship's companion stairway and break the ligaments in the joint of his big toe, a painful injury that for several days left him able to wear only a slipper on the afflicted foot.

Just two days after landing in Buenos Aires, Herbert and Maddie met for the first time a little seven-year-old orphan girl of Scottish origins, Jean Macfarlane, whom they decided to adopt. Herbert remarked in his diary that she was 'very shy and strange poor child', but she quickly settled and became a much-loved member of the Gibson family (24 January 1921).

On 2 February, there was another addition to the clan when Dorothy, Chris's wife, gave birth to Christopher Herbert (familiarly known as Kit), a first grandchild for Herbert and Maddie. Although the delivery was a difficult one, both mother and son came through it unscathed. Three weeks later, Kit was baptized in the Anglican St John's Pro-Cathedral in Buenos Aires (23 February 1921). On the evening of the same day, the baby's father suffered a mishap while partaking of a fairground-type amusement:

> After dinner we drove out to the Japanese gardens and there Chris tried to "walk the treadmill" in a revolving cylinder and got carried up by it and fell very nastily and was tossed about before the man stopped the wretched thing. (23 February 1921)

Fortunately, Chris was left with no more serious injury than an aching head for a couple of days.

During this period, Herbert's already weak financial situation deteriorated further. It is fair to say that, in partnership with his brother Hope, he had invested beyond his means over the previous couple of years, first by buying the Bellavista property and then by acquiring substantial amounts of livestock. Overextending oneself in the precarious economic climate of the early 1920s was an unwise step; no sooner had Hope and Herbert completed their purchases than they were hit by a 'complete snag up in ram and wool prices and depreciation of cattle values' (27 February 1921). Such were the 'financial straits' in which Herbert then found himself that Maddie and Gerald postponed their planned return to England, both to support him and to save him from expenditure which he could, by his own admission, 'no longer face' (27 February 1921). Just days later, news arrived that the entire grape crop on their property at San Rafael, Mendoza, had been lost to hail (1 March 1921). Although the family rallied round, with Chris 'very full of reforms and economy' (4 March 1921), the only remedy was to try to sell land, including some 2,000 hectares of Bellavista and several properties in the Pampa Central region (12 March 1921). With the rural economy in turmoil, buyers were not easy to find and much remained unsold. Attempts to raise revenue by auctioning off cattle were equally unsuccessful; livestock was trading at 'wretched prices' (7 May 1921) and at one disastrous sale beasts from La Tomasa changed hands for prices almost 25 percent lower than those they would have fetched in 1915 (1 May 1921). Next, Herbert was hit by a demand for more than £2,000 from the British tax authorities, a sum he could not afford, but Maddie generously sold some railway shares she owned to help foot the bill (10 May 1921). Unwelcome domestic expenses were also proving a strain on Herbert's finances as first his car went 'wrong in the innards' (27 March 1921) and then frosts caused pipes and water pumping equipment to burst at his Bellavista home (20 June 1921). On the plus side, however, Herbert finally felt able to accept a seat on the Buenos Aires board of Liebigs', the position he had previously declined as being incompatible with his status as Wheat Commissioner, with an annual salary of £1,000 (26 April 1921).

Unlike many directorships that demand little more than attendance at the occasional board meeting, the Liebigs' post required Herbert to adopt a thoroughly hands-on approach. It is unlikely that a man of his temperament would have been content with a back-seat role anyway, and he threw himself into his new task with typical vigour. In early June, he travelled to Fray Bentos in western Uruguay to undertake a tour of the company's *estancias* and processing factories in that area. For the next few months, he was very fully occupied with both Liebigs' and Gibson Brothers business, as well as his relatively few remaining duties as Wheat Commissioner. In October, he toured Liebigs' properties in

Argentina's subtropical northern zone where he viewed, among other things, the 'yerba gardens' in which *mate*, the typical green tea of the region, was produced. By mid November, the whole family was assembled at Bellavista, for both Clem and Cosmo had now come out from England and Chris and Dorothy were visiting from La Tomasa. Having all his nearest and dearest around him pleased Herbert no end and he concluded the latest volume of his diaries in happily thankful mood:

> And this, being the first day since one in Nov. 1908 when we were at the Tomasa all under the same roof on the eve of departing for England, that we are all again safely gathered in the Argentine under one and our own rooftree, – and being too the third anniversary of the Armistice, is a fitting date to close this volume, giving thanks to God who has brought us through these past thirteen years and a great war, and has returned us in safety and health once again to engage in the wholesome life of making His Earth produce and be glad. (11 November 1921)

At this time, there was an outbreak of sheep stealing at Bellavista. First, it was discovered that 150 lambs had gone missing (12 November 1921), and then Gerald had a narrow escape after surprising two rustlers red-handed:

> This morning about half past ten Gerald came on two dogs evidently rounding up sheep. His dogs ran forward and he followed when two men sprang up from behind the fence and lept [*sic*] on to their horses. One rode away at once but the other before doing so drew a revolver and took careful aim at Gerald who was still riding towards him. Gerald dropped his body down to the horse's shoulder and the bullet whizzed over him narrowly missing him. (17 December 1921)

On Christmas Day, the police launched an operation to round up the suspected felons. A total of nine local residents were detained, including the proprietor of the neighbourhood store. Plenty of evidence of their crimes, including a number of guns, sheepskins and meat, was seized, leading the police to conclude that the gang had been 'robbing sheep every night' (25 December 1921).

1922 was a mostly unremarkable year in Herbert's life. Between the family firm and Liebigs', routine business matters dominated his time. The links between the Gibsons and Liebigs' were growing ever stronger, as first Herbert sold his family's remaining lands in Paraguay to the larger concern, and then his youngest son Cosmo secured employment on one of its properties at Colón, a town in the northern Argentinian province of Entre Ríos, adjacent to the Uruguayan city of Paysandú. Chris, meanwhile, continued to run La Tomasa, Clem was employed in the Buenos Aires office of Gibson Brothers (but seems to have spent more time playing cricket), and Gerald became bookkeeper at the Linconia *estancia* after suffering a fall from his horse and generally proving to be ill suited to the more vigorous aspects of ranch life.

The year was, however, to end on an inauspicious note, as the first signs of a new source of worry became visible within the family. Initially, it appears to be nothing more serious than a minor outbreak of marital discord between Chris and Dorothy, and Herbert is quick to lay the blame, rather precipitously as it turns out, at his daughter-in-law's door. He writes of Dorothy, who is again pregnant, being 'not well' and complains that she gives 'little thought to anything but her own wants and woes' (28 December 1922). Within a matter of days, it emerges that Chris is suffering from a drink problem, but still Herbert sides with his son and hints that Dorothy's flaws are to blame: 'Old Chris has a battle to fight but I know he will win. I hope Dorothy will yet awake to the true meaning and duty of home life' (3 January 1923). Although the situation seems to settle for a while, this unfortunate episode provides a foretaste of the spectre that will haunt Chris in the years to come.

On 12 May, Dorothy gave birth to twin boys, who were duly christened Newman Herbert and Bruce Herbert. Although Bruce appeared to be a normal, healthy child, Newman was weak and it soon became clear that something was seriously amiss. By November, Herbert described him as 'slightly better but very fragile' (12 November 1923) and only three days later his condition again deteriorated:

> Newman had a very bad turn at 3 a.m. this morning and I had to ring up D^r. MacLean who prescribed hot bath and castor oil. He suffers terribly in these attacks caused by indigested food which is the seat of the trouble. MacLean came again in the morning and again prescribed and spoke hopefully. (15 November 1923)

Next, Dr MacLean decided that 'Newman was getting insufficient nourishment from his wet nurse' and decreed that he should be given 'Nestle's condensed milk as an auxiliary stimulus' (21 November 1923). This was to no avail, however, and the infant's state rapidly became critical and a second opinion was sought:

Newman had a very bad night indeed. Asked D[r.] MacLean to agree to a consultation with D[r.] Iribarne. The consultation took place at six o'clock and D[r.] Iribarne conveyed to me the sad tidings that there was no hope of recovery, and all that could be done was to alleviate his sufferings and endeavour to nourish him with mother's milk from an enema. All day his temperature has been rising and this evening it is at 104°. He is practically unconscious, and each 3 hours chloral is administered to tranquilize the internal convulsions. (29 November 1923)

Strangely, given the seriousness of his son's condition, Chris was not in attendance and Herbert had to wire for him to come in to Buenos Aires from the camp at once. In the meantime, he struggled to do all he could to help poor Newman, despite the certain knowledge that it would be in vain:

Spent the major part of the day in the futile effort to find a wet nurse willing to allow her milk to be taken to nourish little Newman, knowing full well that it was at best but attempting to prolong a fading life. (30 November 1923)

Sadly, there was to be no miracle recovery: 'All through the day he lay unconscious, with a temperature of 108°, labouring with breathing and past receiving any stimulant or nourishment, and so at 8.50 p.m. he passed tranquilly into eternal sleep' (30 November 1923). Chris did not arrive until the following morning, having been delayed by flooded roads. Herbert, who described himself as 'sorely afflicted' by the loss (30 November 1923), took charge of arranging the funeral, which consisted of a small, sombre affair at the cemetery, Newman's 'little coffin […] covered with white flowers' (1 December 1923).

On a happier note, plans were being made for the marriage of Gerald to Miss Ursula Robson. Ursula and her mother travelled out to Buenos Aires from England for the wedding in order to save the Gibsons the 'great expense of a journey home' (8 August 1923). According to local custom, the couple were first married at a civil ceremony (13 May 1924) and then in church the following day:

The wedding took place in St. John's Pro-Cathedral at 4 p.m., Archdeacon Hodges officiating. Hope gave Ursula away. She looked very pretty indeed in a gold and ivory Anne Boleyn sort of a bridal dress, and so too did her bridesmaids, Inez Methven, May Bridges and little Jean [Macfarlane, the adopted daughter of Herbert and Maddie].

Cos was best man, and Chris and Clem the sidegrooms. Among many present was M^L Riddle the American ambassador. The reception was held afterwards at the Phoenix Hotel, and was a great success, dancing being kept up to 8 p.m. (14 May 1924)

Other notable occurrences that year included Herbert beginning to be troubled by gout in his toes (16 September 1924), Hope suffering an intestinal haemorrhage (25 September 1924), from which he made a reasonable recovery, the suicide of one of the Gibsons' ranch workers (1 September 1924), and the marriage of Lorna Gibson, a daughter of Herbert's late brother Ernest, to Francisco 'Paco' Boote (9 October 1924). Earlier members of the Boote family had made their mark in Argentina as pioneers of photography, the brothers Samuel and Arthur Boote both becoming distinguished practitioners of the art in Buenos Aires during the late nineteenth century. In due course, Lorna and Paco would go on to become the proprietors of Los Yngleses, and the *estancia* remains in the hands of their descendants today.

The year ended with Clem distinguishing himself once again on the cricket field, playing 'most brilliantly' and scoring 54 of Argentina's 72 runs in the second innings against Chile, and thus winning the match (28 December 1924). This performance, highly creditable indeed for a bowler, was eclipsed in the next game of the series, in which he 'knocked up 96 in amazing style' (3 January 1925). Around the same time, Cosmo received his call-up for two years compulsory service in the Argentine Navy, a fate he was able to avoid by having a 'friendly naval doctor' declare him physically unfit (4 January 1925).

1925 was to be a busy year for Herbert. Liebigs' business took up a considerable portion of his professional life. In March, he visited Uruguay to view possible sites for a new Liebigs' factory at the foot of the Cerro, the hill overlooking Montevideo around which many meat-processing works were located (12 March 1925). The next day, he called on the President of the Republic, Ingeniero José Serrato, at his private residence for talks, and then attended a meeting with the directors of the Banco Comercial (Commercial Bank) (13 March 1925). The following month, he received authorization from Liebigs' London board to proceed with the purchase of an existing factory at the Cerro to convert into their new plant (2 April 1925).

Another matter that took up much of Herbert's time was an impending visit to Argentina by the Prince of Wales. In company with other leading members of the British community, Herbert played a prominent role in arranging the Prince's tour and presented plans to the British ambassador, Sir Beilby Alston, for a three-day excursion for the Prince and his entourage to the northern provinces of Entre

Ríos and Corrientes (30 April 1925).

The Prince of Wales reached South America in mid August, landing first at Montevideo (14 August 1925) and crossing to Buenos Aires three days later. His arrival in Argentina was greeted with much pomp and ceremony, the streets being 'thronged' with great crowds (17 August 1925) and elaborately decorated with lights:

> The illuminations of the city are magnificent. It is said they cost $6000 p. hour. The Plaza de Mayo, the Plaza de Congreso, and the Avenida de Mayo which stretches between them, are all a blaze of tens of thousands of red, blue, and white electric globes; while such devices as "Welcome", and the Prince's feathers, afford splendid masses of light and colour. The city is decorated with British and Argentine flags to an incredible extent. (18 August 1925)

For the next few days, Herbert lived in a whirl of social engagements associated with the Prince's visit: grand receptions at the embassy and in hotels, elaborate lunches and dinners, the opening of the Argentine Rural Society's annual show, and an ostentatious service at St John's Pro-Cathedral presided over by the local bishop dressed 'in the fullest of canonicals with a mitre like a huge gilded paper bag and his whole robing distinctly Romanish' (23 August 1925). Then, at the end of the month, the official party, accompanied by numerous local dignitaries, set off on a luxurious train for the whistle-stop tour of Entre Ríos and Corrientes that Herbert had arranged. The trip focused on visits to ranches and meat-processing plants, such as the 'Anglo' freezing works at Zarate and Liebigs' factory at Santa María. In keeping with his reputation as a fun-loving bon vivant, the Prince also found time for leisure activities, such as taking part in an impromptu horse race and dancing with 'several of the local belles' at the Mercedes Social Club (31 August 1925). The hectic pace took its toll on Herbert, however, and he felt increasingly unwell as the trip progressed: 'Far from having recovered from the "grippe" it has got worse each day and I am thankful to have completed the tour without collapsing or revealing my condition' (2 September 1925). Notwithstanding his own discomfort, Herbert hailed the tour as an 'unqualified success and a great triumph for Liebigs' (2 September 1925).

Throughout 1925, Herbert grew increasingly concerned about the behaviour of his third son, Gerald. The first signs of a problem manifest themselves in a rift between Gerald and his mother-in-law, Mrs Robson, who has remained with the Gibsons since her daughter's marriage. Initially, Herbert is inclined to attribute the difficulty to Mrs Robson's rather neurotic disposition, but it soon emerges that her complaints are not without foundation. At the beginning of May, Mrs Robson suffers 'one of her periods of misanthropy' and shuts herself in her bedroom for ten days (1 May 1925), during which time she wrote a letter to Herbert complaining that Gerald's 'abusive and aggressive behaviour had become intolerable' (3 May 1925). By later in the month, she is 'still "sporting her oak" [i.e. hiding behind closed doors] and refusing to come to meals, or to see Ursula and Gerald' (21 May 1925). Then, Cosmo mediates in the dispute, winning Herbert's admiration for his initiative and perception: 'Cos off his own bat tackled the situation this evening with M$^{rs.}$ Robson; made Ursula and Gerald go in and see her; and effected a reconciliation. Cos displays an understanding beyond his years in matters such as this' (23 May 1925).

After Cosmo's intervention, the situation seems to have settled for a while, helped also by the news in July that Ursula was expecting her first child. By the beginning of August, however, the cracks in the relationship between Mrs Robson and her daughter and son-in-law were wider than ever, and she once again confined herself to her room. On 9 September, she emerged and confronted Herbert with her grievances:

> This morning M$^{rs.}$ Robson, who has not been 'on view' since the commencement of last month, and remains in her room, came to the library and 'went off the deep edge' as the moderns put it. To sum up, she has secluded herself as she could not countenance the slothful and empty life Gerald and Ursula are leading, and any remonstrance she makes is met with rudeness by Gerald. They lie in bed to all hours of the morning; have their breakfast served in bed; Gerald often turns out in a dressing gown and bedroom slippers; he drinks too much; he gives Ursula brandy though in her present condition she should have no stimulant; he allows Aristides [an employee] to come up and talk to him through the bedroom window, and of evenings takes him into the drawing room and gives him cocktails; he does no work, and Ursula is too young and under his domination to realize the slothful and unhealthy life they are both living. (9 September 1925)

Although Herbert is reluctant to believe the worst of his son, he recognizes that there is a basis of truth in Mrs Robson's assertions:

Thus M⁶˙ Robson. Though highly strung hysterical and an abnormal woman, I fear there is alas much truth in these charges, though conceivably exaggerated and made with a distorted vision. I cannot spy on Gerald to learn the truth. I cannot tell him M⁶˙ Robson has made these charges. It is another source of anxiety and worry added to all the other burdens I bear. (9 September 1925)

In early November, Gerald suffered a more tangible disorder, namely appendicitis. After the inevitable operation, he developed an abscess under the wound that had to be drained, the source of much pain. While this period of illness undoubtedly had a negative impact on his work, it was insufficient excuse for the manner in which he had neglected his duties as the Linconia bookkeeper for some months. By the end of the year, Herbert began to realize the true extent of Gerald's slackness and had to devote considerable time to 'trying to get at all the details of accounts etc which Gerald had failed to enter or record' (19 December 1925).

As if Gerald's tribulations were not enough for Herbert to bear, Chris's problems had also resurfaced. By the latter part of 1925, however, he seemed to be winning the latest round in his battle with the demon drink and was 'simply wonderfully fit and well-looking' and had taken to smoking a 'briar pipe' and drinking 'nothing but water' (10 November 1925). Around the same time, poor Herbert was deeply concerned to find himself and Hope in the all too familiar situation of being asset rich but cash poor: 'Our financial position preoccupies him [Hope] (as it does me) for though we have possessions we owe much' (16 October 1925). Herbert could do little to alleviate matters in the adverse economic climate of the time, as he deemed that both the Linconia and Bellavista (now renamed Moeraki) properties were 'unsaleable' (16 October 1925). As Christmas approached, however, he received a telegram bearing news of a welcome boost in the form of a £1,000 bonus from Liebigs' as a token of their 'high appreciation' of his 'valued attention to [the] Company's interests' (21 December 1925). Herbert observed that he 'never needed a remittance more sorely', adding that 'when the clouds darken there has again come a gleam' (21 December 1925).

Despite the hint of optimism on which 1925 concludes, it is not long before Herbert again has occasion to lament his situation, remarking wistfully, 'What a different old age mine is to what I had dreamed!' (20 January 1926). On 17 February, his spirits were temporarily lifted by the arrival of Ursula's baby, his first granddaughter, Diana Madeleine Wilson Gibson. Bad news quickly followed good: less than two weeks later, he was distressed to discover that Chris had checked in to a nursing home following a relapse:

> Poor Chris arrived in town this evening and came to me after dinner having put up at Dr John Halahan's Home. I took him out for a drive, and he told me his story. He had left town on the 12th [February] resolved on total abstention, but had arrived at Linconia to find much to worry him, and above all Dorothy's inconstant and fickle behaviour in his absence. He had lost his control and been drinking, and he had come up to town to put himself in Halahan's hands to recover his self-control and return to total abstention. (1 March 1926)

The persistent nature of Chris's problem is only underlined by the fact that the reason he had returned to Linconia was precisely to escape the 'snares and temptation of Buenos Aires [...] fearing he would be unable longer to resist and fall back again to excess of alcohol' (12 February 1926). It seems that wherever he found himself the lure of the bottle was simply irresistible. Herbert was heartened somewhat by an optimistic prognosis from Dr Halahan and prayed for his beloved son's recovery: 'Please God Chris will finally become whole, and his appreciation of the responsibilities of life will awaken' (3 March 1926). Sadly, this was not to be the case and alcoholism would continue to plague him throughout life.

By May, Herbert's lot had improved little. On top of his personal difficulties, he was much troubled by the political situation at home and the perils it posed for his interests there, with Britain in the grip of the General Strike:

> The threatened strike has broken out in the United Kingdom in all its tragic magnitude. A state of Emergency has been proclaimed in the King's name. The Prime Minister [Stanley Baldwin] has spoken with all the gravity and sobriety that mark him as a man of strong and balanced qualities. The outlook is most grave. (3 May 1926)

It was against this background that Herbert finally took the decision to put the Moeraki property on the market in an effort to alleviate his desperate financial situation (9 May 1926). Despite the near impossibility of selling land in Argentina at the time, it seemed that a buyer might be found in the person of Alvan Reid, the husband of Hope's daughter Gladys. Unfortunately for Herbert, however, Reid dragged his heels in the matter, before finally resolving that 'Moeraki did not suit him either by purchase or lease' (1 December 1926). It was to be a further twelve months before a buyer was found, a landowner by the name of Miguel Castellar, the sale going ahead despite a last-minute hitch in the negotiations:

An arduous day. Castellar had come to sign the transference of Moeraki, but being a petulant and quick tempered man took umbrage at a remark of Don Pascual's [an employee of the Gibsons], and tore up his cheques, declaring that nothing would induce him now to buy the place. In the afternoon his "escribano" [notary] came to see me, asked me to accompany him to Castellar's office, and here the incident was smoothed, the transference signed, and Moeraki is sold. (26 December 1927)

Returning to mid 1926, there seemed to be a chink of light on the horizon insofar as Gerald's situation was concerned, for he had now returned to England and, according to a telegram sent by Maddie, 'had at last got a job' (14 July 1926). Less than a month later, however, Gerald cabled Herbert to announce that the post 'had fallen through', but that he had other jobs 'in view' (9 August 1926). This was to become a familiar tale with Gerald; every venture he turned his hand to at this time ended unsatisfactorily, in one case bringing considerable inconvenience and shame to his long-suffering father, as we will see shortly.

A couple of interesting meetings served to lift the gloom of 1926 somewhat for Herbert, the first a luncheon at the British Embassy with 'Prince Mahamud Ali, the nephew of the King of Egypt, a nice looking man [... who] wears a huge emerald ring' (27 May 1926). The second event also took place at the legation and perhaps catered more to Herbert's taste, being a gathering of 'Argentine men of letters' to discuss the translation into Spanish of recent works on the diplomatic ties between Britain and Argentina and a proposed history of South America (4 June 1926). Among the distinguished guests present were Antonio Dellepiane and Emilio Ravignani, two of the nation's most illustrious historians.

By the latter part of the year, Chris had once again slipped under the influence, leading his despairing yet still devoted father to describe him as a 'mere shell with no interest in life and no longer capable of doing more than a little office work, reading trashy novels and soaking' (26 November 1926). Herbert adds that he had 'seemingly no strength of will to abstain from alcohol, and the smallest quantity is a veritable poison to him'. Another concern is that the manager of Moeraki, E O Runnacles, a longstanding employee of the Gibson family, was no longer capable of executing his duties in an effective fashion, with the result that he would have to retire and Clem would take over the running of the *estancia* from his base in the Buenos Aires office:

Runnacles is past work; his memory is failing, his eyesight bad and he won't wear spectacles, and he gets muddled and has lost all conception of efficient management. At his best he was a poor manager tho' a good worker with his own hands. (10 December 1926)

Herbert's sense that all around him was running to rack and ruin was only compounded by the blatantly dishonest conduct of a local election: 'Municipal elections at Ajó and much coming and going of cars. The Radical Party though greatly in the minority practised every device and fraud, substituted the votes in the urns, and nominally won the elections' (26 December 1926).

Fortunately, the New Year dawned on a slightly brighter note. Chris was 'totally abstaining' once again, which was probably just as well considering the hazardous drive that Herbert and he undertook from Linconia to Santo Domingo rail station:

> Chris and I, with Gabino Bravo as gate opener and for emergencies, left for Santo Domingo at 5.15. The rains have made the roads very muddy and greasy, and our progress to the Palenque was very heavy going. Some 5 miles beyond Pueyrredon's estancia, at a pass where the only road is the sloping side of the canal bank at an angle of perilous acuteness the car skidded into almost fathomless mud. The manager, Arambide, saw our distress, and kindly sent two horses to hale us out. The road along the canal was truly a heart racking performance, little wider than the car itself and muddy so that it skidded from side to side. Chris' splendid eye and hand steered us through all these perils. At the "Colorada" estancia road we again got bogged in a quagmire and were pulled out by two horsemen whose timely arrival came to our rescue. After that the road was easier and we arrived at Santo Domingo at 10 a.m. Chris swung round and started home again. (3 January 1927)

Thus we can observe that, despite the arrival of the automobile, travelling in Argentina's rural hinterland had become little easier than in Herbert's youth, especially in times of wet weather.

Also in January, a side representing the MCC was touring South America and played a three-match series against the Argentine national team, which was captained by Clem. Herbert was in frequent attendance at the matches and was also active in entertaining the visitors. The series ended in dramatic style: in the rain-interrupted final match, Argentina were deprived of a draw by being bowled out for 101 in their second innings, just 'one minute before stumps were to be drawn' (22 January 1927). Later that evening, at a dinner in the Jockey Club, Clem was presented with a silver cigarette box by the MCC.

In February, Chris suffered a brief relapse, his quick recovery of self-control attributed to a rather bizarre 'remedy':

> Clem arrived back in the evening from Linconia with good news of Chris who has had another failure but, seemingly, a sort of sunstroke he got has reawakened his mental perception from the predisposition he has had these past years to give way at certain periods to a crave for stimulant. He himself writes me that this sunstroke combined perhaps with the condition he was in when he had it, has "rolled away a mental cloud that has obscured his perceptions" since he was blown up in his O.P. [Observation Post] beyond Dickiebush in May 1918; and he feels he has now once again the balance that will enable him to control and overcome these periods of crave for stimulant. Pray God it is so! (16 February 1927)

And thus we come to a better understanding of Chris's alcohol problem, namely that it may have been induced by his experiences during the Great War. Chris's latest improvement came just in time for the arrival of a new addition to his family; on 27 February, Dorothy gave birth to a son, Ian Herbert Gibson.

In March, Herbert set sail for Southampton on board the RMSP *Arlanza*, one of his fellow passengers being none other than Rudyard Kipling. On reaching England, he discovered that Gerald had continued to lead a somewhat dissolute lifestyle, having acquired a modest poultry farm and incurred considerable debts in the process. On first seeing the establishment, Herbert immediately discerned that it was 'not a very profitable enterprise', but consoled himself with the thought that 'at least it gives him occupation' (8 April 1927). The venture seems to have caused considerable worry to Gerald's wife, Ursula, for she was 'in bed with a sort of nervous break-down caused by anxiety about her and Gerald's none too well ordered monetary affairs' (6 April 1927). It was not long before Herbert began to realize that Gerald's situation was far worse than he had feared, as the following extracts from his diary reveal:

> After lunch I went round to see Mrs. Baker who had lent Gerald money and been unable to recover it. (29 May 1927)

> Further news is reaching us of Gerald's money affairs and making us most anxious as I am unable to prevail on him to tell me the truth and he is sinking deeper in the mire of a slothful and improvident life. (31 May 1927)

> With still further knowledge of the quagmire of debt Gerald and Ursula are wallowing in, Maddie and I motored up to Beeston, missing Gerald who was "out" as usual, but I had a long earnest talk with Ursula, whose state of health too is greatly adding to our anxiety, and she promised to prevail on Gerald to come and tell me the truth. (3 June 1927)

> The poor boy [Gerald] has at last opened his eyes to his foolishness and misguided ideas, and told me what I desired. He has of course many debts and has been for long evading them by giving cheques that are dishonoured on presentation. (4 June 1927)

For a short spell, it appeared that Gerald had resolved to put his house in order and he led his father to believe that he would soon be taking up employment as a bailiff on an estate near St Albans. Like most of Gerald's schemes, however, this came to naught, and Herbert persuaded him that the best course of action would be to return to Argentina (29 July 1927).

In the midst of this turmoil, Ursula gave birth to the couple's second daughter, named June at Herbert's suggestion on account of being born on the longest day (22 June 1927). By early August, Gerald's insolvency had reached crisis point, and yet he still refused to tell his father the truth about his predicament:

> The whole of my day engaged in endeavouring to ascertain Gerald's debts which he continues to conceal from me, although there are now summonses out against him. (3 August 1927)

> Learned […] of new debts of Gerald's of very considerable magnitude, and went to see him but he had been absent all day. (4 August 1927)

> Gerald absent from home and Cos and I unable to find him. In the afternoon the county borough bailiff called at Gerald's house when I was there, and I was able to find out the nature of his pending summonses. Went with him to the County Offices to pay off a debt for which a distraint on the poultry yard had been made, and here I found Gerald whom I took home. Spent the remainder of the day going round banks etc. to ascertain Gerald's debts, and think I have now got on to them all. (5 August 1927)

> Another day spent practically on nothing else than attending to Gerald's affairs. (6 August 1927)

> Spent the afternoon and evening in attending to Gerald's affairs. A truly sad and cheerless day to end the past two months of anxiety. (10 August 1927)

The next day, Herbert and Maddie, with their adopted daughter Jean, Cosmo, and Gerald with his family set sail for Argentina. Gerald's recent difficulties and the embarrassment they had caused were still very much on Herbert's mind:

> We sailed at noon, turning our backs on home where for the past two months Madeleine's life and mine have been clouded by Gerald's dissoluteness, slowly revealed to us as his creditors brought its proofs and the terrible revelation of his evasions and the untruths they led him to. Pray God he will start anew in the Argentine. All Eastbourne, alas, knows the story. (11 August 1927)

On reaching Argentina, yet more bad news of a family nature awaited Herbert, as Chris's marriage was close to collapse, on account of Dorothy having an affair, and he had turned to drink once again:

> I had a long talk with Chris this morning. He is very much shaken by the events of the past two months. His narrative is that he returned [to Linconia] in early June from his visit to Mr James M. Hickson the faith healer, much strengthened and feeling that he could resist the lure of drink. Shortly after his return he realised that Dorothy was making improper overtures to Hall. The latter left Linconia about mid July intending to return to England. Dorothy told Chris shortly afterwards that she had symptoms of becoming pregnant and for this and for an ailment of pink eyes she must go to town. On her way up she wired back to him that it was her intention to go to the Plaza Hotel (where Hall was staying) and not the Phoenix. This news, Chris says, broke down his self control and he resorted to stimulant. Dorothy went to a nursing home where under treatment her pregnancy was removed – the parvula of a female child, – and thence she went to the Plaza Hotel. After some time, obtaining no satisfactory answer to his question when she was going to return home, Chris went to town. […] He found her at the Plaza Hotel in Hall's company and she

openly avowed her intention of living under his protection. There was a scene that night. Chris to save appearances kept company with Hall and Dorothy, but I gather that he himself was drinking. That night she attacked him [with an electric lamp stand or some other heavy object, we subsequently discover], Chris told her that if she summoned Hall he would leave the hotel and her. She did so, and he left, and between drink and misery he knows little of the ensuing days except that he had drifted somehow to the company of a streetwoman he had once known and that she took him home and nursed him through some days of semi consciousness.

As Herbert was still away while all this was going on, Hope and Clem had intervened in an attempt to resolve matters. A settlement of sorts was reached, by which Dorothy agreed to return to Linconia with Chris for the time being, while Jack Hall would remain in Buenos Aires, with the intention of eventually leaving with Dorothy and marrying her once she had got a divorce. According to Chris, however, Dorothy then changed her mind about Hall and decided to have no further dealings with him. Chris's wish was that she should return to her native Canada for 'at least a year' to spend time with her own family, but without any form of judicial separation taking place. Herbert agreed that this was the 'proper course' and it was decided that Maddie would reside at Linconia to take charge of the household and look after her grandchildren during Dorothy's absence (11 September 1927). In the end, Dorothy did indeed travel to Vancouver, accompanied by her youngest son, Ian (26 September 1927).

Given the family tribulations that he had endured, it is not surprising that Herbert described 1927 as a 'year that has had but few pleasant experiences for me' (31 December 1927). For a couple of weeks at the start of 1928, the outlook seemed rather brighter: Gerald had, apparently, realized the error of his erstwhile ways and resolved to begin afresh, and we hear little about Chris's problems. During the second half of January, Herbert was much involved with a visit to Argentina by Lord Bledisloe. After accompanying Bledisloe and his party on an *estancia* visit, he found himself caught up in a dramatic incident on the railway while travelling back to Buenos Aires:

> At 10 p.m. we had all assembled in the restaurant car for dinner when we felt the brakes put violently on. The car began to jump and throw things off the tables. This grew more violent and we were conscious we were derailed when happily the train came to a standstill. Looking out of the window by my side I could see that we were on the edge of

an embankment 10 ft high, with a deep ditch of mud and water below it. The coach in front of our restaurant car was lying over at a dangerous angle, but those behind had not left the line. Presently we learnt that the locomotive had run first into 2 horses and then into a cow, and the latter's body had got entangled under the engine and thrown it off the line and down the embankment. Its couplings had broken, and this, and the effective brake the upturned engine had put to the train's velocity, its buffers ripping up the side of the tender and following derailed vans, had arrested us and saved us from being overturned down the embankment to certain death for us all. (18 January 1928)

Not all were so lucky, however. The driver, stoker and the railway company's General Superintendent of Locomotives were all trapped beneath the engine and only a 'faint groaning' could be heard. Two of the passengers, Mr Eddy, a director of the railroad, and Dr Dye, the Commercial Attaché of the American Embassy, courageously mounted a rescue attempt, digging under the locomotive with their hands. Only the stoker was still alive, but he too succumbed shortly after. The shocked passengers were stranded until a replacement train reached the scene at 3 am, and finally reached Buenos Aires eight hours later.

By mid February, Chris had embarked on yet another downward spiral. Herbert wrote with regret that Chris had 'unwisely broken his pledge' and was 'quite unable to abstain and giving way to drink' (14 February 1928). Within a few days, Chris had again given up alcohol, but was 'terribly shaken and downcast' (20 February 1928). Although beside himself with worry, Herbert remained sympathetic throughout, describing Chris's 'sad affliction' as 'not a vice but truly a malady' (20 February 1928). By the beginning of the next month, however, Chris had 'broken down again' and injured his ribs in a drunken 'affray' (5 March 1928). Shortly afterwards, his sad condition was compounded by a letter from Dorothy in which she asked for a divorce. Over the next few months, the familiar pattern repeated itself time and time again: after a short period of abstention, Chris gave way to temptation. On one occasion, he disappeared for a couple of days and was finally found by Herbert in a room in the Alvear Palace Hotel 'in a sad state of helplessness though not inebriated apparently but under the influence of past excess and sleepless nights' (4 June 1928). In the end, it was decided that he should travel to England to seek treatment there, and he set sail, accompanied by Maddie, at the beginning of August. There was one more dramatic incident before their departure, in which a car driven by Chris and with Maddie as passenger overturned while swerving to avoid a 'big black dog' that had run into the road (30 July 1928). Chris and Maddie were trapped in the wreckage, but Clem, who had been following in another vehicle, fetched help and managed to extricate them. Considering the nature of the accident, their injuries were relatively minor, Chris suffering nothing more than a broken rib and Maddie a contusion to the head that left her in considerable pain and somewhat concussed.

Also on Herbert's mind at this time was the condition of his sister-in-law, Hope's wife, Agnes. She had been in declining health for a number of years, suffering from, amongst other complaints, diabetes. By mid July, she had developed 'symptoms of a most grave condition of the liver' (14 July 1928) and within a month had deteriorated to the point that the doctors held out 'no hope for her recovery' (12 August 1928). Her death on 2 September, therefore, came as no surprise, but prompted Herbert to reflect on his own mortality, for Agnes was only two and a half years older than him. Hope, meanwhile, whose own health had given cause for concern for some time, seemed to lose all sense of purpose with the death of his wife. His daughter Connie took him on a short sea cruise in an attempt to boost his spirits, but he returned in a much-depleted state:

> Hope has arrived very seriously ill with distention of the bowels, liver completely disordered and general condition of health very disquieting. Dr John Halahan and Dr Vickerman both called in and as a first step drew off the fluid accumulated in the bowels. (22 September 1928)

Despite the best efforts of the two doctors, Hope continued to slide downhill and plainly lacked even the will to recover: 'Hope is slowly losing ground, [...] he does not rally and expresses with wonderful composure that he has no wish to survive his wife and hopes to rejoin her' (1 October 1928). By the next day, 'his liver and kidneys [were] ceasing to function', yet he remained 'very tranquil' and conversed with his daughters about his approaching end, an 'event he [awaited] without fear or regret' (2 October 1928). By the end of the week, the doctors expressed the view that Hope had little time left and Herbert sadly bade a final goodbye:

> This evening I had a little chat with him, he was very composed though weak and far spent; his spirit was cheerful and one could see that his mind was at rest. We embraced and took farewell with deep emotion. (5 October 1928)

Hope lingered for a few days more, before passing away in the early hours of 10 October. His funeral the next day, which took place at his house and then in the British section of the Chacarita cemetery, was attended by a 'very large gathering' drawn from both the English-speaking community and wider Argentine society (11 October 1928). An obituary in *The Standard* attested to the high regard in which he was held by his peers:

> Few men were better known in this city than Mr. Hope Gibson. A shrewd and successful business man, his many sterling qualities and upright character earned him the respect of all, and his loss will be deeply deplored by a vast circle of friends and business acquaintances.[120]

Unsurprisingly, Hope's death affected Herbert deeply. For much of their adult lives, the two men had lived in near association, as brothers, friends and business partners. Herbert ends his diary entry for 11 October with a heartfelt reflection on their relationship:

> Thus closes the last chapter of a close union with a brother who, more than any of my father's family, has been near to me. Since he first came out, in 1889, with his wife Agnes and his little babe Connie, or "Tonie" as we then called her, we have been very united in all our family and worldly affairs. He has always been the unselfish comrade, more thoughtful for my weal than his own. A truly kind hearted and good man, gone to his rest, rejoined please God with his wife whom he loved so dearly, and leaving the world poorer by the loss of his genial presence.

In some sense, Hope's death brought down the curtain on one of the most depressing periods of Herbert's life. From this point onwards, things gradually began to look brighter, especially insofar as Chris was concerned. He returned with Maddie from England at the end of October, apparently determined to regain control of his life, and was reunited with Dorothy and his sons. In an effort to start afresh, the family took up residence in Montevideo for a spell, living in a house on Avenida Brasil in the suburb of Pocitos. Gerald, too, seemed to be leaving his self-indulgent past behind, but suffered an unfortunate mishap while playing Santa Claus on Christmas Day:

---

120 'Obituary: The late Mr. Hope Gibson', *The Standard* (Buenos Aires), 11 October 1928.

> In the afternoon we had a Christmas tree and this was the scene of a grave accident that might have proved fatal. Gerald, as Santa Claus, with a big cotton-wool beard, got too close to one of the drooping candles, towards the end of the present giving. He went up in flames. Cosmo ran to his rescue and he too had his garments fired. Gerald displayed great courage and presence of mind; and in thirty seconds the flames were extinguished. Dearest Maddie, as capable as ever in moments of need, assisted by Ursula, had both boys in oil and cotton wool very speedily. Gerald was badly burnt on throat, neck, chest and both hands; Cosmo on the stomach and one hand. (25 December 1928)

The doctor was summoned at once and took more than three hours to dress their burns. Gerald, in particular, suffered great pain in the ensuing days and also developed a kidney complication. Although his condition had improved somewhat by New Year, this episode cast a long shadow over the family's festive celebrations.

Leaving the Christmas Day drama to one side, Herbert went forward into 1929 in more positive mood than he had been for some time. The financial worries he had experienced for most of the past decade were considerably relieved by a new banking arrangement, which permitted him an overdraft of up to $450,000. 'This', Herbert recorded in his diary, 'relieves me of the embarrassing position I have been in during nine years of heavy indebtedness to my own firm, restores my independence within that firm, and saves me a considerable difference in interest' (10 January 1929). During this period, he began to regain the drive that seemed to have been missing from his life for some time, his sense of purpose renewed by the prospect of what would become one of his greatest achievements. The possibility of staging a major British commercial exhibition in Buenos Aires had first been raised the previous year with the intention of arranging the event for some time in the latter part of 1930 or early in 1931. By April 1929, plans were advancing rapidly and Herbert was a member of a delegation from the British Chamber of Commerce that visited the Casa Rosada, Argentina's presidential palace, to brief President Yrigoyen on the scheme:

> Had a very busy day including a visit, in delegation of the Br. Ch. of Commerce to the Casa Rosada where we had an audience with the President and informed him of the project, and progress achieved, of the British Empire Industrial Fair to take place in Buenos Aires at the end of next year. Sr. Irigoyen [*sic*] received us most cordially and promised us every support from his government. (4 April 1929)

The trade fair, which will be discussed in detail separately, would take up much of Herbert's time and energies over the next two years. While his efforts as the exhibition's chief organizer left him near to exhaustion by its end, its success was, without doubt, the crowning glory of Herbert's career, both boosting his prestige and earning him numerous accolades, foremost among which was the award of his baronetcy.

In April, Herbert and Maddie sailed to England, where Herbert embarked upon his usual round of meetings and visits. The highlight of their trip was a holiday in Scotland, during which they based themselves at Fisher's Hotel in Pitlochry, an establishment that survives today. They spent their first few days exploring the local countryside, visiting Ballinluig, Dunkeld, Aberfeldy, Loch Tay, and the Queen's View overlooking Loch Tummel. While Maddie remained in Pitlochry, Herbert then made the first of two interruptions to his break, travelling to Hull to give a speech about trade with Argentina. He then spent a couple of days in London, dealing with business matters, before returning to Scotland. After only two more days of relaxation, during which the couple walked to the small village of Moulin above Pitlochry and took a drive to Blairgowrie, Herbert ventured south once again, this time heading for Harrogate to attend the Royal Show. On his return to Perthshire, Herbert and Maddie spent a few more pleasant days touring the region by car, including a trip through Glenshee to Braemar and thence on to Balmoral and Ballater, and a visit to Loch Earn and St Fillans, before they left Pitlochry for Edinburgh, where they put up at the Caledonian Hotel. In the capital, Herbert called upon Ballingall & Fraser, the Gibson family's Scottish lawyers, and visited the 'Lodge of Edinburgh (Mary's Chapel) N⁰· 1, of which [he] became a Brother in Dec 1888',[121] which, he goes on to tell us, was the 'oldest in the United Kingdom' (19 July 1929).

By late August, Herbert and Maddie were back in Buenos Aires, where they were delighted to see their grandchildren once again. Of the offspring of Chris and Dorothy, Herbert wrote: 'Kits is well and a truly beautiful boy. Bruce is backward and almost simple minded and with no boyish vitality. Ian is a sturdy rogue' (12 September 1929). Bruce, of course, was the surviving twin of Newman, who had died in infancy, and would not enjoy a long life either, passing away in 1935 at the age of twelve.

Having been appointed a director of the Buenos Ayres Great Southern Railway in January 1929, Herbert was a member of the four-man delegation from Argentina that travelled to Chile to attend the International Railway Congress in

---

121 Herbert's recollection of the date of his inception into Masonry is flawed: he actually joined the lodge in December 1887. See Chapter 4, p. 97.

Santiago at the end of the year. The party enjoyed a memorable journey across the Andes:

> Left Mendoza at 10 a.m. in the transandine and climbed up on the railway the Andean valleys and gorges by way of Uspallata, Aconcagua and Tupungato, till we reached the tunnel at Las Cuevas. Saw on our way the Puente del Inca [Inca's Bridge]. The tunnel is a few feet short of 10,000 ft. above sea level, but I experienced no mountain sickness. The tunnel is 4000 m. long and two thirds through one passes the frontier and a bell rings. We emerged on the Chilian side at 5.30 p.m. and descended to Los Andes station, but it was dark when we got there. The peaks on both sides were covered with snow. (6 December 1929)

As well as attending several sessions of the Congress and a reception for delegates hosted by the 'President Dictator, Col. now General Ibañez', described as a 'man of medium stature and age, dark, strong face and sparse of speech', Herbert also found time for a visit to Chile's National Library (11 December 1929).

1929 was to conclude on an unhappy note for one member of Herbert's family. Poor Cosmo had for some time been troubled by bouts of tonsillitis and it was decided that an operation was required. This fairly routine procedure appeared to have gone reasonably well at first, but some nine days after the operation Cosmo suddenly suffered a 'hemorrhage [*sic*] of the throat' due to the fact that a 'piece of tonsil, apparently severed during the operation but not removed, had come away' (23 December 1929). He was left much weakened by this unexpected turn of events and went on to suffer kidney, bladder and intestinal trouble and developed jaundice. While he recovered satisfactorily from these complications in the New Year, it was some time before Cosmo regained full health.

And so concluded the 1920s, probably the least fruitful and contented period of Herbert's life. After a promising start to the decade – newly knighted and with his family alongside him in Argentina – Herbert suffered at the hands of the post-war economic malaise, but what affected him most deeply were the various troubles that beset his family. By the dawn of 1930, however, the worst of these seemed to be in the past and Herbert was somewhat reinvigorated by the expectation of playing a leading role in the forthcoming British Exhibition, the focus of our next chapter.

CHAPTER 9

THE BRITISH EXHIBITION

The period from 1930 to 1931 was to prove eventful for Herbert and for Argentina. The start of 1930 was marred by further discord within the Gibson clan, this time between Clem, who was in charge at Linconia, and Gerald, who was also still in residence there. Herbert wrote that the 'friction in the household has reached breaking point' and went on to state that Clem had become 'taciturn', while Gerald and Ursula took 'their meals in their own room' (18 January 1930). Matters had become so bad that Herbert proposed to resolve the situation by sending Gerald and family to live on the Gibsons' vineyard at San Rafael, Mendoza. Cosmo would then have had to leave the service of Liebigs' to take Gerald's place on the staff of Linconia. For reasons that are unclear, however, this plan never came to fruition. Chris, meanwhile, was preparing to take a 'great excursion' to see the Paraguayan Chaco, having returned from Montevideo and now living with Dorothy and his sons in the Buenos Aires suburb of Hurlingham (27 April 1930).

Herbert's already considerable public profile was, if anything, increasing at this time. He had become a frequent visitor to President Yrigoyen whenever issues of concern to Anglo-Argentine relations arose, and had recently assumed the role of acting chairman of the Buenos Ayres Great Southern Railway while the normal incumbent, Fernando Guerrico, was absent through ill health (12 February 1930). This resulted in a considerable increase to Herbert's workload, which he described in a letter to Maddie:

> I have taken over a heavy burden, not one that I cannot bear or that gives me worries and sleepless nights or anything of that sort, but very very constant duties. [...] The reading and signing of each day's routine business from lawyers, managers and other departments which must come before me represents 1½ to 2 hours. I have practically a daily meeting with my colleagues Messrs MacRae, White & Labarthe, to talk of subjects of interest or importance as these arise [...]. I have the

regular fortnightly meeting of the Board which I have already got down to 2 hours, – it was 3 and sometimes 4 with M<u>r.</u> Guerrico who dealt more comprehensively with themes than I have occasion or motive to do. Then I have meetings with <u>all</u> the Chairmen [of the other railway companies], not fixed but about one a week. Then there is the meeting of all the railway representatives supposed to be monthly but frequently convened for emergency subjects. Then I have to go and see Cabinet Ministers, and sometimes the President, and other functionaries both here and at La Plata. (17 May 1930)

After a Chamber of Commerce luncheon in early May, Herbert recorded that one of the principal guests, the vice-president of the Argentine Rural Society, had paid him a particularly pleasing compliment, avowing the regard in which he was held in his adopted land: 'In speaking of me Bruzone very nicely said that, whatever name I was known by to my fellow countrymen, with all my Argentine friends I was "Don Heriberto"' (7 May 1930).

All the while, initial preparations for the forthcoming British Exhibition continued and Herbert, as chairman of the British Chamber of Commerce in Argentina, was in the very thick of it. Arrangements had been made for the band of the 2nd Battalion of the Cameron Highlanders to take part in the Exhibition and one of Herbert's first major responsibilities was to inspect the barracks belonging to the Ministry of Marine where the visiting troops would be lodged (25 July 1930). The Exhibition itself was to take place at the showground in the suburb of Palermo, the venue of the annual Argentine Rural Show. During an early visit to the site by officers of the Chamber of Commerce and the British Embassy, the ambassador, Sir Ronald Macleay, informed Herbert 'very confidentially' that the Prince of Wales himself, the future Edward VIII, would be present to open the Exhibition (31 July 1930). The secret of the Prince's visit was not kept for long; on 4 August, sources in the Argentine government leaked the news to the press, much to Macleay's annoyance. This indiscretion was quickly forgotten, however, as the country was plunged into yet another bout of political uncertainty:

> Government is displaying uneasiness at some unknown plot or conspiracy that is hatching. The private house of the President is guarded by small detachments of police and security agents, and both Government House and the Post Office have also now pickets of troops surrounding them. No one knows what it is all about, but there is a general feeling that there is not only a growing opposition to the

Yrigoyen Govt. arising from its exclusive political activities to the neglect of the business of the Country, but disaffection in the army. (29 August 1930)

Always a contentious individual with bitter opponents on both left and right, Yrigoyen now cast a sorry figure, weakened by old age, surrounded by sycophantic advisers and widely perceived to be out of touch with the country's situation. Plotters within the military, led by General José Félix Uriburu and among whose number figured a young captain by the name of Juan Domingo Perón, had been toying with the idea of a coup for some months, but had so far lacked the confidence to make their move. Early September found Yrigoyen laid low by influenza and, no longer fit to exercise executive authority, he handed over power to Dr Enrique Martínez, the acting vice-president. This development galvanized the rebels into action. The next day, Herbert recorded that 'troops from the Campo de Mayo were advancing on the city', marking the outbreak of revolution (6 September 1930). He responded by sending home all the staff from Gibson Brothers and promptly retired to the offices of the Southern Railway, from where he watched events unfold. The rebels met with little opposition on their march, Yrigoyen himself having fled the city. Uriburu led his forces down the Avenida de Mayo, the principal thoroughfare of Buenos Aires, and was installed in the presidential palace by six o'clock the same evening. Two days later, Uriburu was sworn in as provisional president and named his cabinet. Although there were sporadic clashes between the military and supporters of the ousted Radical Party over the following days, the revolution was accomplished in a relatively peaceful manner; according to Herbert, the 'city [looked] more like a Carnival Feast than anything else' with 'everybody in great jubilation fluttering flags and forming processions' (8 September 1930).

While Herbert welcomed the coup and at first approved of Uriburu's choice of ministers, writing that 'these are almost all my personal friends' (8 September 1930), he quickly became concerned that, despite the change of regime, many were precisely the same individuals who had occupied positions of power under Yrigoyen:

> Everyone, anyway of my own circle and generation, accepts what has happened as a great deliverance from an inept, incapable, corrupt and degraded regime of the Yrigoyen party which had permeated the whole country with a political dictatorship and ruining it. That is so; but the people are the same people […]. (10 September 1930)

Furthermore, he reported that there was already a growing resentment against the military government among some groups that had only a few days before supported the uprising, owing to their exclusion from the new order and Uriburu's failure to deliver on pledges he had made earlier. Meanwhile, Yrigoyen, Herbert notes, was 'in La Plata in the barracks of the 7th Regiment of Infantry, practically as a prisoner' (10 September 1930). History tells us that the former president was later transferred to a jail on the island of Martín García in the River Plate, from where he was released in 1933 only a short time before his death.

Notwithstanding his mixed feelings about the Uriburu regime, Herbert wasted little time in calling on the new president to inform him of the plans for the British Exhibition:

> Had an exceptionally busy day, and in the afternoon, accompanied by Buxton and Chirgwin [respectively the vice-chairman and secretary of the British Chamber of Commerce], called at Government House where the Provisional President General Uriburu granted us an audience. I briefly stated to him the stage of organisation our Exhibition had reached, and he gave us very cordial assurances of the support of his government. (11 September 1930)

This meeting briefly landed Herbert in hot water with Sir Ronald Macleay, for he felt that it pre-empted recognition of Uriburu's regime by the United Kingdom government. At a meeting with Herbert, the ambassador made it plain that he was 'distinctly displeased', criticized the visit as 'impulsive', and even accused the Chamber of Commerce delegation of 'trying to force H.M. Government's hands' (12 September 1930). Herbert, however, managed to pacify him somewhat by explaining the 'real nature' of the audience with Uriburu (12 September 1930). Recognition of the new administration was, in any case, only a matter of days away, coming on 17 September. This cleared the way for Herbert's next meeting with Uriburu, at which the president behaved in a 'very cordial' manner (20 September 1930).

For the next few months, Herbert was much occupied in making arrangements for the Exhibition, which was to open in the middle of March 1931. He found himself moving in the highest circles among both British and Argentine society: in November he lunched with 'J.C.C. Davidson late Chairman of the Conservative Party and son of [his] old friend Sir Mackenzie Davidson' (7 November 1930),[122]

---

[122] Davidson was the chief lieutenant of party leader Stanley Baldwin in the late 1920s. A spectacularly successful raiser of funds for the Conservatives as chairman, he later became known as an active player in the skulduggery of internal party politics, being implicated in the 'dirty tricks' campaign waged by members of the Tory hierarchy against Winston Churchill in the 1930s.

and a few days later invited Elena Alvear de Bosch, wife of Dr Ernesto Bosch, Uriburu's Foreign Minister, to become a patroness of the Exhibition (10 November 1930). The highlight of his preparations came in January, when he briefed the Prince of Wales on the Exhibition's progress: 'Today at one o'clock I had the honour to speak over the Radio Telephone to the Prince of Wales who spoke from his own telephone in St James' Palace, I speaking from the "Transradio" office' (15 January 1931). Their transatlantic discussion, still very much a novelty at that time, was fully covered in the press, an account appearing in *The Standard* the next day:[123]

> The conversation commenced punctually at the hour arranged (1 p.m.) under perfect conditions. When Sir Herbert asked if he had the honour of addressing His Royal Highness, the Prince replied "Prince of Wales speaking". The following is a record of their conversation:
>
> **Sir Herbert:** "The coming of your Royal Highness to the Argentine has aroused most cordial expressions of welcome throughout the country. The memory of your last visit remains fresh, and the ease with which you have subsequently acquired and now speak the Spanish language is referred to with pleasure and admiration.
>
> "In the Cattle Show Grounds of Palermo which Your Royal Highness visited in 1925 there is now uprearing a wonderful fabric reproducing all the beauty of old English architecture. The Canadian Pavilion too, now reaching completion, is a stately building.
>
> "A group of Argentina gentlemen who recently visited the Exhibition grounds remarked that when Your Royal Highness came to see them you would exclaim that you were back in England.
>
> "Everything promises well for the Exhibition which will be one not only of all the best that British industry, art and genius can produce; but also of British thoroughness and efficiency.
>
> "It is felt that this Exhibition will prove the awakening of a new era of British commerce and endeavour in the Argentine and other South American Republics under the leadership of the nation's greatest Ambassador.
>
> "On behalf of the British Chamber of Commerce and the Exhibition Committee I wish you God-speed on your journey and his Divine protection in all your travels by sea and land and air."

---

123 The first transatlantic telephone conversation had been made from New York to London as recently as 1927.

H. R. Highness: "Thanks for your kind message. Please give warm message of greeting to my Argentine friends; I am looking forward with great pleasure to renewing the friendships I formed in the Argentine Republic on the occasion of my visit in 1925. How are these Exhibition buildings progressing?"

Sir Herbert: "The buildings are progressing very well, Your Highness."

H. R. Highness: "Fine. It was very kind of the Rural Society to allow us the use of their grounds at Palermo."

Sir Herbert: "Of course, as Your Royal Highness knows, the economic depression throughout the world is felt here also, but it is recognised that this will give still greater importance to the recognition here that they must 'buy from those who buy from them.'"

H. R. Highness: "I wish you to convey my kindest regards to the Ambassador."

Sir Herbert: "I shall have great pleasure in conveying your gracious message to the Ambassador, who is at present in Mar del Plata."

H. R. Highness: "I am looking forward to seeing you all once more. Isn't this a wonderful line?"

Sir Herbert: "Marvellous! We owe the arrangement of this communication to Com. Lloyd Hirst, the representative of the Marconi Company and Director of the Transradio International."

H. R. Highness: "Thank him for the excellent arrangements."

Sir Herbert: "It is a great honour to be allowed to speak to Your Royal Highness, and all here wish you "bon voyage."

H. R. Highness: "Thank you Gibson. Goodbye."[124]

---

124 'The Prince of Wales' Radio Telephone Conversation with Sir Herbert Gibson', *The Standard* (Buenos Aires), 16 January 1931.

At the beginning of February, Herbert paid a visit to Dr Bosch to seek his permission to borrow the Argentine copy of the Treaty of Amity, Commerce and Navigation signed with Great Britain in 1825 for display at the Exhibition:

> 'Called on the Minister of Foreign Affairs [...] and he readily agreed to lend the 1825 Treaty to the Exhibition and showed it to us with the signatures of George IV, Canning [George Canning, British Foreign Secretary], Rivadavia [Bernardino Rivadavia, Minister of Government and Foreign Affairs of Buenos Aires], Las Heras [General Juan Gregorio de la Heras, Governor of Buenos Aires], M$^{l.}$ Garcia [Manuel García, Under-Secretary in the Buenos Aires Ministry of Foreign Affairs] and Woodbine Parish [British Consul-General].' (6 February 1931)

The treaty occupies an immensely important place in the history of Anglo-Argentine relations; not only did it contain significant clauses to protect the rights and freedoms of British citizens in Argentina, but, in the words of H S Ferns, 'remained the legal foundation of Anglo-Argentine intercourse until [...] the 1930s'.[125]

It soon emerged that the Prince of Wales would be accompanied on his visit to Argentina by his younger brother, Prince George, the future Duke of Kent. Following the success of the tour Herbert had arranged for the Prince of Wales in 1925, he was asked to plan something similar for Prince George on this occasion. Assisted by Chris, he prepared an excursion through the Province of Entre Ríos and across into Uruguay, with which the two princes 'were greatly taken' on their arrival in Buenos Aires (6 March 1931).

With a little over a week to go before the Exhibition's official opening, Herbert spent the days following the princes' arrival in a whirl of last-minute preparations and official engagements. Indeed, it seems that he was expected to be at the beck and call of the royal entourage, as his account of the first Sunday of their visit reveals:

> Their RR. HH. [Royal Highnesses] attended service at St. Andrew's [the Scottish church in Buenos Aires], where Maddie and I occupied the front pew on the north side. Just before the Princes arrived I was summoned to the telephone, and the Embassy spoke through to me that it was his intention to visit the Show Grounds immediately

---

125   H S Ferns, *Britain and Argentina in the Nineteenth Century* (Oxford: Clarendon Press, 1960), p. 113.

after lunch. The Church was thronged, and their RR. HH. when they arrived occupied the front pew on the south side. [...] At the termination of the service and when the Prince rose to leave he came across to me and told me he was going to the Ex Service Club for five minutes and thence to the Show Grounds.

Dearest Maddie helped me by getting out of church amongst the first after the Princes left and we got our car almost at once and speeded to our flat. There I left her and I continued to the Embassy where I saw Lloyd Thomas the Secretary of the Prince and told him that I was continuing to the Show Grounds. Arrived there I sent a message for Bellasis [Mr Brian Bellasis, manager of the Exhibition] and he presently appeared, but none too soon, for scarcely had he joined me at the gates before the Princes drove up accompanied by a few members of their staff. The visit was a complete success and the Prince of Wales expressed himself most gratified with the organisation, and the comfort with which he had been able to visit it. (8 March 1931)

Poor Herbert was unexpectedly recalled to the Embassy at six o'clock the same evening for discussions about alterations to the princes' itinerary. Unfortunately, these changes compromised the tour he had planned meticulously for Prince George and left Herbert with little choice but to advise that it be scrapped.

The final days before the opening of the Exhibition on 14 March are occupied with almost non-stop meetings. By the time the great day arrives, one gets the impression that Herbert is much wearied by all his efforts, but he manages to play a full part in the ceremonies:

> After a busy morning lunched early, changed, and to the Show Grounds at 1 o'clock. Very hot day, otherwise pleasant.
>
> Their Royalties and Staff arrived at 2.20 p.m. at the Cerviño & Sarmiento Gate where I received them and accompanied them to H.M.G. [His Majesty's Government] Pavilion, and returned to receive and accompany the President [General Uriburu] and his staff there. The Personages went through the various pavilions as far as the Railway one, and thence to the Official Stand. All the Stands crowded. Great enthusiasm.
>
> After the Band of the Cameron Highlanders had played the Argentine and British anthems, I made my brief address to the Prince and to the President. The Prince then spoke, an excellent speech in

both Spanish and English, which was broadcasted throughout the world. Then the President spoke, a poor speech badly delivered. (14 March 1931)

That evening, Herbert presided over a Chamber of Commerce banquet, at which both he and the Prince of Wales spoke again. At 11 pm the Prince and his party went on to a ball, but a tired Herbert and Maddie returned home after just a short while. The day seems to have passed most satisfactorily and Herbert recalls with gratification that the Prince had been 'very pleasant' to him throughout (14 March 1931).

A lengthy report of the Exhibition's opening was carried in *The Times* two days later, in which a few details of Herbert's speech were provided:

> BUENOS AIRES,
> March 14
>
> The British Empire Trade Exhibition was opened to-day in the Rural Society's grounds at Palermo, Buenos Aires, by the Prince of Wales, who made two speeches, the first in English and the second in Spanish. Sir Herbert Gibson spoke after him and President Uriburu after.
>
> The weather was ideal. There was a guard of honour of British sailors and the band of The Cameron Highlanders played the Argentine National Anthem, "God Save the King", and "God Bless the Prince of Wales." A flight of pigeons of different colours signalised the opening. [...]
>
> Sir Herbert Gibson, opening the proceedings, recalled that five years ago the Prince of Wales had seen in the same place the annual live stock show held by the Argentine Rural Society, at which, as a British farmer, he had been able to see the splendid cattle descended from British herds.
>
> "More than any other [he said], the art and craft of husbandry formed the first tie to unite the British and Argentine people, and has continued to draw them closer in their ancient and historic friendship."
>
> After thanking the Argentine people and the President of the Republic, in Spanish, for their aid in the exhibition, he then asked the Prince of Wales to declare the exhibition open.[126]

---

126 'Buenos Aires Exhibition: A Successful Opening', *The Times*, 16 March 1931.

After transcribing fully the words of the Prince of Wales and General Uriburu, the report recorded that 'the Prince of Wales's speech was successfully broadcast by the B.B.C.', his voice coming through 'clearly and distinctly', but that 'atmospherics interfered with the speech of Sir Herbert Gibson'!

With all his engagements, many of which required him to speak in public, it is little wonder that Herbert developed a 'complete loss of voice' in the days following the opening ceremony (17 March 1931). Meanwhile, he continued to attend the meetings, dinners and banquets associated with the Exhibition, but, on one occasion, had to get an acquaintance to deliver a speech on his behalf (18 March 1931). Things quietened down a little with the departure of the two princes for Montevideo on 21 March, by which time Herbert appears to have been thoroughly exhausted and incubating a heavy cold. A week later, he received a generous telegram of thanks from the Prince of Wales, who was by then aboard ship en route to Rio de Janeiro:

> "I am so very appreciative of all your kindness and assistance to me during my visit to Buenos Aires which contributed so largely to the success of the inauguration of the Exhibition and to the advancement of friendly relations and trade expansion between the British Empire and the Argentine" Edward P. (28 March 1931)

Herbert replied with characteristic courtesy and modesty:

> "I thank your Royal Highness most humbly and gratefully for your gracious message, though far beyond my deserts, and rejoice with loyal pride that your memorable visit to this country has culminated in the wonderfully impressive inauguration of the Exhibition where the speech of its Royal Patron has stirred the souls of all who heard it both present and throughout the world. Under so inspiring a Royal leadership nothing but success can now attend British endeavour in this Republic and Continent. With deepest respects I wish your R. H. and Prince George Godspeed in your homeward voyage." (28 March 1931)

At this point, it is appropriate to dedicate a few lines to describing the Exhibition itself and some of its highlights. While the showground was mostly taken up by the displays of numerous commercial enterprises, perhaps the centrepiece of the Exhibition was a scaled-down replica of St James' Palace, the London residence of the Prince of Wales, reproduced in meticulous detail. Among other sundry attractions figured the Golden Arrow car in which Don Kaye had recently set a new world land speed record, a model of the Transandine Railway, an enormous map of the world on which all parts of the British Empire were lit up in red, and a pavilion dedicated to promoting the Canadian nation. The commercial exhibitors were too numerous to list them all here, but among the better-known names represented were Aquascutum, Commercial Union Assurance, Dunlop, the Edinburgh & Leith Flint Glass Works, Gordon's Gin, Holland & Holland of New Bond Street (the renowned shotgun manufacturers), John Robertson & Sons of Dundee (whisky distillers), Rolls Royce, the Royal Bank of Canada, Royal Enfield (makers of cycles and motorcycles), and Slazenger. On the entertainment front, the pipe band of the Cameron Highlanders, commanded by Captain Fairfax Lucy, proved to be a tremendous hit with visitors. Before returning to Britain, the Camerons played in front of the presidential palace in central Buenos Aires, saluted President Uriburu, and then laid a wreath on the memorial to General José de San Martín, a hero of Argentina's struggle for independence, in the square named after him.

The Exhibition was a huge success in terms of visitor numbers: by the end of March, more than 600,000 had passed through the gates (31 March 1931) and by the time it closed almost a month later the tally stood at an impressive 1,500,218 (27 April 1931). On the final evening, Herbert and Maddie entertained a party of family members at the Exhibition restaurant, before observing the closing ceremony, which was marred somewhat by a 'downpour of rain' (27 April 1931). At the end of the proceedings, the band of the Cameron Highlanders sounded the Last Post in total darkness, before marching past the central stand in a blaze of light, at which point Herbert took the salute.

Although Herbert had been deeply engrossed in the Exhibition for the past few months, almost to the exclusion of his other business activities, there had been one development he could not ignore. On 4 April, Fernando Guerrico, chairman of the Southern Railway, had died following a long illness. Herbert was among a number of railway luminaries who delivered orations at Guerrico's funeral. As acting chairman during Guerrico's absence, it was only natural that Herbert should fall heir to the post on a permanent basis, being duly appointed on 6 April. This meant that there was to be no respite for Herbert from his busy schedule, since he moved straight from the hectic round of activities related to the Exhibition into another equally demanding and responsible role. While clearly drained by all his recent labours, Herbert was not a man to shirk his duties and he embraced the new position with typical enthusiasm.

In the weeks following the closure of the Exhibition, Herbert found himself showered with honours in recognition of his role in its apparently outstanding success. First, the British Chamber of Commerce in Buenos Aires resolved to present him with a portrait, to be painted by Hubert Olivier (8 May 1931). After a series of sittings in Olivier's temporary studio in the gallery of the museum in the Exhibition grounds, the portrait was finished within just twelve days. The day before it was unveiled, Herbert received news of his greatest accolade from Sir Ronald Macleay:

> Sir Ronald asked me to the Embassy and told me, very charmingly, that H. M. the King was graciously pleased to confer a baronetcy on me.
>
> !
>
> I asked Sir Ronald to convey to H. M. that I humbly recognised in his gracious message his wish to symbolize the approval the Exhibition had deserved of him, and regarded the honour as one to my colleagues of whom he had selected me as their representative; and it was much honour to me, and I accepted it. – Something like that anyway. I was at a loss just how to express my feelings which were very much the same as when Lord Crawford told me in the latter half of 1918 that I had been selected for the honour of decoration as a K.B.E.
>
> I think it will please my dear wife and make her happy, and I think it will please my sons too, and that is what matters most to me. (19 May 1931)

Official notice of Herbert's baronetcy duly appeared in the next honours list, his name featuring alongside one of Britain's foremost composers:

> The papers this morning published the list of honours bestowed on the King's birthday. No new peers; 4 baronets of whom I am one, Sir E. Elgar is another; and the other two received the honour, one for founding and endowing the Pangbourne Hospital, the other, a Director of Arts in Aberdeen for his service to science. So I am in good company with one philanthropist and two intellectuals. (3 June 1931)

He resolved to incorporate two of the places he held dearest into his new title, thus becoming Sir Herbert Gibson of Faccombe and Linconia, a title that neatly encapsulates his twin national identities. In the days following the announcement of his honour, Herbert was deluged by 'stacks of cables, telegrams, letters and cards of congratulations' (5 June 1931), requiring him to play 'truant from church' the next Sunday 'in order to really get through acknowledgments' (7 June 1931).

He certainly did not let his absence from weekly worship go to waste, writing some 69 letters and 33 cards in the course of the morning!

The following Friday, 12 June, was, in Herbert's own words, a 'memorable day' for him. First, he lunched at the British Embassy in distinguished company, the other guests including José Evaristo Uriburu, Argentina's ambassador to London, the papal nuncio and the Marquesa de Salamanca. He next attended a gathering at the Chamber of Commerce, where he was presented with a 'beautiful silver salver' inscribed with the signatures of the whole organizing committee of the Exhibition. Then, in the evening, Herbert was the guest of honour at a banquet in the City Hotel, at which the portrait painted by Olivier was formally presented to him. Sir Ronald Macleay paid such generous tribute to Herbert in his speech that the latter was, by his own admission, struggling to control his emotions while replying. The day's events were recorded in detail in an article in *The Standard* the next day:

> Honoured by His Majesty the King in the Birthday Honours List; in the afternoon presented with a silver salver by the committee of the British Exhibition, further honours were in store for Sir Herbert Gibson last night, when at a banquet given by the British Chamber of Commerce, at the City Hotel, that organization presented him with a portrait of himself, in oils, done by Mr. H. A. Olivier. The man who was at the head of the Trade Fair and did so much for its success; the man who is chairman of the British Chamber of Commerce in Argentina; the man who is always ready to take up work that will benefit the British community and British Trade, takes these honours very modestly, and this was apparent last night, when, before an array of the leading lights in Buenos Aires, and with the British Ambassador, Sir Ronald Macleay, in the chair, Sir Herbert was overwhelmed with the reception he received.[127]

The report carries a transcript of Sir Ronald's tribute to Herbert, some of which is worth reproducing here to demonstrate the esteem in which our subject was held:

> In offering what our Argentine friends call this "demonstration" to Sir Herbert to-night, we have I think two principal objects in view. One is to thank him and the other is to congratulate him. We want to thank him from the bottom of our hearts for the masterly manner in which

---

127 'Honours Fall Fast – But Deserved', *The Standard* (Buenos Aires), 13 June 1931.

he has guided the activities of the Chamber during his period of office and we want to thank him for the splendid lead he gave us in being, what I think nobody here will contest, the real initiator of that truly grandiose project – the British Empire Trade Exhibition.

We want to thank him for his vision, his courage and unfailing optimism and for the perseverance, tact and persuasive eloquence which enabled him to smooth away asperities, to overcome difficulties and to inspire his colleagues, in the British Chamber of Commerce and his collaborators on the London Committee with the same enthusiasm and an equally sturdy confidence. There is no need for me to-night to recount the glories of our Exhibition, to dwell on its principal features or to attempt to forecast its results on the expansion of our trade with this great and growing country. […]

I opened my remarks by saying that we not only wanted to express our gratitude to Sir Herbert we also wanted to offer him our sincerest congratulations. And surely we have every reason to do so, as it must have given immense pleasure and satisfaction to everybody present here to-night and indeed to all Sir Herbert's friends in this country and at home to read in their morning papers on the 3rd. of this month that His Majesty, the King, had been graciously pleased to recognise the services done by Sir Herbert in connection with the promotion and organization of the British Empire Trade Exhibition in Buenos Aires by conferring upon him the honour of a Baronetcy. I think that you will all be as delighted as I am that His Majesty's recognition of Sir Herbert's services should have taken the form of an hereditary honour. The Gibson family have now been established "radicado" I believe is the right word, in this Republic for many years and they have all done yeoman service to their own country by displaying in their relations with the Argentines those qualities of honour, straightforwardness, fairplay and sportsmanship together with what I may call an attitude of cultured sympathy with their surroundings which we are proud to think are the hallmark of an English gentleman. It therefore seems to me highly fitting that the honour now conferred on the most distinguished member of the family should pass on to subsequent generations, and that the memory of his services both to his own King and country and to the Argentine be thus kept alive in the persons of his descendants. I am happy to say that so far as I can judge at present there is very little fear of the honour going out of the direct line.

A further presentation was made to Herbert at a luncheon in the City Club just over a week later, this time by the Honorary Grand Committee of the Exhibition, a group composed of distinguished representatives of Buenos Aires business and society. In the words of a press report in *The Standard*, Herbert's gift consisted of a 'very handsome silver and gold shield in bas-relief',[128] but the recipient himself seems to have been less impressed, claiming that it looked like a 'tombstone' (20 June 1931). Indeed, Herbert did not even trouble to take the memento home, and merely hung it on his office wall! Even if the token of their esteem was less than magnificent, the warm tribute paid by Dr Ramón Cárcano on the committee's behalf was more than adequate, a few extracts from which are quoted below:

> Sir Herbert Gibson incarnates a singular condition. He is an Englishman in England and an Argentine in Argentina, to the reverse of the generality of men, who outside of their country, are foreigners everywhere. [...] He loves the land of his birth not so much because it is his fatherland as because it is a free country, and that is why he also loves Argentina. [...]
>
> At the back of the English spirit there is always a little humour and also a little spleen. Sir Herbert's humour is well known, but up to the present we know nothing about his spleen. Without any bad intention, I hope that he will preserve the first-named quality for the Argentines and the other for his compatriots. [...]
>
> He is a philosopher and a moralist. He unites justice with moderation and serenity with ardour. Loyal in his conduct, he meditates and acts with good judgment. He knows the capacity of the public wellbeing, which develops when not dominated by self interest. The British Exhibition is an exponent of his practical idealism, which induces him to love high purposes and serve useful objects.
>
> The Honorary Committee, which has, in the present case, been really honorary, because it has confined itself to enjoying the triumph, resolved to offer him a memento, and, to-day, on presenting it, repeats the definition of which he was the object: 'Sir Herbert is a wonderful man.' Let us drink to his health. (*The Standard*, 21 June 1931)

One of Herbert's final public engagements stemming from the Exhibition was to attend a prize-giving ceremony for children who had entered an essay competition:

---

128 'Shield Presented to Sir Herbert Gibson', *The Standard* (Buenos Aires), 21 June 1931.

> At 5.30 p.m. to "La Razón" [that is, the offices of *La Razón* newspaper] in whose "Salón de Actos", with Dr. Angel Sojo in the chair a distribution was made of prize books presented by the Chamber of Commerce to the successful school children who had competed in the "La Razón" concourse for the best essays on the British Exhibition. Of course the essays were obviously written by the children's parents and schoolteachers, with the exception of one or two by children of British parentage; and one precocious Argentine kid of diminutive stature read a speech full of words as long as himself. (1 August 1931)

Up till this point, it would seem that the Exhibition had been an unmitigated triumph. Soon, however, there was a meeting of the Demobilizing Committee, 'at which the unpleasant fact was confirmed that there [had] been a loss of over $200,000' (6 August 1931). Less than a month later, the final deficit was established at the not inconsiderable sum of $269,000 (2 September 1931). Although we learn relatively little of this matter from Herbert's diaries, it was evidently of concern to him as principal organizer of the Exhibition and somewhat tarnished its aura of success. Without knowing the full circumstances surrounding the loss, perhaps we can speculate that financial prudence, never Herbert's strongest suit it is fair to say, had simply fallen by the wayside in favour of laying on a lavish spectacle. Little blame seems to have attached to Herbert personally, however, and he was soon re-elected to the chairmanship of the Chamber of Commerce, an office he had held without interruption since September 1927 (8 October 1931).

Financial concerns closer to home were also on Herbert's mind, as he struggled to find a solution to the difficulties in which Alice Gibson, widow of his late brother Ernest, had become mired. Los Yngleses, which she and her daughters had inherited, was generating insufficient income to cover its costs and meet mortgage interest payments, and was operating with a floating debt of between $70,000 and $80,000. In a bid to rescue the situation, Herbert embarked upon a detailed study of the Yngleses accounts and entered into a lengthy correspondence with the *estancia*'s agents in Buenos Aires, Lockwood & Company. Tackling the debt was his main priority, but the only way he could see to achieve this was by selling off all the livestock and leasing the land. Alvan Reid, who was married to Hope Gibson's daughter Gladys, occupied the neighbouring Palenque property and expressed an interest in either renting Los Yngleses or amalgamating the two ranches on a co-partnery basis. While Alice was willing to consider liquidating the livestock and renting out the lands, she insisted upon retaining the Yngleses homestead as her residence. Herbert, quite reasonably, viewed this arrangement as unworkable, as the homestead included the 'sheep dip, the cattle yards, and all the plant necessary to the business end of the estancia' which 'would be of no use to the resident of the homestead while they would be required by the tenant'.[129] Alvan Reid, meanwhile, would only consider leasing the Yngleses lands or entering into a partnership agreement if he could reside with his family at the ranch house and 'could not contemplate an agreement affording Mrs. Ernest Gibson or her daughters either permanent or occasional residence there'.[130] Reid's position was not due to 'unfriendly or unkindly feeling', but simply because he was 'convinced that under such an agreement difficulties and unpleasantness would inevitably arise on both sides'.[131] Despite all Herbert's work in computing the different options open to her, Alice Gibson remained 'sorely perplexed' by the whole matter.[132] In the end, procrastination seems to have won the day, as she deferred confronting her financial crisis and resolved to struggle on as best she could. Sadly, the affairs of Los Yngleses were to return to trouble Herbert in the final months of his life, by which time he described them as being in a 'sad muddle' (6 June 1934).

Aside from matters pertaining to Los Yngleses, Herbert spent most of October and November occupied with his usual programme of meetings connected to the business of Gibson Brothers, the Southern Railway and Liebigs'. Between engagements, he managed to find time to attend the cinema with Chris, where father and son viewed *Cimarron*, a 'film of the wild and woolly west covering the period 1889 to 1930' (11 October 1931), and to record with satisfaction the 'crushing victory' of the National Government in the UK general election (28 October 1931). Less happily, after a period of heavy rain and bitter cold, he noted that 600 sheep had been lost at Linconia and that 'all the grape crop' at San Rafael, Mendoza, had been 'destroyed by frost' and other fruits 'very badly damaged if not indeed also totally destroyed' (9 November 1931).

At the end of November, Herbert embarked upon the voyage to Britain for a well-deserved break. On arrival, he was met by Maddie and they went together for the first time to the property where she had established their latest English base, a cottage by the name of Red Tiles in the hamlet of Netherton, close to their former residence of Faccombe Manor. Herbert fell in love with the new house straight away:

---

129 Herbert Gibson to Messrs Lockwood & Company, 23 September 1931.
130 Herbert Gibson to Messrs Lockwood & Company, 29 October 1931.
131 Herbert Gibson to Messrs Lockwood & Company, 29 October 1931.
132 Herbert Gibson to Messrs Lockwood & Company, 29 October 1931.

> A delightful abode. Its exterior a four square building with no architectural pretensions, but the interior with cosy low-ceiled rooms, and mysterious passages where staircases ascend and turn halfway up, to right and left, leading to the rooms of the upper storey. Dear Maddie has furnished the house beautifully with everything appropriate and homely. She has converted the steeps and slopes of the land belonging to it into a charming garden with banked paths and crazy pavements. Truly a charming home made beautiful by her cunning hand. (15 December 1931)

Christmas greetings cabled from Argentina brought with them a piece of good news in which Herbert undoubtedly took great pride: the appointment of his second son, Clem, as the *Intendente* (Mayor) of General Lavalle, a position, if we recall, occupied by Herbert for a number of years.

And so 1931 drew to a close, certainly one of the busiest, but also most rewarding, years of Herbert's life. There can be no question that he took great satisfaction from the achievements of the British Exhibition and was immensely proud, in his quiet, understated way, to have been honoured with a baronetcy. The concerns about his immediate family that had blighted much of the 1920s appeared to have subsided, or at least been pushed to the back of Herbert's mind, leaving him free to pursue to the fullest extent his work for the Exhibition, a project which could almost have been tailor-made for a man of his cross-cultural background, energetic disposition and organizational ability. Reading his diaries, I entertain not the slightest doubt that he revelled in the whole experience, in spite of the demanding schedule he was often required to follow. In fact, we could say that the end of 1931 found our subject a much more fulfilled individual than he had been for some time, if understandably rather fatigued.

Photograph taken in 1860s by George Corbett, showing Thomas Gibson (tall, bearded figure standing by wagon) and his brother Robert (figure holding pole) marking out the boundaries of Los Yngleses. Clementina Gibson, Thomas's wife, stands in the background with children. Baby Herbert is in her arms.

Thomas Gibson (seated) with three of his sons (Herbert on right)

Top: Herbert and Maddie
Bottom: Herbert (seated) with his sons standing behind (from left to right, Cosmo, Gerald, Chris and Clem)

Top: Gibsons' house at Linconia
Bottom: Herbert and Maddie's 'cottage' at Bella Vista

CHAPTER 10

MAN OF LETTERS, 1911–1934

In Chapter 5, we examined some of the earlier manifestations of what may be termed Herbert's intellectual output and thus acquired valuable insights into the development of his interests and ideas around a range of themes. As we saw, discourses of a fairly practical nature on rural affairs figured prominently in his writings from that time, but by no means to the exclusion of more scholarly, even philosophical, topics. From 1911, it was the latter to which Herbert turned his attention more frequently, a shift of emphasis in keeping, perhaps, with the status he was attaining as a serious contributor to the more learned circles of Argentine society.

At the end of July 1911, Herbert began to publish in *The Standard* a series of articles of an anthropological character under the title 'The First Inhabitants of Argentina'.[133] In the initial instalment, he reviewed some theories as to the origins of South America's indigenous peoples, considering both their racial characteristics and the superficial affinities of certain Amerindian tongues to the Semitic and Ugro-Altaic language families of the Old World (27 July 1911). In his second contribution, he further examined the issue of language, before beginning to survey the different tribes found within Argentina and its closest neighbours, beginning with the inhabitants of Tierra del Fuego (3 August 1911). In succeeding articles, Herbert continued his investigation of the various aboriginal peoples, describing the customs and characteristics of groups including the Patagonians (10 August 1911), the Araucanians of Chile (17 & 24 August 1911), the Pampeans of central Argentina (17 August 1911), the Charrúas of Uruguay (24 August 1911), the Guaranís of northern Argentina and Paraguay (31 August 1911), and the tribes that dwelt in the Chaco region (7 & 14 September 1911). His tenth and final instalment was dedicated to the best-known native civilization of the southern continent, the empire of the Incas, whose sphere of

---

133 'The First Inhabitants of Argentina', a series of ten articles published weekly in *The Standard* (Buenos Aires) between 27 July and 28 September 1911.

influence had extended well into the territories that would later become Argentina's north-western provinces (28 September 1911). Herbert demonstrated a sound knowledge of the history and oral traditions of the Incas and concluded his study with a brief assessment of the influence of their Quechua language on South American Spanish.

While this series of articles ended up being the most significant manifestation of Herbert's lifelong passion for anthropology, he also made a number of smaller contributions to the topic. These included an article on 'The Indian Settlements in the Paraguayan Chaco' published in the *South American Missionary Magazine* in 1916 and two pieces that appeared in the *Buenos Aires Herald* in the early 1920s, one a lengthy letter to the editor and the other the text of a lecture he delivered.[134] In fact, Herbert harboured ambitions to write a much more extensive anthropological work in his autumn years, but sadly the numerous business commitments that kept him fully occupied until shortly before his death precluded this.

The history of Latin America was another topic on which Herbert continued to write and speak knowledgeably. Naturally enough, the relationship between Britain and the countries of the River Plate was one of the aspects that interested him most, a topic he pursued in a lengthy article published in 1914. Based on a lecture Herbert gave in London to the Royal Colonial Institute on 10 February that year, it constituted a comprehensive survey of Anglo-Argentine connections from the British 'invasions' of Buenos Aires and Montevideo at the beginning of the nineteenth century to the present moment.[135] In it, he made a great deal of British influence upon the political, industrial and agricultural development of Argentina, with particular emphasis on railways and the pastoral sector, and painted a largely attractive picture of the country. Clearly, one of his aims was to stimulate British interest in Argentina and to attract settlers and investment to her shores. He concludes that the country had never offered 'greater opportunities to capital and industry than at the present time', but warns that only 'men of education, energy, and intelligence' should seek their fortunes there, for it was 'not a country for misfits, no matter what their social claims may be' (p. 227). The section of this piece that dealt with the early history of British involvement in the region was reprinted in *The British Magazine* almost eight years later.[136]

---

134 'The Indian Settlements in the Paraguayan Chaco', *South American Missionary Magazine*, October 1916, 121-126; 'Primitive Man: Dr. Wolfe's Discoveries', *Buenos Aires Herald*, 14 December 1922; 'Myths of South America: When the Sun Fell Down', *Buenos Aires Herald*, 21 September 1923.

135 'British Interests in Argentina', *The United Empire Journal*, March 1914, 211-229.

136 'The British in the Countries of the River Plate 1806-1823', *The British Magazine*, January 1922, 17-25.

In February 1917, Herbert delivered a lecture on 'The Argentine People' to a large audience at King's College, University of London.[137] In it, he offered a wide-ranging introduction to the anthropology, history and culture of his adopted land, once again with the intention of stimulating British awareness of Argentina and thereby promoting the inward movement of both monetary and human resources. He opened with a review of the current state of Anglo-Argentine trade relations, criticizing British businessmen for their tendency towards 'absenteeism', whereby they were content to remain in the United Kingdom and delegate the representation of their firms in South America to local agents. Such an attitude contrasted sharply with that of earlier investors in the region, Herbert argued, recalling with nostalgia the era when 'men with affairs abroad went there in person [...] established residence and directed their businesses themselves' (p. 5). In consequence, the influence of men such as his own father and uncles was 'not only a commercial but an intellectual force, for they enjoyed the friendship of the statesmen and leading citizens of those countries' (pp. 5-6). While advances in communications had made it feasible to run an enterprise at long range, Herbert did not view this as a desirable development, for it had led to a decline in the 'personal relations between British communities in South America and the peoples of that continent' (p. 6). Indeed, he concluded, the British were now 'more aloof and out of touch with the South American nations' than they had been fifty years before. The negative implications of this extended beyond the social realm and had, Herbert asserted, led to a weakening of Britain's trading position in the region. On a more optimistic note, however, he perceived a reawakening of interest in the United Kingdom 'to increase not only the commercial but the intellectual exchange with Spanish-speaking nations', one effect of which had been the recent establishment of a Chair of Spanish within the University of London (p. 8). This was welcomed warmly by Herbert, who considered that 'by the study of the Spanish language, and the knowledge of both Spanish and Spanish-American literature, one's world is widened, one's mental vision enlightened, and one's intellectual possessions enriched' (pp. 8-9).

Much of the remainder of Herbert's lecture was dedicated to a compelling account of South American history, starting with the pre-Columbian era and then proceeding through the colonial period, with particular emphasis, of course, on the Argentine situation. Curiously, he does little more than mention in passing the defining moments of Argentine nationhood – the revolution of 1810 and declaration of independence six years later – save to say that the

---

137 'The Argentine People: A Lecture Delivered at King's College, University of London by Herbert Gibson on Thursday, February 22, 1917' (London: Humphrey Milford & Oxford University Press, 1917).

British invasions of 1806 and 1807 had 'probably accelerated' the demise of Spanish colonialism in the region (p. 22). Having cited the 'very ample provision' made for education in Argentina and the consequently good levels of literacy among her citizens (p. 29), Herbert stated that the 'Argentine is a voracious reader of newspapers' and talked of the vibrancy of the nation's press culture (p. 34). Lastly, he offered a brief introduction to Argentine literature, including a discussion of the gauchesque genre and its greatest example, José Hernández's *Martín Fierro*.[138] In keeping with the celebratory tone adopted throughout much of the lecture, Herbert's conclusion painted an overwhelmingly positive picture of Argentina as a well-rooted nation that could look to the future with assurance:

> Eight millions of people are there, engaged in developing the country's resources, cultivating its soil, harnessing its water-courses, plumbing its minerals, and gathering the wealth of its forests. Their activity extends beyond that to the questions of social order; the housing of workpeople and the amelioration of the conditions of the poorer classes; to national education, thrift, and provision for old age; to the best average welfare of the national family. [...] There is an atmosphere of cheerfulness in the Argentine, and a spirit of *bonhomie* in ordinary business life, that is infectious. The Argentine people are warm-hearted; in the history of their political life they have been quick to forgive and forget. But they are, too, shrewd and practical; in any question of general social or national interest they 'sense' its bearings with ready perception. These are the outward traits of a nation that has long since 'found itself', that looks out on its future with confidence, and in its inner domestic life displays the qualities of an imaginative and kindly people. (pp. 46-47)

Herbert could certainly be criticized for presenting an image of Argentina as seen through rose-tinted spectacles, but perhaps he could be excused for overplaying the country's advantages when viewing it from the context of war-ravaged Europe. In any event, if his purpose was to engage British interest in Argentina, how better could he have done so than by offering a glowing endorsement of the nation's current direction and future prospects?

---

138 *Martín Fierro*, a long narrative poem first published in two parts in 1872 and 1879 respectively, is often regarded as Argentina's national epic. Taking its inspiration from the oral poetry favoured by the gauchos, it gives eloquent testimony to the changes rural Argentina was undergoing at the time of its composition and serves as a eulogy to a dying lifestyle, that of the free-spirited, itinerant cowhand.

In Chapter 5, we saw that another historical topic of interest to Herbert was that of the Jesuit missions in Paraguay (see p. 132). In 1928 he turned his attention once again to the record of the Society of Jesus and delivered a lecture at the headquarters of the Asociación Argentina de Cultura Inglesa (Argentine Association of English Culture) entitled 'Jesuit Historians and Travellers in South America', the full text of which was reproduced in the *Buenos Aires Herald*.[139] In it, he traced the history of the Jesuits' missionary work from their arrival in Brazil in 1549 until their expulsion from the continent in 1768. In keeping with the tone set in his address of 1904 to the English Literary Society, Herbert again took a benign view of the Jesuits' enterprise, speaking admiringly of the way they had established their settlements, and celebrating their achievements in intellectual fields, such as historiography, mathematics and medicine. In his conclusion, he hailed the 'immense value of [...] Jesuit contributions to Argentine History', a not uncontroversial point of view given the suspicion with which the conduct of the Society of Jesus in South America is often regarded.

Moving on from Herbert's works on aspects of Latin American history, he made a couple of noteworthy contributions to what we might broadly term the realm of philosophy or morality. The first to be discussed here appeared in 1923 in *The Pathfinder*, the magazine of the St Andrew's Scots Church in Buenos Aires.[140] Herbert took both inspiration and the title of his piece from a speech given by Stanley Baldwin shortly before his accession to 10 Downing Street:

> When Mr. Stanley Baldwin, now the Prime Minister, returned from the United States six months ago, to render account of his mission for the settlement of the debt of nearly nine hundred million sterling that Great Britain had contracted there to assist her Allies, he made a speech in the House of Commons that marked him at once as the man to whose sober and great hearted guidance the destinies of his country might safely be entrusted. [...]
>
> Mr. Baldwin, at the close of a speech on so uninspiring a theme as finance, a speech remarkable for its lucidity and wholesome doctrine, gave a slogan of four short Anglo-Saxon words to his countrymen. – "*Faith, Hope, Love, – and Work.*" (pp. 1-2)

Baldwin's message of 'faith in the future; hope for a torch; love of one's fellows for a motive; – Work, earnest unremitting work for a way' clearly struck a chord

---

139 'Jesuits in South America: Sir Herbert Gibson's Lecture', *Buenos Aires Herald*, 15 July 1928.
140 'Faith, Hope, Love, – and Work', *The Pathfinder*, October 1923, pp. 1-4.

with Herbert, who hailed it as 'something new from a politician' (p. 2). In the years immediately following the Armistice of 1918, the people of Britain had, according to Herbert, been made a number of vague, and as yet unfulfilled, promises by their political masters, who had pledged 'rich and rare fruits' and a 'home for heroes' (p. 2). Baldwin, however, recognized that only through selfless cooperation and hard work could citizens expect to share in a brighter future:

> The times were past for waiting; there was no wizard laden with spoils to furnish homes for war weary disappointed men; the only fruit must be earned by the sweat of the brow; the nation must rouse itself and work as it had never known in this generation. (p. 2)

While Baldwin's words had been intended for domestic consumption, Herbert argues that they were equally valid 'to a Church Magazine whose readers are scattered up and down this wide Pampa, seven thousand miles away' (p. 3). In particular, he contends, Baldwin's ideal would serve as an antidote to the pernicious economic doctrine that had gained currency in the years after the Great War, namely that 'each nation should limit its production to its own needs' (p. 3). According to the theorists who espoused this view, countries should aim to produce only a small surplus above their domestic needs to exchange for any commodities that could not be manufactured at home. Herbert, on the other hand, unequivocally rejected this 'selfish independence' and slated attempts by nations able to produce much more than their requirements to limit supply and thus oblige the people of war-shattered Europe to pay over the odds for imports (p. 3). In the particular case of Argentina, he considered it downright immoral to impose artificial restrictions on the yield of her abundant terrain just to drive up prices in the marketplace:

> We read in the daily press the most amazing projects to force half-starved Europe to pay more for the food we send there. Not a word of the ways and means to produce food at a cheaper cost. Mr. Baldwin's slogan is up to us as well; here where food is plentiful, want unknown, and employment for all. The man who sits on fertile land and fails to put his very soul into producing its greatest yield, betrays his trust. There is no such thing as possession in this world; every man is the Trustee of his fellow men for whatever he holds. (p. 3)

Rather than putting economic self-interest first, therefore, working hard for the common good is the more appropriate course for a world that is 'slowly rising again from its shattered ideals and false gods and racial prejudices' (p. 3). By so doing, one embodies the core values of faith in, and hope for, the future and gives practical expression to one's love for humanity. In taking Baldwin's speech from its domestic context and applying it to the realm of world trade, Herbert was, in effect, elevating it from the status of practical advice to a nation seeking to rebuild itself for its own advancement to a message of universal idealism.

In another article intended for the consumption of Argentina's British community, Herbert turned his attention to the topic of 'Education and Ideals'.[141] Resisting the view of education as synonymous with scholarly attainment, he argued that its primary goal should be to inculcate ideals for living into society's youth. With this in mind, he explored the preference among the Anglo-Argentine community for their children to receive a 'British' schooling rather than be integrated into the local education system. Thinking in purely pragmatic terms, the education available in Argentine schools was probably of better calibre and greater relevance, Herbert proposed, than that offered in the British-style establishments:

> Between education and scholarship there lies a wide difference. Many a splendid man has made the world richer for having lived there, and has gone to his grave without the solace of knowing that triangles and parallelograms of the same altitude are one to another as their bases. If only learning and erudition are sought for, they are to be obtained in a greater degree in the many excellent Schools and Colleges of this Country than could be claimed for the modest curricula of our British schools here.
>
> As a preparation for a professional or commercial career in this country, it is even doubtful if it is right to take a boy from the environment that is always to be his, deprive him of the course of instruction set out by the National Board of Education, and teach him from English text books. The call of the soil will rebel within him if he is over "anglicised" in that direction. His mentality, and even his language, is subject to the subtle influence of Nature, – for ever acclimatising her children to their surroundings, and blending within them new variations of type and language. (p. 41)

Of course, Herbert acknowledged, it was easier to justify a British schooling for those who would 'remain as foreign as their parents' by virtue of being temporary residents in Argentina, but the 'greater majority' of the English-speaking

---

141 'Education and Ideals', *The British Magazine*, August 1925, pp. 39-43.

community did not fall into that category (p. 42). The reasons why most families continued to send their offspring to British schools ran much deeper, therefore, than mere practical concerns:

> What they seek for is not to alienate the loyalty and the duty of their children from the country of their birth; but to have them taught the same principles that have stood themselves in good stead, and which they truly believe to be the foundation of loyalty and duty to every rightful cause. (p. 43)

Put another way, the alumni of British schools will have been educated, in the metaphorical sense, 'to play cricket' (p. 43). Having received such an education, Herbert contends, one would be equally well prepared to contribute to either British or Argentine society:

> If destiny takes them back to the country of their origin, they return equipped to play their part there; if they remain in the country of their birth, and finally merge into complete national life, they will play their part here all the better. Never were the ideals of individual responsibility, self-discipline, honourable dealings, and chivalry, which lie at the core of a British education, more in need of cultivation, than in these present times of negation to all the sheet anchors that have withheld men from evil ways, and moored them to sound principles. (p. 43)

When taken together, 'Faith, Hope, Love, – and Work' and 'Education and Ideals' offer a compelling insight into Herbert's view of the individual's role within society. To summarize, while one should always seek to better oneself, personal gain should not be the motive; rather, everyone must recognize that they live in connection with others, hold faith in human progress, and display the highest standards of conduct when interacting with their fellows. Living in accord with such values is more than just desirable; it is an essential part of doing one's 'duty'. Such an attitude was not, of course, particularly original – being more or less the foundation upon which Western, Judeo-Christian morality rests – but I think it is fair to say that Herbert articulated it with considerable eloquence. It would be easy to dismiss Herbert's words as too idealistic to serve as useful guidance to his readers were it not for the fact that he always strove to abide by them himself. As we have seen in previous chapters, courtesy, generosity of spirit, self-control, and a belief in the essential goodness of humankind were key traits of his character.

In addition to his writings of an intellectual quality, Herbert was by no means a stranger to penning works of a less weighty character. Foremost among these were the poems he crafted under the nom de plume of Corin, a number of which appeared in the pages of the *Buenos Aires Herald*. Some of these dealt with serious topics, but in a more light-hearted fashion than would have been possible in a conventional article; others were entirely frivolous in nature. An example of the former type, published in August 1921, poured scorn on a recent statement by the Prime Minister, in which Lloyd George had failed to overturn the law that denied citizenship to children of British parentage born outside the Empire, in spite of the sterling service many such individuals had rendered to the land of their ancestors during the Great War.[142] An eloquent yet stinging attack on an anomaly of considerable concern to Argentina's British community, 'The Reward' revealed the betrayal felt by those who had willingly left behind the security of South America to answer the call to arms from Europe:

> July of nine fourteen! He won't forget
> The date: the stirring news: the slogan cry—
> "Blood overseas calls blood"! He hears it yet,
> And wondering asks himself:—'was it a lie?'
> Hot-footed home they sped, that gallant set,
> And some went west. And some who did not die
> Returned to hear, in this their land of birth, it
> Asked by their 'alien' kin:—"was England worth it?"
>
> A priceless jest! When fools from overseas
> Were met at landing-stage, and swiftly sped,
> No time to lose,—by way of O.T.C.'s,
> Straight to the B.E.F.—While "civies" read
> Of sterner sacrifice:—the price of cheese;
> A tax on cinemas; a rise in bread,
> And sandwich-men displayed for their perusal,
> "Don't fret about the war.—Business as usual."
>
> Who won the war?—Ring out the glorious dead,
> Asleep in Vlamertinghe's field of crosses.
> Ring out the alien brood who fought and bled
> To save their motherland,—nor heeded losses.
> Versankt! They have no vote!—Proclaim instead

---

142 'The Reward', *Buenos Aires Herald*, 4 August 1921.

The funk-hole crow; the profiteering bosses;
The politicians strutting round like pullets,
Prating of killing Huns with silver bullets.

You splendid ship of fools with souls inspired!
Odd hounds from litters pupped in foreign lands!
They kept their own skins whole and gladly hired
You alien kin, to hold their flabby hands.
They "did their bit",—to cushy jobs retired;
They bravely flapped the flags and played the bands,
And when the stunt was done:—these purple Neros
Kicked out your sons, and kept their home for heroes.

Other contributions by Corin included 'To Mr. W. L. B.', a humorous ditty written to mark the visit to Argentina by W L Bradbury, the editor of *Punch*, and 'A Roundelay' composed to mark the thirteenth birthday of a young acquaintance. The closing stanza of the former ends with a self-deprecatory allusion to the stereotypically dour, humourless mien of the Scots:

Though palaces are oft prepared
For those who hither roam:
To you all doors are opened wide,
For yours is every home.
Yet lest you find our people dull,
And slow to see a joke;
Remember, Sir, the Scotch were first
To settle midst this folk.[143]

Leaving his poetry to one side, Herbert also proved to be an able author of children's tales. Originally nothing more than bedtime stories invented for the entertainment of his first-born, Chris, six pieces went on to be published under the title *Chunga Tales*. Four of them first appeared in the *St. Andrew's Gazette*, the journal of the St. Andrew's Society of the River Plate, between September and December 1901, but it was not until September 1935, some nine months after Herbert's death, that all six became available in a single volume.[144] The book was compiled by

---

143 'To Mr. W. L. B.', *Buenos Aires Herald*, 25 February 1926.
144 'The Kongkong', 'Tommy and the Meerminx', 'Casimiro', and 'The Cangrejoo' were published in the *Gazette*; 'When the Sun Forgot to Shine' and 'Angels Unawares' joined them in *Chunga Tales*, ed. by Sir Christopher Gibson (published privately, 1935).

Chris Gibson after coming across his father's manuscripts while revising some old papers.

Although the stories are quite varied in theme and style, four feature fabulous or unusually named creatures. 'When the Sun Forgot to Shine' is set on an Argentine *estancia* during a spell of extremely wet weather, with the result that the whole property becomes overgrown with enormous weeds. Giant toodstools appear and even the wild animals acquire unnatural proportions. A *mulita* – a type of small armadillo – that was kept as a children's pet turns into something quite monstrous:

> We kept it as a pet in the little run where the rabbits used to be before an opossum got over the wire netting one night and finished them. It was three days after the sun forgot to shine, when we went to see how our *mulita* was getting on. We couldn't make out at first what had got into the run; but when it turned its great scaly back to us, we saw that the *mulita* had grown too. He was as big as the kitchen table now, with a rough hairy shell on him like the side of an elephant covered with scrubbing bristles. Suddenly, from under the shell, a great head like a turtle's was thrust out. We rushed off screaming and told father, who went and looked for himself. Then we saw him go back to the run with a big axe, and we were told not to go there again. But Manish and Mendoza and Sixto were sent off with spades that afternoon, to bury something. (pp. 11-12)

Next, a huge, dinosaur-like beast is sighted. It had a scaly neck 'that towered higher than the wool-hoist at the end of the shed', 'great, bulging eyes', the body of a 'huge lizard, craggy with knots and shiny as if it were wet' and on its front legs were 'great fingers with long claws' (p. 16). Shortly, another terrible apparition is seen on the *estancia*:

> A head as large as a coal sack, shaped something like a pig's with little twinkling eyes and a nose like an elephant's would be when it first started to grow; a wide-open mouth with no teeth above but all ribbed inside; a neck not very long but bendy and fat; a huge body reminding us of the pictures of a hippopotamus; great arms and three-fingered hands with claws like horns; a long, broad tail covered with lines of scales that ran up over the back – a beast so huge that everything beside it seemed to shrink and look insignificant – we saw it stretch out its paw to gather the stem of the great aloe. It struck at the

trunk; the great branch bent over to it; the cruel, hungry mouth closed upon the shoot – and we watched no more. (p. 21)

At this, the terrified children flee back to the house where their father orders the doors and windows to be barricaded. A thunderstorm of apocalyptic scale breaks out during the night and continues all through the next day, during which one of the monsters attempts to break into the house. By nightfall, the storm subsides and the following morning the sun makes its reappearance. There is no sign of the great weeds or beasts and the natural world has returned to normal. What became of the monsters is a mystery, although the remains of one are discovered some time later:

> Where the great reptiles went was never known […]. All that we can tell is that a few months later we were having a lovely ride through a paddock with old Mendoza, and Don [the pet dog] capering in front of us. Presently the dog stopped in front of a brown heap, and began growling and barking. We rode up to it and saw that it was a huddled pile of rough skin, with a great piece of bone sticking out of it. (pp. 27-28)

'The Kongkong' lives in a hole in a riverbank beneath a weeping willow. He has a 'delicate nose', a 'moustache' and 'dainty little paws' and likes to keep himself clean (p. 68). One day, a noisy bird appears in the willow and disturbs the Kongkong's sleep. The bird, it turns out, is called the Songsong and proceeds to build a nest in the tree. Although the Kongkong is not altogether enamoured of his new neighbour at first, he takes a keen interest in the construction of her nest. Later, when she has laid eggs, he starts bringing her assorted bugs and grubs to eat. When her eggs finally hatch, he even becomes cross, thinking she has broken them! On one occasion, the Songsong is late in returning home from gathering food for her chicks and the Kongkong grows concerned. The calls from the 'dear little fluffy balls' in the nest become so weak that the Kongkong thinks they are going to starve and so he catches a 'splendid, big, fat Bongbong' for them to eat (p. 82). Just as he is feeding the chicks the Bongbong, the Songsong arrives back and is overcome with gratitude for his kindness (p. 82). When the time comes for the Songsong family to fly the nest, the Kongkong misses them greatly. The following spring, he is overjoyed when the mother Songsong and all her chicks return to the willow to nest once again.

Along similar lines, 'The Cangrejoo' is a charming tale about a strange creature that hatches from eggs laid in a sandy beach. It possesses a pink and white shell with a 'row of black dotty warts on either side', four hairy arms, two feelers and two hind legs covered with a 'sort of shell-armour' (pp. 94 & 97). Seeking to make his home inside an empty seashell, the Cangrejoo is frightened by the noise coming from within. A wise catfish, however, explains the mystery of why the 'voice of the sea' can be heard to emanate from such shells and the Cangrejoo is finally able to settle peacefully into his new abode (p. 106).

The final tale to feature an unusual being is 'Tommy and the Meerminx'. Young Tommy is out fishing on the lake one day when he is lured from his boat into the water by the meerminx, a sort of young, mischievous mermaid of attractive appearance and personality. At first, Tommy is scared because he cannot swim, but soon discovers that he has grown a fish's tale in place of his legs and is able to move with ease in the meerminx's underwater world. She shows him all sorts of wonders, but then they quarrel and Tommy longs to return home. At this point, he wakes up lying in the bottom of his little boat. Although the whole episode seemed very real to Tommy, it was clearly nothing more than a dream.

Of the two stories yet to be discussed, one – 'Casimiro' – possesses the quality of a fairy tale. A young girl, Candida, lives with her grandfather, Miralejos, on the estate of the wicked Duke Casimiro. After seeing Candida in the forest one day, Casimiro resolves to marry her and gains Miralejos's consent. The duke soon discovers that his new bride is a spirited girl who stands up to his bullying. After her grandfather's death, Casimiro tries to make her disclose the location of the bags of money Miralejos was reputed to have owned. Although Candida genuinely knows nothing of their whereabouts, he locks her in a room with a barred window and tells her she will starve there unless she reveals where the money bags are hidden. It is unlikely to be an empty threat, as the reader is led to believe that Casimiro's previous wife suffered a similar fate. In her cell, Candida finds a brass button hidden behind a portrait of her unfortunate predecessor; she presses it and straight away the great bell in the castle tower begins to ring – something it should do only when a member of the family dies. Casimiro panics and races to the tower in an attempt to stop its ominous pealing, leaving Candida to witness the outcome of his folly:

> Candida looked up at the tower. An awful sight met her eyes.
> There was the Duke high up in the tower belfry, clinging to the great tongue of the bell. As the bell swung first to one side and then to the other, the tongue with its human burden fell heavily upon the thick bronze sides, and brought out a sound like metal struck with a muffled hammer. As Candida remained looking up, horrified at the

> sight, she saw the Duke's arms relax, and the great bell swung him far out, away into space, over the battlements of the tower. His body, turning and twisting in its flight, fell at last with a heavy, sullen thud on the grass slope stretching below the terrace; and there it lay in a huddled mass, silent and still for ever. (pp. 130-131)

Shortly afterwards, during the demolition of Miralejos's cottage, his hoard of 'sacks and sacks full of golden pieces and florins' is discovered in the roof space, making Candida the 'richest person in the country' (p. 132). She puts her newfound wealth to good use by restoring the late Duke's castle and the rest of his run-down estate, becoming known to all as 'the good Lady Candida' (p. 132).

Our final tale – 'Angels Unawares' – is set on an *estancia* managed by one William Graham, a Scotsman. The ranch is a frequent stopping-off point for passing drifters and one day John, a countryman of the manager, turns up, having 'lost' his ship at Bahía Blanca, and does some odd jobs around the place to earn his keep. The manager is not surprised when he departs suddenly, for that is only to be expected from a vagrant, but John eventually returns and becomes the ranch handyman. He is adored by all, especially Graham's children and the *estancia* cat, which takes up residence in his quarters. He proves himself adept at all sorts of tasks and even manages to mend a wind-driven water pump when everyone else had failed. One day, Graham's son Frank falls while climbing up to the dovecote and dislocates his shoulder, but the resourceful John and the boy's mother manage to put it back into its socket. John and Frank later stage a magic lantern show for all the *estancia* people and John sings to great acclaim. That same night, however, he informs Graham that he must leave for Buenos Aires the next day to join a new ship. In tribute to John's good character, Graham resolves that there will always be a 'meal and a bed' for every tramp who calls at the ranch (p. 66).

When taken together, the *Chunga Tales* reveal their creator's vivid imagination and flair for storytelling. 'When the Sun Forgot to Shine' is perhaps the masterpiece of the collection and is of such quality that it could almost have flowed from the pen of Horacio Quiroga, the great writer of short stories for both adults and children who spent the majority of his life in the northern Argentine province of Misiones. Like so many of Quiroga's tales, Herbert's show that nature can be an unruly force over which humankind possesses no control; when faced with its more hostile manifestations, the only course is to weather the storm and hope for the best, as any attempt to confront its terrifying power is futile. Everything will work out in the end so long as one obeys that golden rule; as

Quiroga's works frequently demonstrate, failure to accept this reality ends only in frustration or even tragedy. Happily, the protagonists of 'When the Sun Forgot to Shine' act wisely and avoid such a fate.

Herbert's son Chris inherited some of his father's literary inclination and ability and went on to publish two books about his travels and experiences in the Chaco region of Paraguay. The first, titled *Gran Chaco Calling* and subtitled *A Chronicle of Sport and Travel in Paraguay and the Chaco*, documented Chris's adventures in the territory during the early 1930s, drawing in particular on two lengthy excursions in 1930 and 1932.[145] A fair portion of the book is devoted to Chris's passion for angling and it contains a number of photographs of his impressive catches, including one of 25 dorado taken in just two hours of fishing. Chris recorded his experiences in a quite informal, lively style, with the result that *Gran Chaco Calling* is an entertaining read. We know that Herbert made some contribution to the volume, but exactly how much is unclear since he received no acknowledgement in its pages. In his diary entry of 11 February 1933, Herbert mentions having written a chapter for Chris's work, so his input to the finished product may have been quite considerable.

Chris's second book, *Enchanted Trails*, takes its inspiration from the regular visits he went on to make to the properties administered by Gibson Brothers both on their own account and on behalf of clients in northern Argentina, Paraguay, and the Brazilian Matto Grosso.[146] These excursions, typically lasting between one and three months, were a highlight of Chris's existence, to the extent that he attributes them with having 'saved [his] reason' through bringing welcome relief from an 'existence permanently tied to a desk' in Buenos Aires (p. 15). As well as describing the ranches he toured and the activities that took place on them, the book contains abundant references to the opportunities available in Paraguay for the sporting fisherman and even includes an appendix on 'Fish of the Ríos Paraguay, Alto Paraná and Alto Uruguay'.

Having now reviewed a broad selection of Herbert's writings and speeches from both the earlier and later periods of his life, we can safely say that he was a man of ample intellect, endowed with an intense curiosity in the world around him, a fertile imagination, keen powers of observation and a solid mastery of language. Indeed, one is left to wonder how much more significant his accomplishments in intellectual fields might have been had circumstances been different. As we learned before, Herbert had always held literary ambitions, but laid

---

145 Meredith H. Gibson, *Gran Chaco Calling: A Chronicle of Sport and Travel in Paraguay and the Chaco*, (London: Witherby, 1934).

146 Sir Christopher Gibson, *Enchanted Trails* (London: Museum Press, 1948).

these largely to one side in order to pursue the necessities of the family business; it is unfortunate that even in his latter years he was unable to take a step back from the demands of commerce and truly give free rein to his more creative impulses. Had his wealth and health permitted, there is every reason to believe that Herbert could have left a much greater literary legacy.

CHAPTER 11

THE FINAL YEARS

Herbert's sojourn in the United Kingdom following his exertions of 1931 continued until April of the following year. While he was able to use this time to recover some of the considerable energies he had expended on the British Exhibition, it was far from being a complete break. As ever, he kept up quite a full schedule of appointments in connection with the business of both Gibson Brothers and Liebigs'. Other engagements included a series of meetings with the Prince of Wales, during which they discussed the establishment of a scholarship scheme that would enable Oxford undergraduates to visit Argentina, a project in which the Prince took a 'personal interest' (12 January 1932). In mid March, Herbert was the principal guest at a luncheon of the Royal Empire Society during which he 'spoke for 20 minutes on the bonds of union between Argentina and Gt. Britain', and later the same day he attended a dinner of the Honourable Company of Master Mariners at the Mansion House (15 March 1932). His characteristic generosity was very much to the fore during his stay in Britain, best exemplified by the purchase of a ring with a 'canary diamond set as a marquise' for Maddie during a shopping trip to the Burlington Arcade (27 January 1932).

When the time came to return to Argentina, Herbert was greatly saddened to leave behind the 'beautiful cottage home' Maddie had established at Netherton and he departed 'with a very heavy heart' (2 April 1932). Little of note occurred during the ensuing months, save for Herbert being admitted to a rather exclusive-sounding circle that met regularly for lunch at the Jockey Club:

> Lunched with Dr Frias at the Jockey Club and the Wednesday knights of the Round Table; a party of all ages, politics, and vocations [...] who were all most entertaining. I sat between Dr Cullen, a one-time Cabinet Minister, and [Ramón J.] Carcano. After luncheon I was declared a knight of the round table. (18 May 1932)

In June, Herbert received the welcome news that Maddie intended to come from England to join him in Buenos Aires, having got over a particularly severe bout of arthritis:

> The airmail brought from my best beloved the mighty news that the new treatment she was having for arthritis had so much relieved her that she had resolved to come out to me [...]. This happiness submerged all worldly matters in my thoughts, and my soul is singing. (21 June 1932)

Poor Herbert had to be patient, however, as the fondly anticipated reunion with his dear wife did not take place until the end of October, when she finally reached Argentina accompanied by their adopted daughter, Jean, and Cosmo.

In September, Herbert had undertaken a reorganization of the management of Gibson Brothers, admitting both Chris and Clem as full partners of the firm. Around the same time, Clem became engaged to Marjorie Anderson, a member of another Argentine-Scottish family. At first, this news brought great joy to Herbert, who held both Clem and his fiancée in the highest regard, describing the former as a 'very sterling fellow, worthy of the best of wives, God bless him' (4 September 1932) and Marjorie as an 'intelligent and vivacious girl, full of conversation, well read and up in all the events of the passing hour' (22 September 1932). Moreover, she made an 'excellent "opposite" to the silent Clem' (22 September 1932). Unfortunately, however, the engagement did not run an entirely smooth course and by February 1933 matters seem to have reached crisis point. Herbert records:

> This evening after Maddie and Jean had gone to bed poor Clem came up from the Andersons' flat where he had been since he dined with us, sadly upset and broken by what had evidently been a stormy time with Marjorie who followed him. They went back and I presently went down to the ground floor where I found them in darkness. Marjorie spoke of their "not being able to get on together, and perhaps it would be best for them to break the engagement off", but they asked me to return to my flat which I did sorely distressed and my heart aching for poor Clem who is of such a sweet nature and manly honest character that I cannot conceive any woman falling out with him. (17 February 1933)

Regrettably, the discord between Clem and Marjorie turned out to be more than a minor tiff and continued to give Herbert cause for concern. Nearly three months after the episode described above, he recorded:

> Poor Clem is in a sad plight through his engagement to Marjorie Anderson for whom he has never had any attachment and as time goes on finds he has nothing in common with her, but has the feeling that he cannot ask her to break the engagement and that it is his duty to marry her if she so desires. Maddie and I are greatly grieved for him. (13 May 1933)

The ever-honourable Clem did indeed stick to his word and the marriage went ahead. In accordance with Argentine law, it was celebrated first in a civil ceremony on 22 June before receiving religious sanction at St John's Pro-Cathedral two days later. Under the circumstances, it was not a particularly joyous occasion and the decision was made to have an 'absolutely quiet ceremony' attended by only the closest family members and no invitations were sent out (24 June 1933). Even Clem's adopted sister, Jean, did not attend the ceremony for, in Herbert's words, 'her heart [was] very sore that her beloved big "brother" Clem [was] going to be married' (24 June 1933). In spite of this inauspicious start to wedded life, the union proved to be more fruitful and enduring than many; Clem and Marjorie had three sons – Geoffrey (born 1934), Clement (born 1936), and Thomas (born 1943) – and were separated only by Clem's death in 1976.

Around the same period, Cosmo also appeared to be on course to become a married man, having proposed to Venetia Mirrieless in October 1932 while in England. The Mirrieless family travelled out to Argentina for a spell, but returned home again in April 1933, leaving Cosmo 'heartbroken' as he was 'very much in love' (5 April 1933). We hear nothing more of Cosmo and Venetia until the end of August, when Herbert describes the circumstances that were to bring their relationship to a premature end:

> Found [...] letters from dearest Maddie of which the latest was by airmail dated 15th August and gave me the news, with the letters she had received from M$^{rs.}$ Mirrieless and Venetia that "for financial reasons and Venetia's health which her doctor thought would be impaired if she went to a sub-tropical climate" she had agreed with her parents, in order to assuage them, to cancel her engagement to Cosmo but with the stipulation that it was not final, and she might exercise her own wish, to which they agreed, and it was her intention to stick to Cos. (29 August 1933).

Herbert felt that there was more behind this decision than had been stated, recording that 'it was obvious before she left that M*rs.* Mirrieless did not enjoy her visit and had set her mind against the engagement', while her husband, a 'good simple man, thinks in these matters as she wishes him to think'! (29 August 1933). Irrespective of the true reasons behind it, the split was to prove final and Cosmo would eventually go on to marry another girl.

Chris too was a source of worry to his parents around this time; in March, he had taken a 'small glass of beer' and suffered the 'poisonous reaction the least drop of alcohol [had] on his nervous system', leading to fears of a relapse into alcohol dependency (24 March 1933). Within the extended family, Herbert was also troubled by the conduct of Paco Boote – husband of his niece Lorna – who seemed intent on having his say in the running of Los Yngleses, causing some distress in the process to his mother-in-law, Alice. From the pages of Herbert's diary, it is clear that he had little time for Mr Boote; on one occasion, he complained that during a visit to the races with Maddie and Jean they were 'bored [...] inordinately' by Paco (15 April 1933), who then 'wearied' Herbert 'with his garrulous comments on the management of the Yngleses' during a 'long visit' a few days later (20 April 1933).[147]

Away from family affairs, Herbert was heartened by the signing of a new convention between the governments of Argentina and the United Kingdom, which, in essence, served to update the treaty of 1825 and shelter Argentina from some of the effects of a British trade policy designed to favour territories that were part of the Empire. The convention was agreed after lengthy talks in London between a delegation headed by Argentina's vice-president, Julio Roca, and representatives of the UK government led by Walter Runciman. The so-called Roca-Runciman agreement was quite controversial in Argentina, as many politicians with nationalist or socialist leanings bitterly opposed it on the grounds that it ceded excessive power to British firms, especially in sectors such as the meat trade and public utilities. Within the country's Anglo community, however, the renewed formalization of links between the two nations was welcomed warmly. When news reached Buenos Aires that the two delegations had arrived at an agreement, Herbert was authorized by the Executive Council of the Chamber of Commerce to cable messages of congratulation to the chief negotiators and to the Prince of Wales, who had shown keen interest in the deal's progress (27 April 1933). One month later,

---

147 It was unusual for anyone to be treated so harshly in the diaries. According to other accounts, Paco Boote was a congenial and respected member of the Anglo-Argentine community. Perhaps his relatively humble origins weighed against him in Herbert's estimations; his grandfather, John Boote, had been a simple *puestero* at Los Yngleses. In later years, however, Paco went on to play a creditable role in the administration of Los Yngleses and quite probably saved the *estancia* from ruin.

Herbert was part of a welcoming committee that met members of the returning Argentine delegation as they disembarked at Buenos Aires, and was pleased to have the opportunity of shaking Roca's hand (26 May 1933). A few days later, Herbert was one of around 1,200 guests who attended a celebratory luncheon in the Central Hall of the Stock Exchange, an event addressed by both President Justo, who gave a 'vibrant and constructive' speech, and Vice-President Roca (3 June 1933).

Despite turning seventy on 8 July 1933, Herbert displayed little inclination to reduce his level of activity. He continued to play a full role in the various companies he was involved in, chiefly Gibson Brothers, Liebigs' and the Southern Railway, and also kept up his schedule of public appearances, such as speaking at gatherings of the Chamber of Commerce. Just after arriving in England at the end of October, however, the first indications of a decline in his health began to manifest themselves, starting with nothing more sinister than a bout of backache, which Herbert initially attributed to a 'chill' (27 October 1933). That night, he was unable to sleep as the pain was 'so acute' and remained in bed all the next day, his distress alleviated somewhat by a hot water bottle and 'belladonna plaster' (28 October 1933). Dr Savoy, the local 'lady doctor' was summoned and prescribed for both lumbago and, perhaps more significantly in light of future developments, what Herbert described as 'my trouble of uric acid' (28 October 1933). His suffering continued for more than a week before finally abating somewhat. By 19 November, the pain had returned as bad as ever, this time in the left hip joint, leaving him barely able to walk, before moving to the right groin two days later and forcing confinement to bed once again. Dr Savoy clearly recognized that the location and mobile nature of Herbert's discomfort indicated something more serious than a routine back problem, and sent him to consult a Harley Street specialist, who reached a 'somewhat discouraging diagnosis':

> To Harley St. to consult Dr Douthwaite a specialist to whom Dr Savoy has advised me to go. He made a very thorough examination, and with respect to the pains in my limbs etc. derived from uric acid he proposes to give me diathermic treatment when I am in town. He finds however that the prostate gland is enlarged and while expressing himself averse to a recourse of surgery he wishes to have a further examination in consultation with a surgeon, and is to arrange for one when I come to town. (29 November 1933)

Nowadays, with our enhanced awareness of medical matters, the combination of pain in the lumbar and pelvic regions with enlargement of the prostate should set alarm bells ringing, as it may well indicate a malignancy that has metastasized to the bones. In such cases, the fact that the cancer has already spread means that surgical removal of the prostate often serves little purpose. In this light, Herbert's relief at the outcome of his next appointment can be understood as misplaced:

> In the afternoon to the consulting rooms of a surgeon, Mr Andrews of 41 Harley St., at which Dr Douthwaite was also present, and I was thoroughly examined more especially with respect to the 'prostata'. Mr Andrews found no occasion to pass a catheter and at the termination of his examination no occasion either for surgical intervention, – nor, he said to me, need I ever be subject to an operation for the prostata, – and the outcome of the whole somewhat trying "vetting" was satisfactory. (5 December 1933)

My interpretation of Mr Andrews' prediction is less positive than Herbert's, for it is likely to have been influenced by his recognition that the ailment had progressed beyond the stage at which surgical intervention would be appropriate. The fact that the surgeon seems to have refrained from giving Herbert a frank statement of his condition is not at all surprising, as the prevailing view among medical professionals at this time was that it was wholly counterproductive to inform a patient of a terminal prognosis.

To his credit, Herbert did not seem to dwell excessively on his condition, despite the fact that he must have been in considerable discomfort much of the time. On the contrary, he pressed on with everyday activities for as long as he possibly could. In December 1933, he took pleasure in reporting the acquisition of new dentures to replace the set he had been fitted with two years earlier and which had 'really defaced' him (8 December 1933), and derived much satisfaction from the news that Chris's first book, *Gran Chaco Calling*, had been accepted by a publisher subject to the excision of a 'few familiar episodes not interesting to the general public' (18 December 1933). Before returning to Argentina, he also paid a visit to the Prince of Wales at St James's Palace, where he was received with the 'customary graciousness' (19 December 1933). On setting sail for Buenos Aires ten days later, little did Herbert realize that this would prove to be the last of his many transatlantic voyages.

By the end of March, poor health was beginning to impinge on Herbert's capabilities to a significant extent. Severe pain that left him unable to sleep and lameness that made walking very awkward afflicted him with increasing frequency and were associated by his Argentine doctors with the prostate. Suppositories were prescribed for his lumbar pain and an enema proved necessary to relieve stubborn constipation (2 April 1934). A short while later, he began to experience difficulty in passing water and soon found it necessary to attend his doctor's surgery on a regular basis to have his bladder cleared by catheter. Chris's health was also causing concern and he had to submit to surgery for the 'fistula and hemorrhoids [sic] from which he [had] been suffering for more than a year' (28 May 1934).

From late May, Herbert's diary entries gradually become shorter and more routine, reflecting his growing infirmity and the consequent reduction in his daily programme. On a happier note, he records the birth of Clem's first son, Geoffrey: 'At 10.30 p.m. Marjorie gave birth to a fine boy, to Clem's great relief and happiness' (11 June 1934). Thankfully, Herbert was well enough to attend the baptism of his newest grandson a little more than a month later: 'Today at 3 p.m. Geoffrey, Clem's child, was baptized by the Rev. M$^{r.}$ Evans at St. John's pro-Cathedral the godparents being Jimmie Gunther and M$^{rs.}$ Strachey (a daughter of the Ronald Leslies)' (20 July 1934). Later in the day, Herbert attended his doctor's surgery to have his 'bladder drawn as usual'.

Herbert's diaries come to an abrupt end after 12 August. His final entries are very brief, but contain no hint of the impending cessation of his almost lifelong habit. He certainly seems to have been living quite quietly for the previous couple of weeks, although he had continued to go to his office on an almost daily basis. We know, however, that around this time the pain in Herbert's back and hips became crippling and confined him to his Buenos Aires apartment, where he would remain until his death at the end of the year. Just a few days after his last diary entry, he wrote to Compton Mackenzie, the famous author who would go on to pen *Whisky Galore* (1947), giving his apologies for being unable to meet him on his arrival in Buenos Aires:

> My dear Mr. Compton Mackenzie
> I am very disappointed indeed to find myself somewhat crippled with arthritis and under doctor's orders to remain at home for the next few days. I had hoped to go on board this evening to welcome you, and to be present at the luncheon that Dr. Herrera Vegas is giving in your honour at the Jockey Club, but I am afraid that I must abandon any idea of attending any meetings for a few days. (16 August 1934)

We could surmise, therefore, that while Herbert remained capable of dictating his correspondence, he had given up writing for himself and was thus no longer able to record his daily thoughts and activities. Alternatively, he may simply have felt that his experiences were no longer worth describing now that he was reduced to a humdrum existence of lying in bed and receiving medical treatments. In a letter of 25 October to Charles Adeane, an old acquaintance in England, he wrote:

> My dear Adeane,
> I have indeed been remiss in my correspondence with you since I returned to this country. For one thing I have been somewhat in the docotr's [sic] hands all the time, and during the last two months have had to reconcile myself to treatment in my house, but am glad to say with good results and my medico is well pleased with my progress. Another reason, I had truly little to write you of interest as things have been, as you can well imagine, dull and uneventful.

Notwithstanding his evident physical frailty, Herbert remained mentally alert and lucid until close to the end. In one of his final extant letters, he wrote to Sir Hilary Leng, his close friend and fellow luminary of the British business circle in Buenos Aires, proposing that a wedding gift should be made to the Duke of Kent:

> My dear Hilary,
> Lying on the broad of my back and thinking of things I have felt that some wedding gift from our Community here, – its intrinsic value perhaps of less importance, – should be made to the Duke of Kent. Accompanying his brother the Prince of Wales he visited us here in 1931 and won all our hearts. I do not know quite how it can be initiated. [...] Would you set the ball rolling? (29 November 1934)

Just one month later, Herbert passed away, surrounded by his closest family. Argentinians awoke the next morning to find their leading newspapers full of warm tributes to the man who had done so much to promote good relations between their country and Great Britain. The most impressive homage was to be found in *The Buenos Aires Herald*, which devoted its main headline and much of its front page to the news of Herbert's passing under the banner 'British Community Loses its Leader' (29 December 1934). Indeed, Herbert's death took precedence in the *Herald* over such notable stories as Albert Einstein's new assertion that the universe might be infinite and the latest developments in the Lindbergh baby trial.[148] One theme ran throughout all of the obituaries, namely

---

148 In 1932, the two-year-old son of Charles Lindbergh, the renowned American aviator, had been kidnapped and murdered. It took some time for the authorities to apprehend the kidnapper, hence the fact that his trial was only getting underway at the time of Herbert's death.

that Herbert had dedicated his life to public service and had been a true friend of the Argentine nation. More than one of the tributes quoted from a profile of Herbert that appeared in *Comercio Nacional* earlier that year, in the course of which it was stated that 'la República Argentina no hubiese podido desear mejor diplomático, ni mayor gran amigo' ('the Argentine Republic could not have wished for a better diplomat nor a greater friend', 1 June 1934).

In accordance with normal South American practice, the funeral was held as quickly as practicable, at 10.30 the morning after his death. The service, which took place in the British section of the Chacarita cemetery, was widely reported in the next day's press. Canon J T Stevenson of St John's Pro-Cathedral officiated, with the assistance of the Rev. Douglas Bruce of the St Andrew's Scotch Presbyterian Church, at what was, by all accounts, a simple yet impressive ceremony. The list of mourners reads like a Who's Who of Argentina's British community, in the company of distinguished representatives of the local populace. Orations were delivered by Dr Leguizamón, for many years a close friend and associate of Herbert, and Dr Cosme Massini Ezcurra, President of the Argentine Rural Society. Leguizamón's address included the following passages that leave little doubt as to the affection and respect in which the deceased was held:

> With the demise of Sir Herbert there disappears the most eminent of the Argentine Republic's adopted sons. His patrician virtues, his irreproachable moral standing, his gifted talent and his sincere and proved 'Argentinismo' throughout a long and fruitful life, have given to his personality the dignity of a national figure.
>
> Sir Herbert was a vigorous example of the illustrious sons of the Victorian era. His aristocratic bearing and the gentlemanly air of his affable manner, had opened the world's pathways to him and gained for him the respect and sympathy of all who knew him.
>
> The outstanding characteristics of his personality were unmistakeable; tall, slender, with a clear-cut head, a high brow and clear and deep eyes over a prominent nose – and gave one the impression of a close investigator of everything that is given to man to know and also somewhat of a visionary who is searching out the definite designs of the Supreme Powers.
>
> Sir Herbert's great spiritual value lay in the marvellous equanimity of his clear intelligence and in his vast store of general knowledge. He possessed, to a degree given to but few, the highest qualities of the Anglo-Saxon race, and he was, as such, reflective, serene, prudent and firm, while, in addition, he had acquired, as the result of his

lengthy residence in the Argentine, the best qualities of the National character; clear sighted sagacity in analysis and in controversy, talent and grace in intimate and literary intercourse, and, above all, a pitying clemency for all humanity.

He had attained in his untiring zeal for select reading a marvellous knowledge on innumerable subjects. He knew and loved our country life amidst which surroundings he passed the happy years of his youth; he possessed an inexhaustible treasury of the traditions of the Pampa, and its country life and customs were linked up in his memory with the persistent efforts of the three generations of the Gibson family established in the Argentine; he zealously studied the social, economic and political problems of the present era and when discussing them demonstrated an extraordinary spirit of understanding.

He had at his command a perfect knowledge of the English and Spanish languages and versed as he was in the classics of either language, it was second nature to him, thanks to his prodigious memory, to quote alike and with rare appositeness a passage from Shakespeare or a maxim from Martín Fierro.

Gentle in speech, an opportune and subtle "raconteur", precise and keen in observation, bounteous and benevolent in stimulating charitable actions – it was always pure delight to hear him in his fluent and eloquent oratory, both in improvisation and in his polished and prepared periods. […]

But the cherished preoccupation of his whole existence and one which embodied the purest desires of his being was always to strengthen the bonds of friendship and economic cooperation between the Argentine Republic and Great Britain inasmuch as both Nations shared the same place in his affections.

Leguizamón's eloquent and heartfelt farewell seems to capture Herbert's essential qualities perfectly, and is thus a fitting point for us to bid adieu to the man we have come to know so well through recalling his life story. If this biography achieves just one thing, let it be that Herbert's example inspires present and future generations of Britons and Argentinians alike to further the longstanding ties between their two great nations in a spirit of peace and friendship.

BIBLIOGRAPHY

Documentary sources

Donaldson, Boswell Secundus (Boz), Memoirs, 2 vols
Gibson, Geoffrey, 'The Chivalrous Shepherd'
Gibson, Herbert, 'Administration Notes', 5 vols
Gibson, Herbert, 'Agricultural and General Notebooks', 7 vols, 1885–1934
Gibson, Herbert, Private and business correspondence, 1895–1934
Gibson, Herbert, General diaries, 16 vols, 1879–1891, 1908–1934
Gibson Herbert, 'Diary of Herbert Gibson. Church Army Commissioner for 2nd (and subsequently also for the 5th) Army, Arras, 23rd April to 14th September 1917'
Gibson, Herbert, 'Notes on Anthropology, Languages, etc.', 5 vols
Gibson, Robert, 'A Journal of a Voyage from Liverpool to Montevideo and Trip Thence to Buenos Ayres in 1826–27'
National Library of Scotland (NLS), MS 10326 (Correspondence, chiefly from members of the Gibson family in Glasgow and between George and Robert Gibson, with some formal documents and miscellaneous papers, 1816–1842.)
NLS, MS 10327 (Correspondence, 1844–72. This consists of a series of letters, 1844–51, from Thomas Gibson in Ajó to Robert in Buenos Aires, reporting on the day-to-day running of an estancia; and a second series, 1847–72, from Matthew Dunnett in Glasgow to his relations Thomas and Jessie Gibson. There are also some papers concerning the estancia and the family collected by Sir Herbert Gibson.)
NLS, MS 10328 (Legal and financial papers concerning the sale and purchase of property in the province of Buenos Aires, together with sketch maps, powers of attorney and other miscellaneous papers, 1825–93.)

Published works by Herbert Gibson (in chronological order)

'Farming in the Argentine as a Field for Capital and Labour', Chamber of Commerce Journal, 10 August 1892, 186–92 (reprinted in South American Journal, 3 September 1892, 257–61)

'The History and Present State of the Sheep-Breeding Industry in the Argentine Republic' (Buenos Aires: Ravenscoft and Mills, 1893)

'The Cultivation of Lucerne in Argentina', Journal of the Royal Agricultural Society of England (3rd series) 6 (1895), 675–684

'Informe sobre la producción de manteca y queso; Informe sobre la exportación de ganado en pié y de carne congelada y fresca en el Reino Unido' (La Plata: Talleres de Publicaciones del Museo, 1896)

'Cattle Breeding in the Argentine', Stockbreeder's Magazine, April 1899, 54–63

'Horse-breeding in the Argentine', Stockbreeder's Magazine, May 1899, 147–155

'Sheep-breeding in the Argentine', Stockbreeder's Magazine, June 1899, 334–342

'Sistema de señales para el ganado ovino' (Buenos Aires: La Agricultura, 1899)

'Informe presentado á la Sociedad Rural Argentina por Heriberto Gibson, delegado de la Sociedad ante el Congreso Comercial Internacional de Filadelfia' (Buenos Aires: Jacobo Peuser, 1900)

'Protection', Review of the River Plate, 22 December 1900, pp. 6–8

'Reflexiones económicas', La Patria (Dolores), 11, 29, 30 August, 13, 15, 16 September, 28 October 1903

'Civic Duty', Buenos Aires Scotch Church Magazine, May 1905, pp. 1–3

'British Representation', letter to the Editor of The Standard (Buenos Aires), 10 June 1906

'Santiago de Liniers – Count of Buenos Aires', Buenos Aires Herald Weekly Edition, 13 March 1908

'Maundy Thursday', Buenos Aires Herald, 16 April 1908

'The Duty of Happiness', Buenos Aires Scotch Church Magazine, April 1908

'British Disunity in the Argentine Republic', The Standard (Buenos Aires), 7 July 1908

'The Value of Manure', Buenos Aires Herald, 13 August 1908

'Las escuelas prácticas de ganadería y agricultura', lecture to the Union Club of Azul, 11 October 1908

'The Progress of Alfalfa-growing in the Argentine', Pastoralists' Review, 16 November 1908

'Argentine Stock-Breeding Reviewed – Records of the Past: Possibilities of the Future', Buenos Aires Herald, 1 January 1909

'Water Storage in the Pampa Central: Suggested Solution of a Present Day Problem', Buenos Aires Herald, October 1910

'Argentine Meat and the "Beef Trust": View of an Estancia Owner', The Times, 7 April 1911

'The First Inhabitants of Argentina', a series of ten articles published weekly in The Standard (Buenos Aires) 27 July–28 September 1911

'British Interests in Argentina', The United Empire Journal, March 1914, 211–229

'The Indian Settlements in the Paraguayan Chaco', South American Missionary Magazine, October 1916, 121–126

'The Argentine People: A Lecture Delivered at King's College, University of London by Herbert Gibson on Thursday, February 22, 1917' (London: Humphrey Milford & Oxford University Press, 1917)

'The Reward', Buenos Aires Herald, 4 August 1921

'The British in the Countries of the River Plate 1806–1823', The British Magazine, January 1922, 17–25

'Primitive Man: Dr. Wolfe's Discoveries', Buenos Aires Herald, 14 December 1922

'Myths of South America: When the Sun Fell Down', Buenos Aires Herald, 21 September 1923

'Faith, Hope, Love, – and Work', The Pathfinder, October 1923, pp. 1–4

'Education and Ideals', The British Magazine, August 1925, pp. 39–43

'To Mr. W. L. B.', Buenos Aires Herald, 25 February 1926

'Chunga Tales', ed. by Sir Christopher Gibson (published privately, 1935)

Articles in newspapers and periodicals (in chronological order)

Fream, W., 'The Cultivation of Lucerne in England', Journal of the Royal Agricultural Society of England (3rd series) 6 (1895), 684–690

'Mr. Herbert Gibson's Report', Review of the River Plate, 24 November 1900, p. 6

'Editorial Note', Review of the River Plate, 22 December 1900, p. 8

'Shakespeare v. Bacon', Buenos Aires Herald, 6 November 1902

'The Baconian Cypher in Shakespeare's Plays', Buenos Aires Herald, 6 November 1902

'English Literary Society. Lecture by Mr. Herbert Gibson', Buenos Aires Herald, 16 June 1904

'Sunday Rest – Mr. Herbert Gibson's Address at Meeting held in Beranger Hall on Tuesday Night', The Standard (Buenos Aires), 3 September 1905

'Commemoration of the Spanish Royal Wedding', The Standard (Buenos Aires), 31 May 1906

'The Revolution of 1810 and After' (a report on Herbert Gibson's lecture to the St Andrews Debating Society), Buenos Aires Herald, 31 July 1906

'Jesuits in South America: Sir Herbert Gibson's Lecture', Buenos Aires Herald, 15 July 1928

'Obituary: The late Mr. Hope Gibson', The Standard (Buenos Aires), 11 October 1928

'Old British and American Firms', The Standard (Buenos Aires), 1 May 1930

'The Prince of Wales' Radio Telephone Conversation with Sir Herbert Gibson', The Standard (Buenos Aires), 16 January 1931

'Buenos Aires Exhibition: A Successful Opening', The Times, 16 March 1931

'Honours Fall Fast – But Deserved', The Standard (Buenos Aires), 13 June 1931

'Sir Herbert Gibson Bt. K.B.E.', Comercio Nacional, 1 June 1934

'British Community Loses its Leader', Buenos Aires Herald, 29 December 1934

'La obra pictórica desconocida de Tomás Gibson y la estancia Los Ingleses en el Tuyú', La Prensa (Buenos Aires), 15 May 1938

Published volumes

Bethell, Leslie, (ed.), 'Argentina since Independence' (Cambridge: Cambridge University Press, 1993)

Crawley, Eduardo, 'A House Divided: Argentina 1880–1980' (London: C. Hurst, 1984)

Dodds, James, 'Records of the Scottish Settlers in the River Plate and their Churches' (Buenos Aires: Grant and Sylvester, 1897)

Fletcher, Ian, 'The Waters of Oblivion: The British Invasion of the Río de la Plata, 1806–1807' (Tunbridge Wells: Spellmount, 1991)

Gibson, Sir Christopher, 'Enchanted Trails' (London: Museum Press, 1948)

Gibson, Meredith H., 'Gran Chaco Calling: A Chronicle of Sport and Travel in Paraguay and the Chaco', (London: Witherby, 1934)

Graham-Yooll, Andrew, 'The Forgotten Colony: A History of the English-Speaking Communities in Argentina' (London: Hutchinson, 1981)

Hennessy, Alistair and John King (eds.), 'The Land that England Lost: Argentina and Britain, a Special Relationship' (London: British Academic Press, 1992)

'Provincia de Buenos Aires, Intendencia de General Lavalle: Memoria, años 1897 y 1898' (Buenos Aires: Jacobo Peuser, 1899)

'Provincia de Buenos Aires, Intendencia de General Lavalle: Petición y memoria elevada al Superior Gobierno de la Nación solicitando el dragado de la barra del Riacho de Ajó' (La Plata: Talleres de Publicaciones del Museo, 1897)

Ferns, H. S., 'Argentina: Part of an Informal Empire?', in The Land that England Lost: Argentina and Britain, a Special Relationship, ed. by Alistair Hennessy and John King (London: British Academic Press, 1992), pp. 49–61

'Britain and Argentina in the Nineteenth Century' (Oxford: Clarendon Press, 1960)

Miller, Rory, 'Britain and Latin America in the Nineteenth and Twentieth Centuries' (London and New York: Longman, 1993)

Nahum, Benjamín, 'Manual de historia del Uruguay', (Montevideo: Ediciones de la Banda Oriental, 1994)

Pedemonte, Juan Carlos, 'Los presidentes del Uruguay', 4th edn, (Montevideo: Ediciones de la Plaza, 1992)

Shumway, Nicolas, 'The Invention of Argentina' (Berkeley: University of California Press, 1991)

Slatta, Richard W., 'Gauchos and the Vanishing Frontier' (Lincoln and London: University of Nebraska Press, 1992)

Smith, Adam, 'An Inquiry into the Nature and Causes of the Wealth of Nations', ed. by Kathryn Sutherland (Oxford: Oxford University Press, 1993)

Stewart, Iain A. D. (ed.), 'From Caledonia to the Pampas: Two Accounts by Early Scottish Emigrants to the Argentine' (East Linton: Tuckwell Press, 2000)